**FREE MONEY**
for
**MATHEMATICS AND**
**NATURAL SCIENCES**

# FREE MONEY
## for
# MATHEMATICS AND NATURAL SCIENCES

### SECOND EDITION

## LAURIE BLUM

PARAGON HOUSE PUBLISHERS
New York

Published in the United States by

Paragon House Publishers
90 Fifth Avenue
New York, New York 10011

Copyright © 1987 by Laurie Blum

All rights reserved. No part of this book may
be reproduced, in any form, without written permission
from the publisher unless by a reviewer who wishes to
quote brief passages.

**Library of Congress Cataloging-in-Publication Data**

Blum, Laurie.
    Free money for mathematics and natural sciences.
    Rev. ed. of: Free money for science students. 1st ed.
c1985.
    1. Science—Scholarships, fellowships, etc.—United
States—Handbooks, manuals, etc. 2. Science—United
States—Socieities, etc.—Directories. 3. Mathematics—
Scholarships, fellowships, etc.—United States—Handbooks,
manuals, etc. 4. Mathematics—United States—Societies,
etc.—Directories. 5. Federal aid to higher education—
United States—Handbooks, manuals, etc. 6. Student aid—
United States—Handbooks, manuals, etc. I. Blum, Laurie.
Free money for science students. II. Title.
Q183.3.A1B58    1987    507'.9    87-8912

ISBN 0-913729-83-3

# INTRODUCTION

Would you like to have enough money to attend any college or university you want, regardless of how much it cost? Of course you would.

How many impoverished or would-be students have not applied for financial aid because they decided in advance that they had no chance of success?

There really are hundreds of millions of dollars—perhaps more than a billion dollars—given away *free* to students. There are also low-cost loans and many other ways that mean that, yes, you can afford to go to school. Many of these sources fund students regardless of their financial need or academic excellence.

Do you just walk up, hold out your hand, and expect someone to put money in it? Of course not. It takes time, effort, and thought on your part. You're going to have to find out who is giving away money. You're going to have to fill out applications. You may meet with frustration or rejection somewhere down the road. The odds, however, are in your favor that you will qualify for some sort of financial aid.

The hardest part has always been finding the sources of money—which is why I wrote this book. Sure, there are many books that explain how students can attempt to locate sources to fund their education; several are extremely expensive and largely unavailable reference books, while others have some student scholarship information, but it's combined with things like contests, awards, and prizes for professionals.

In this country more than 24,000 foundations give grants; an impossible number for anyone to wade through—nor is there any reason why you should. For this book, I've taken the scholarship and grants that apply to as many students (undergraduate and graduate) as possible.

The listings are divided into three categories. I wanted to make this book as easy to use as possible; because I find it tedious to use an index, this book has been set up in a manner that eliminates the need for one. Check all three categories to see which grants apply to you. The geographic listings apply to where you live, and in many cases, where you go to college. The miscellaneous section is based on such restrictions as ethnic origins, religious affiliations, and hobbies. Subject listings apply, for the most part, to your major or intended major field of study. Regardless of your field of study or your geographic location(s), you can qualify for at least some of the grants in this book.

I have included, wherever possible, the total amount of money that is awarded to students, the number of scholarships or grants given, the average size of an award, and the range of monies given. Do not be dissuaded from applying if the average award is only $200 (because the same material you put together for one application can be used for most, if not all, of the other applications, you will hopefully apply for a number of scholarships and grants). You might get more, you might get less. But remember, this is free money!

# HOW TO APPLY

Applying for grants and scholarships is a lot like applying for school: it takes work, some thought and organization—but at this stage in your life, you know what you have to do. You've done it before.

## vi·INTRODUCTION

First comes the sorting-out process. Go through this book and mark off all the listings that may give you money. Pay close attention to the restrictions, and eliminate the least likely grants). You might get more, you might get less. But remember, this is free money!

## HOW TO APPLY

Applying for grants and scholarships is a lot like applying for school: it takes work, some thought and organization—but at this stage in your life, you know what you have to do. You've done it before.

First comes the sorting-out process. Go through this book and mark off all the listings that may give you money. Pay close attention to the restrictions, and eliminate the least likely foundations. Although none of the foundations in this book require an application fee, the effort you'll have to put in will probably limit you to no more than eight applications (if you are ambitious and want to apply to more than eight foundations, bravo, go right ahead). Write or call the most likely foundations to get a copy of their guidelines. (In cases where the contact's name is not listed, begin your letter: To Whom It May Concern.) If you call, just request the guidelines—please don't interrogate the poor person who answers the phone!

Grant applications, like college applications, take time to fill out. Often you will be required to write one or more essays. Be neat! You very well may prepare a top-notch proposal, but it won't look good if it's done in a sloppy manner. Proposals should always be typed, double-spaced please, and be sure to make a copy of the proposal. I've learned the hard way that there is nothing worse than having the foundation not be able to find your proposal, and having to reconstruct it because you didn't keep a copy. Sometimes an interview is required. (Well, you probably had some interviews when you were looking at colleges, right?) You may be asked to include personal references. Be sure to get strong and numerous references. Remember, you have to sell yourself, convince the grantors to give money to you and not to someone else. Above all, don't panic. Follow the instructions, and all will be well.

## DEFINITIONS

The word *minority* in this book refers to people who are black, Mexican, American Indian, Puerto Rican, or female Americans. If a listing doesn't specifically say that it's for graduate students, then it is only for undergraduates.

## FEDERAL MONEY

Historically, Federal aid has been a mainstay for the student seeking college money. It remains one of the first sources of money you should pursue. Apply for financial aid. The process is not complicated, but you must fill out the applications to be considered. Again, it is well worth your time and effort to explore the resources available to you. The U.S. Department of Education offers five main student-aid programs, some of which are grants which do not have to be paid back, others are loans which must be paid back with interest. These programs include Pell Grants, Supplemental Educational Opportunity Grants (SEOG), College Work–Study (CWS), 10-15 hrs/wk., minimum wage or higher, National Direct Student Loans (NDSL), and Guaranteed Student Loans (GSL)/Plus Loans. Undergraduates can receive money from all of these programs. Graduate students can receive money from the CWS, NDSL, and GSL programs.

In order to qualify for Federal student aid:

1. You must be attending school at least part-time (six credits).
2. You must be a U.S. citizen or permanent resident alien.
3. You must show financial need.
4. You must maintain a satisfactory academic record (which basically means that you can't flunk three out of the four classes you are taking; if you receive a grade of C, your financial aid will not be cut off).
5. You cannot be in default of a previous Federal student loan, or owe a refund on a Federal grant that you have been awarded.
6. You have signed a statement of registration compliance indicating that you have either registered with the Selective Service or that you are not required to register. You must also sign a "statement of education purpose" saying that you will only use the money for school or expenses related to school.

Be sure to check with the financial aid office at the school you attend or the schools you are planning to attend, as not all of these programs are offered at every school.

*Pell Grants:* provide help to undergraduate students and do not have to be paid back. The maximum award is $2,100 per year. The amount you receive is based on your financial need, on whether you are a full-time or part-time student, and on the cost of your tuition, food, housing, books, and supplies.

*Supplemental Educational Opportunity Grants:* like Pell grants, are available to undergraduate students to help pay for their college education. This money does not have to be repaid. You can receive a maximum of $2,000 a year depending on your financial need, the availability of SEOG funds at your school, and the amount of other financial aid you are receiving.

*College Work-Study:* under this program, the Federal government each year grants funds to colleges so that they can pay students who work for them. CWS provides jobs on campus for undergraduate, as well as graduate, students who have financial need. Your pay will be at least the current minimum wage. The number of hours you work is regulated by your school, taking into consideration how heavy a work load you can handle. You may be eligible for a CWS job even if you are a part-time student.

*National Direct Student Loan:* a National Direct Student Loan is a low-interest loan (five percent as of the writing of this book) to help defray the cost of your college education. There are loans for both undergraduate and graduate study. An undergraduate may borrow up to $6,000 and a graduate student up to $12,000 (this includes any money you may have borrowed from NDSL for undergraduate study). You are obligated to begin repaying this loan six months after you either graduate, withdraw from school, or take fewer than six credits. You can take up to 10 years to repay your loan. The amount of your payment depends on the amount you borrowed, but usually you must pay a minimum of $30 per month. If you become ill or are unemployed, your repayment period may be extended or deferred.

*Guaranteed Student Loan:* a Guaranteed Student Loan is a low-interest loan made by a lender such as a bank, a savings and loan association, or a credit union. The interest rate is eight percent. As an undergraduate, you can borrow up to $2,500 a year; as a graduate student, up to $5,000 a year. The maximum you may borrow as an undergraduate is $12,500; as a graduate student, you may borrow $25,000, including any GSL loans you may have taken out as an undergraduate. You cannot borrow more than the cost of your expenses (tuition, food, housing, books, and supplies) while you are attending school, minus any other financial aid you receive. If your income or your parents' income is above $30,000, you must show financial need. There is a "service charge" for borrowing under the GSL plan. You must pay a 5½ percent fee, which is deducted from your loan before you receive it. This is given to the Federal government to help reduce the government's costs of subsidizing this program. You must begin to repay your GSL six months after you leave school or drop below half-time status. The minimum monthly payment is $50. Repayment is usually over a five year period, but may be extended to up to ten years. Under similar conditions, as with the NDSL, you may defer your repayment.

*Auxiliary Loans to Assist Students* (ALAS): these are loans for undergraduate students who are financially independent of their parents, and loans for graduate students. An undergraduate may borrow up to $2,500 a year; as a graduate student, up to $3,000 a year. The maximum you may borrow as an undergraduate is $12,500; as a graduate student, you may borrow $15,000, including (for both undergraduate and graduate students) any money you borrowed under GSL. The annual interest rate is 12 percent; you make these interest payments while still in school. You must pay a ¼-percent fee, which is deducted from your loan before you receive it. You must begin to repay your ALAS six months after you either leave school or drop below half-time status. Repayment is usually over a five-year period, but may be extended to up to ten years. Under similar conditions, as with the GSL, you may defer your repayment.

*Parent Loans for Undergraduate Students:* PLUS loans are made by the same lenders as the GSL lenders, at the higher loan rate of 12 percent. Parents may borrow up to $3,000 per year up to a maximum of $15,000 for each child who is a dependent, an undergraduate student and who is enrolled at least part-time (six credits). Nondependent undergraduates may borrow up to $2,500 a year. However, undergraduates cannot borrow more than $2,500 a year on a PLUS loan and a GSL, or the total undergraduate limit of $12,500. Graduate students may borrow up to $3,000 per year, with a maximum of $15,000. This amount is separate from GSL limitations. Unlike GSL borrowers, you do not have to show financial need; however, you may have to undergo a credit analysis. A PLUS borrower must begin repayment within 60 days of taking out the loan. There are no deferments for parent borrowers; however, those deferments available to GSL borrowers, are also available to PLUS borrowers who are either independent undergraduate students or graduate students.

You will need a copy of your tax return from last year or your parents' tax return. If you have not completed your tax return, you may estimate the financial information on your return, but you will have to verify this information once your tax return is completed. Remember, Federal aid does not automatically continue from one year to another. You must reapply each year.

Your financial aid office at school should have the necessary forms. If it does not, or if, as a high-school student, you are unable to obtain these forms, call the Federal Student Aid

Information Center at (301)984-4070. They will be happy to answer any questions you might have about these programs.

## OTHER SOURCES OF MONEY

Although you have probably been told this many times, you really ought to check with the various organizations you belong to (Boy Scouts, fraternities, etc.), places of worship you attend, and employers you have worked for. Thousands of corporations have programs where they will pay for all or part of their employees' or children of employees' school expenses. Your hobbies or talents may qualify you for prizes or awards. Did you know that if you have a sense of humor you can qualify for the Laurel and Hardy comedy grant? If you are a veteran or the child of a veteran, don't work your way through college—you probably qualify for some scholarship money. The single largest scholarship for men and women is the one presented by the Army, the Navy, the Marine Corps, and the Air Force ROTC program. An ROTC Scholarship can be worth a total of $33,000 for four years. The GI bill was the historic beginning of Federal financial aid. Money for veterans and relatives of veterans is an inducement to keep America strong, a strategy to have a better-educated military, and a reward for serving one's country.

Many millions of dollars in athletic scholarships go unclaimed each year simply because no one applied for them or because the athletic departments couldn't find enough qualified applicants.

Before you reject this category because you are not a 250-pound left tackle or do not have the backhand of Chris Evert-Lloyd, consider the following:

Until the late 1970s, it was all too common for colleges to have multi-million-dollar training facilities for the football and basketball teams, while the women's volleyball team practiced on a muddy lot with a clothesline stretched between two poles. A law that took effect in 1978 decreed that schools must provide male and female athletes with "equal benefits and opportunities." That means separate—but equal—practice facilities, equipment, number of coaches, number of games *and* scholarship money.

In the late 1970s and early 1980s, the sports pages were filled with tales of academic abuses committed by outstanding athletes. There are now restrictions on how poorly the star quarterback can do academically before he is asked to leave school. One of the results of these scandals is the limit imposed by a school on how many scholarships can be awarded in the "major" sports (football, basketball, track and field, softball), with requirements that money be distributed among women athletes in these sports, as well as in archery, badminton, bowling, crew, frisbee (yes, there is a scholarship currently available at the State University of New York at Purchase, albeit just one), handball, synchronized swimming (this is a sport only available to women athletes; did Esther Williams stereotype us all?).

Schools are not restricted in how they spend their recruiting time and effort, only their scholarship money. Consequently, they will often devote a considerable amount of time and effort seeking out the best basketball and football players, but pay little or no attention to seeking out the best archery, bowling, or lacrosse athletes. If someone happens to turn up and ask for

## x•INTRODUCTION

scholarship money, fine. If not, the money goes back into the general fund. No big deal. Wide World of Sports hasn't yet paid a dime for the rights to collegiate riflery!

And finally, be sure to request information from your high-school guidance counselor and the financial aid office at each school you have applied to. They can explain what scholarships or other forms of aid the university offers.

## ONE FINAL NOTE

By the time this book is published, some of the information contained here will have changed. No reference book can be as up-to-date as the readers (or the authors) would like. Names, addresses, dollar amounts, telephone numbers, and other data are always in flux. Most of the information will not have changed. Good luck.

# ALABAMA

### Alabama Commission on Higher Education
One Court Square, Suite 221
Montgomery, AL 36197 (205)269-2700

**Restrictions:**
None

---

### Alabama GI and Dependents Educational Benefit Act
Alabama Department of Veterans Affairs
P.O. Box 1509
Montgomery, AL 36192 (205)261-5126

**$ Given:** Tuition for 18-36 months of study.
**Contact:** Department of Veterans Affairs.

**Restrictions:**
Must have parent who died in line of duty or who is MIA or died of disability incurred while serving. Parent must have had AL residency. Student must study in AL.

---

### Alabama Student Assistance Program—Student Incentive Grants
One Court Square, Suite 221
Montgomery, AL 36197 (205)269-2700

**$ Given:** 7,200 $300 (minimum) scholarships per academic year. Renewable maximum per award $1,500.
**Contact:** Participating Institute or above address.
**Deadline:** Application period January 1-November 1, no deadline.

**Restrictions:**
Resident of AL. Must attend participating institute in AL.

---

### Alabama Student Grant Program
One Court Square, Suite 221
Montgomery, AL 36197 (205)269-2700

**$ Given:** 6,000 $600 (max.) scholarships per academic year. Renewable.
**Contact:** Associate Director for Student Assistance, address above.
**Deadline:** Apply January 1—September 15; deadline January 15, February 15, April 15.

**Restrictions:**
No Theology or Religion majors. Resident of AL—must supply 5 documents proving residency. For attending eligible private, non-profit institutions in AL. At level of Community College.

## 2·FREE MONEY

| | | |
|---|---|---|
| **The American Legion**<br>Department Adjutant<br>P.O. Box 1069<br>Montgomery, AL 36102 | **$ Given:** 25 $200, 4-year scholarships.<br>**Deadline:** May 25. | **Restrictions:**<br>AL resident, descendant of veteran, financial need. |
| **E. L. Gibson Foundation**<br>201 South Edwards<br>Enterprise, AL 36330 | **$ Given:** 38 grants from $80-$500. | **Restrictions:**<br>Residents of Coffee County, AL for health-related study. |
| **James M. Hoffman Scholarship Trust**<br>First National Bank of Anniston<br>P.O. Box 1000<br>Anniston, AL 36202 (205)238-1000 | **$ Given:** 35 awards of $100-$500 per year. Renewable.<br>**Deadline:** June 1, September 1. | **Restrictions:**<br>Graduate of high school in Calhoun County, AL. |
| **Miss Elizabeth D. Leckie Scholarship Fund**<br>604 East Commerce Street<br>Greenville, AL 36037 (205)382-3411 | **$ Given:** 6 scholarships of $1,000. | **Restrictions:**<br>Butler County, AL residents. |
| **Scholarships for Children of Blind Parents**<br>c/o Division of Rehabilitation and Crippled Children<br>State Board of Education<br>P.O. Box 11586<br>Montgomery, AL 36111-0586<br>(205)281-8780 | **$ Given:** Tuition and fees at state supported institutions; 36 months maximum.<br>**Contact:** Carl Monroe | **Restrictions:**<br>Children of blind heads of households with family income less than $3,000. |
| **The William H. and Kate F. Stockham Foundation, Inc.**<br>c/o Stockham Valves & Fittings, Inc.<br>4000 North Tenth Avenue, P.O. Box 10326<br>Birmingham, AL 35202 (205)592-6361 | **$ Given:** 26 grants totaling $22,530.<br>**Contact:** Herbert Stockham, Chairman | **Restrictions:**<br>AL residents. |

# ALASKA

| | | |
|---|---|---|
| **Alaska Commission on Postsecondary Education**<br>400 Willoughby Avenue, Pouch FP<br>Juneau, AK 99801 (907)465-2962 | **Contact:** Margaret Swanson. | **Restrictions:**<br>None. |

**Goldstein Scottish Rite Trust**
P.O. Box 1194
Juneau, AK 99802 (907)586-1185

**$ Given:** 8 grants from $500-$2,000.
**Contact:** James Taylor
**Deadline:** April 1

**Restrictions:**
Needy graduates of Juneau Douglas High School.

---

**Kawabe Memorial Fund**
c/o Seattle First National Bank
Charitable Trust Administration
P.O. Box 3586
Seattle, WA 98124

**$ Given:** 2 grants totaling $4,000; each grant is $2,000.

**Restrictions:**
Residents of AK.

## ARIZONA

**Arizona Commission for Postsecondary Education**
2600 North Central
Phoenix, AZ 85004 (602)252-5793

**Restrictions:**
Loans only.

---

**Dougherty Foundation, Inc.**
3336 North 32 Street, Suite 11S
Phoenix, AZ 85018 (602)956-3980

**$ Given:** Grants total $233,650

**Restrictions:**
AZ residents.

---

**Erwin Fry Foundation**
P.O. Box 610
Sierra Vista, AZ 85636 (602)886-1263

**$ Given:** Varies
**Deadline:** February 15

**Restrictions:**
Residents of Cochise County

## ARKANSAS

**Arkansas Department of Higher Education**
Arkansas State Scholarships
1301 West 7 Street
Little Rock, AR 72201 (501)371-1441

**$ Given:** $100-$300 scholarships per academic year.
**Deadline:** June 24.

**Restrictions:**
AR residents; financial need.

---

**The Harvey and Bernice Jones Foundation**
c/o Jones Truck Lines, Inc.
P.O. Box 233
Springdale, AR 72765 (501)751-2730

**$ Given:** 27 grants totaling $8,075

**Restrictions:**
Given in AR, primarily students in Washington County; financial need.

## 4·FREE MONEY

**Lyon Foundation, Inc.**
65th & Scott Hamilton Drive
Little Rock, AR 72204

**$ Given:** Grants totaling $15,765
**Contact:**
Secretary-Treasurer
Lyon Foundation
P.O. Box 4408
Little Rock, AR 72204

**Restrictions:**
Given in AR.

---

**The Murphy Foundation**
Murphy Building
El Dorado, AR 71730 (501)862-6411

**$ Given:** 14 Grants totaling $28,300
**Contact:** Secretary

**Restrictions:**
Given in AR and LA.

---

**Potlach Foundation for Higher Education**
c/o George C. Cheek
P.O. Box 3591
San Francisco, CA 94119 (415)981-5980

**$ Given:** 180 grants totaling $127,050.
**Deadline:** February 1 for new applications; July 1 for scholarship renewals.

**Restrictions:**
Residents of areas of company operations—primarily AR, ID, MN.

---

**Trinity Foundation**
P.O. Box 7008
Pine Bluff, AR 71611 (501)534-7120

**$ Given:** 22 grants totaling $25,300.
**Contact:** Guidance office of high school.
**Deadline:** April 10 of senior year of high school.

**Restrictions:**
AR residents.

## CALIFORNIA

**Mary M. Aaron Memorial Trust-Scholarship Fund**
P.O. Box 241
Yuba City, CA 95992 (916)673-1836

**$ Given:** 63 grants of $300-$400. Total amount given $38,450.
**Contact:** W.D. Chipman
**Deadline:** March 15.

**Restrictions:**
CA students who attended CA schools.

---

**American Legion Auxiliary-California Auxiliary**
Nurses Scholarships
113 War Memorial Building
San Francisco, CA 94012

**$ Given:** $800.

**Restrictions:**
CA male veterans or wives, widows, children, grandchildren of veterans. CA residents for study in CA nursing schools.

# California · 5

**Avon Products Inc.**
**Scholarship Program**
2940 East Foothill Boulevard
Pasadena, CA 91121

**$ Given:** $2,000 maximum per year; renewable; 3 years
**Contact:** Personnel Manager
**Deadline:** November 1.

**Restrictions:** Resident of Pasadena Unified School District or Monrovia United School District for entire senior year. Top ⅓ of class. Financial need.

---

**Awards for Spanish Surnamed Californians**
**Youth Opportunities Foundation**
8820 Sepulveda Boulevard, Suite 208
Los Angeles, CA 90045 (213)670-7664

**$ Given:** Grants range from $100-$1,000.
**Deadline:** March 1.

**Restrictions:** CA high school seniors who have Spanish surnames.

---

**Bankamerica Foundation Achievement Awards**
P.O. Box 37000
San Francisco, CA 94137 (415)953-3175

**$ Given:** $2,000.
**Deadline:** February 24.

**Restrictions:** CA High school seniors with a GPA of 3.25; see high school counselor.

---

**W.P. Bartlett Trust Fund**
c/o Burford and Moran
141 East Mill Avenue
Porterville, CA 93257

**$ Given:** 21 grants totaling $19,000, average grant $1,000.
**Contact:** William B. Richardson, Secretary.
**Deadline:** February

**Restrictions:** Graduates of Porterville, CA high school district who will attend a CA institution.

---

**Arthur C. Boehmer & Florence Schubert Boehmer Scholarship Fund**
228 West Pine Street
Lodi, CA 95240 (209)369-2781

**$ Given:** 38 grants from $350-$1,200.
**Deadline:** June 15.

**Restrictions:** Students who graduated from school in Lodi Unified School District with preference given to study of medicine, for study at CA institutions.

---

**Borrego Springs Educational Scholarship Committee**
P.O. Box B
Borrego Springs, CA 92004 (619)767-5314

**$ Given:** 15 grants totaling $13,246.
**Contact:** A. A. Burnard, III, Chairman.

**Restrictions:** Borrego Springs high school graduates.

## 6·FREE MONEY

| | | |
|---|---|---|
| **California Department of Veterans Affairs**<br>Division of Veterans Services<br>P.O. Box 1559<br>Sacramento, CA 95807 (916)445-2334 | **$ Given:** 8,000 awards of $2,000 (maximum). Renewable.<br>**Contact:** Director.<br>**Deadline:** Prior to registration for school. | **Restrictions:**<br>Born in CA or 5 years residency. Wife, child or unremarried widow of veteran. Must attend full-time. |
| **California Farm Bureau Federation**<br>**CFB Scholarship Foundation**<br>1601 Exposition Boulevard<br>Sacramento, CA 95815 (916)924-4047 | **$ Given:** 17 awards of $500.<br>**Deadline:** March 1. | **Restrictions:**<br>CA residents meeting admission requirements of a four year college or university in CA. |
| **California Masonic Foundation**<br>1111 California Street<br>San Francisco, CA 94108 (415)776-7000 | **$ Given:** Grants averaging $500.<br>**Contact:** Larry C. Basker, President | **Restrictions:**<br>CA & HI undergraduates. |
| **California Student Aid Commission**<br>1410 Fifth Street<br>Sacramento, CA 95814 (916)322-2800 | **$ Given:** $100-$1,500 maximum, renewable to maximum of $6,000 in 6 year period. | **Restrictions:**<br>Must be child, natural or adopted, of peace or law enforcement officer who has died or is totally disabled or permanently impaired—the accident or injury must be compensable under CA law and have been incurred in line of duty. |
| **California Student Aid Commission**<br>1410 Fifth Street<br>Sacramento, CA 95814 (916)322-2503 | **$ Given:** 500 fellowships from $294-$5,830.<br>**Contact:** College Scholarship Service Box 70 Berkeley, CA 94701<br>**Deadline:** February 11 | **Restrictions:**<br>CA resident. Financial need. No teaching credentials or certificate programs. |
| **California Student Aid Commission**<br>**California State Graduate Fellowships**<br>1410 Fifth Street<br>Sacramento, CA 95814 (916)322-2803 | **$ Given:** Approximately 500 fellowships per year ranging from $288-$5,430.<br>**Contact:** Program supervisor, graduate fellowships.<br>**Deadline:** February 9. | **Restrictions:**<br>Graduate study in CA by residents of CA at schools accredited by California Student Aid Commission. |

# California·7

| | | |
|---|---|---|
| **California Teachers Association (CTA)**<br>1705 Murchison Drive<br>Burlingame, CA 94010 (415)697-1400 | **$ Given:** Ten $1,000 Scholarships. Renewable.<br>**Contact:** Manager, Human Rights Dept., above address.<br>**Deadline:** February 15. | **Restrictions:** High school graduate, above average GPA; member or dependent of member of CTA. |
| **California Teachers Association**<br>**California Teachers Association Scholarships**<br>1705 Murchison Drive<br>Burlingame, CA 94010 (415)697-1400 | **$ Given:** 10 awards of $1,000.<br>**Contact:** Manager, human rights department.<br>**Deadline:** February 15. | **Restrictions:** Member or dependent of member of CTA. |
| **California Student Aid Commission**<br>**Bilingual Teacher Grants**<br>1410 Fifth Street<br>Sacramento, CA 95814 (916)323-4720 | **$ Given:** 1,000 awards of $300-$3,600.<br>**Deadline:** February 1. | **Restrictions:** CA undergraduates and graduates with secondary language competence. |
| **California Student Aid Commission**<br>**Cal Grant "A" Program**<br>1410 Fifth Street<br>Sacramento, CA 95814 (916)322-2290 | **$ Given:** Total of 16,400 grants: 3,740 of $4,600 for independent colleges; 972 of $300 at University of California; $291 average at California State Universities and Colleges.<br>**Contact:** College Scholarship Service, Box 70, Berkeley, CA 94701<br>**Deadline:** February 9. | **Restrictions:** Resident of CA—financial need and academic ability. Must attend approved CA school. |
| **California Student Aid Commission**<br>**Cal Grant "B"**<br>1410 Fifth Street<br>Sacramento, CA 95814 (916)322-2800 | **$ Given:** 7,500 grants; freshmen: non-tuition cost of living expenses, books, supplies, and transportation. Sophomores, juniors, seniors: cost of tuition, living allowance to $1,210. Tuition: $291 at State colleges to $3,520 at independent, $972 at University of California.<br>**Contact:** College Scholarship Service Box 70 Berkeley, CA 94701<br>**Deadline:** February 11. | **Restrictions:** Residents of CA who could not attend college without financial assistance. Must not have completed more than one semester. |

# 8·FREE MONEY

**California Student Aid Commission**
**Cal Grant "C" Program**
1410 Fifth Street
Sacramento, CA 95814 (916)322-5606

**$ Given:** 1,337 awards of $500-$2,000.
**Deadline:** February 1.

**Restrictions:**
CA nursing students.

---

**Vikki Carr Scholarship Foundation**
Box 5126
Beverly Hills, CA 90210

**$ Given:** $200-$1,500
**Contact:** above address
**Deadline:** March 31

**Restrictions:**
17-22 years of age
Mexican-Americans;
Residents of CA.

---

**Collins Pine Co.**
**Almanor Scholarship Fund**
P.O. Box 796
Chester, CA 96020 (916)258-2111

**$ Given:** $1,200.
**Deadline:** September 1.

**Restrictions:**
Chester high school graduates.

---

**Community Foundation for Monterey County**
420 Pacific Street
Monterey, CA 93940 (408)375-9712

**$ Given:** 2 grants totaling $2,000.
**Deadline:** March 30, June 30, September 30, December 31.

**Restrictions:**
Given in Monterey County, CA

---

**The Corti Family Agricultural Fund**
c/o Bank of America N.T. & S.A. Trust Dept.
1011 Van Ness Ave., P.O. Box 1672
Fresno, CA 93721 (805)395-0880

**$ Given:** 136 grants totaling $73,363.
**Contact:** Kern County Supt. of Schools Theresa Corti Scholarship Committee 5801 Sundale Ave., Bakersfield, CA 93309

**Restrictions:**
Kern County, CA high school graduates studying agriculture.

---

**Vincent A. Davi Memorial**
1155 Pine Street
Pittsburg, CA 94565 (415)439-8400

**$ Given:** 4 grants totaling $4,400.
**Contact:** Horace A. Enea.

**Restrictions:**
Students of Pittsburgh CA Unified School District only.

---

**Delta Kappa Gamma**
**Epsilon Pi Chapter Scholarship**
1566 I Street
Arcata, CA 95521 (707)822-0540

**$ Given:** $250.
**Contact:** Maureen Jahannsen.
**Deadline:** May 1.

**Restrictions:**
Residents of Humbolt or Del Norte CA counties or attending Humbolt University or Redwood College.

# California·9

| | | |
|---|---|---|
| **Delta Kappa Gamma**<br>**Chi State Graduate Study Awards**<br>808 University Avenue<br>Sacramento, CA 98525-6725 (916)922-5911 | **$ Given:** 5 Scholarships given. Not renewable.<br>**Deadline:** January 5 | **Restrictions:** Graduate study by women who have been members in good standing of Delta Kappa Gamma in CA for 2 years prior to January 5 of year of application. |
| **The Ebell of L.A. Scholarship**<br>743 South Lucerne Boulevard<br>Los Angeles, CA 90005 (213)931-1277 | **$ Given:** 55 grants totaling $107,000, each grant $175/month for a 10-month school year.<br>**Deadline:** Applications accepted year-round. | **Restrictions:** Sophomores, juniors or seniors attending school in Los Angeles County and residents of L.A. County. Must be unmarried, young, and in financial need. |
| **Fed Mart Foundation**<br>P.O. Box 81667<br>San Diego, CA 92138 (714)282-0690 | **$ Given:** 146 grants of $300.<br>**Contact:** High School in January.<br>**Deadline:** March 15. | **Restrictions:** San Diego CA high school graduate with GPA of 3.5. |
| **Fieldcrest Foundation**<br>c/o Fieldcrest Mills<br>326 Stadium Road<br>Eden, NC 27288 | **$ Given:** Grants totaling $33,000. | **Restrictions:** NC, CA, GA, IL, NJ, VA residents. |
| **Golden Gate Restaurant Association**<br>**David Rubinstein Memorial Scholarship Foundation Awards**<br>291 Geary Street, Suite 600<br>San Francisco, CA 94102 (415)781-5348 | **Contact:** Guy Leonard.<br>**Deadline:** April. | **Restrictions:** Northern CA high school students planning to enroll in hotel or restaurant related courses. |
| **Graham-Fancher Scholarship Trust**<br>1211 Pacific Avenue, Suite 6<br>Santa Cruz, CA 95060 (408)423-3640 | **$ Given:** 20 $50-$1,500. Renewable.<br>**Contact:** Trustee, above address.<br>**Deadline:** Apply April 15-May 15. | **Restrictions:** Resident of Northern Santa Cruz County, CA; graduating from high school in same area. |

## 10·FREE MONEY

**Leon L. Granoff Foundation**
P.O. Box 2148
Gardena, CA 90247 (213)321-2810

**$ Given:** 14 grants ranging from $721-$10,269.

**Restrictions:**
CA high school students. See high school counselor.

---

**George Grotefend Scholarship Fund**
1644 Magnolia Avenue
Redding, CA 96001 (916)244-4600

**$ Given:** 250 grants totaling $70,000, ranging from $100-$400.
**Contact:** Dean M. Dennett.
**Deadline:** May 1.

**Restrictions:**
Undergraduate and graduate students who received their entire high school education in Shasta County, CA.

---

**James B. Grubb Oakland Scottish Rite Scholarship Foundation**
1547 Lakeside Drive
Oakland, CA 94612 (415)451-1906

**$ Given:** 29 grants ranging from $450-$1,800.
**Contact:** Oliver Rothi.

**Restrictions:**
CA college graduates.

---

**A. B. Guslander Masonic Lodge Scholarship Fund**
P.O. Box 67
Willits, CA 95490

**$ Given:** 5 grants of $1,200 each.
**Contact:** Orval R. Archer, Bank of Willits, 145 South Main St., Willits, CA 95490.
**Deadline:** May 20.

**Restrictions:**
Willits High School CA graduates in junior or senior year of college, or graduate school.

---

**Ina & Ray Harris Fund**
110 West Eighth, Suite 1700
San Diego, CA 92101

**$ Given:** Grants ranging from $500-$2,500.
**Contact:** William Yale, Trustee.

**Restrictions:**
San Diego, CA residents attending a CA non-profit school; financial need.

---

**Helms Foundation, Inc.**
P.O. Box 312
Redwood Valley, CA 95470 (707)485-7997

**$ Given:** $325,901.
**Contact:** W. D. Manuel, Assistant Secretary.

**Restrictions:**
Residents of southern CA.

---

**Fannie & John Hertz Foundation**
P.O. Box 2230
Livermore, CA 94550-0130 (415)449-0855

**$ Given:** 120 grants totaling $1,585,419.
**Deadline:** November 1.

**Restrictions:**
Fellowships in applied physical sciences. Scholarships for high school grads in S.F. Bay area, U.S. citizens only.

# California·11

**Thomas and Jennie Hiebler Memorial Scholarship Fund Trust**
c/o California First Bank
P.O. Box 109
San Diego, CA 92112 (714)294-4686

**Contact:** High School Scholarship Committee-Mancos or Montrose.

**Restrictions:** Graduates from Mancos H.S. District or Montrose H.S. District in Colorado who are attending colleges or universities in the state of CA.

---

**Italian Catholic Federation, Inc.**
1801 Van Ness Ave. Suite 330
San Francisco, CA 94109 (415)673-8240

**$ Given:** 100 scholarships of $250.

**Restrictions:** CA graduating seniors of Italian ancestry and Catholic faith.

---

**Japan Studies Scholarship Foundation Scholarship Award**
1737 Post Street #4/5
San Francisco, CA 94115 (415)921-7221

**$ Given:** 4 awards of $500 and 5 awards of $100.
**Contact:** Ms. Hisako Takahahi.
**Deadline:** May 15.

**Restrictions:** Students living north of Fresno and San Luis Obispo, CA.

---

**Japanese American Citizens League (JACL)**
1765 Sutter Street
San Francisco, CA 94115 (415)921-5225

**$ Given:** $350-$5,000 per year.
**Contact:** National Youth Director at above address. Send self-addressed stamped envelope for information.
**Deadline:** October 1 to July 31.

**Restrictions:** CA residents of Japanese ancestry or member of JACL.

---

**Ruth Jenkins Scholarship Fund**
c/o Bank of America Trust Department
P.O. Box 1947
La Jolla, CA 92037 (619)230-5871

**$ Given:** 3 grants totaling $4,600 (high $3,600, low $500).
**Contact:** D. Towne, Trust Administrator
**Deadline:** May 31.

**Restrictions:** Black student residents of San Diego, CA.

---

**Jessie Klicka Foundation**
c/o Bank of America, N.T. & S.A.
P.O. Box 1631
San Diego, CA 92112

**$ Given:** Grants ranging from $750-$2,500, average grant $2,000.
**Contact:** Thelma M. Dewar, Secretary, 3550 3rd Ave., Suite 2A, San Diego, CA 92103.
**Deadline:** April 15.

**Restrictions:** Graduates of San Diego, CA city and county high schools.

## 12•FREE MONEY

**Achille Levy Foundation**
c/o Bank of Achille Levy
P.O. Box 5190
Ventura, CA 93003-9956 (805)656-6035

**$ Given:** 15 grants totaling $15,000.
**Contact:** Robert L. Mobley, Vice Chairman.

**Restrictions:** Residents of Ventura County, CA.

---

**Mabelle McLeod Lewis Memorial Fund**
P.O. Box 3730
Stanford, CA 94305

**$ Given:** 11 grants totaling $95,200; high $10,000, low $3,000.
**Contact:** Phyllis Stephens, Executive Secretary.
**Deadline:** January 15.

**Restrictions:** Advanced doctoral students studying literature, history, philosophy, art, languages, at northern CA institutions.

---

**Luso-American Education Foundation**
P.O. Box 1768
Oakland, CA 94604 (415)452-4465

**$ Given:** Scholarship to study in Portugal.

**Restrictions:** CA Portuguese language students.

---

**Marin Educational Foundation**
**Marin Educational Grant**
1010 B Street, Suite 300 (Albert Building)
San Rafael, CA 94901 (415)459-4240

**$ Given:** $200-$2,000.
**Deadline:** April 1.

**Restrictions:** Residents of Marin County, CA.

---

**Mexican-American Business & Professional Scholarship Association Scholarship Program**
P.O. Box 22292
Los Angeles, CA 90022 (213)265-8764

**$ Given:** $100-$1,000.
**Contact:** Roberto Zuniga.
**Deadline:** May.

**Restrictions:** Mexican-American undergraduate students from Los Angeles County.

---

**Norton Simon Inc.**
**Foundation For Education**
11 West Colorado Boulevard
Pasadena, CA 91105 (213)449-6840

**Deadline:** January 15.

**Restrictions:** CA residents.

---

**Oakland Scottish Rite Scholarship Foundation**
1547 Lakeside Drive
Oakland, CA 94612 (415)451-1906

**$ Given:** Grants averaging $1,200.
**Deadline:** March 31.

**Restrictions:** Northern CA high school graduates.

## California · 13

**Pacific Gas and Electric Company**
215 Market Street, Room 1300
San Francisco, CA 94106 (415)972-1338

**$ Given:** Thirteen $1,000 awards per year. Renewable to 4 years. Four $1,000 runner-up awards, not renewable.
**Deadline:** October 31.

**Restrictions:**
High school senior in good standing who resides or attends school in PG & E CA territory. Interviews necessary.

---

**Esper A. Petersen Foundation**
c/o Bertha Matthews
4241 Kirk Street
Skokie, IL 60076 (312)677-0049

**$ Given:** Grants totaling $25,349.
**Deadline:** January 1.

**Restrictions:**
CA, IL residents.

---

**Ramona's Mexican Food Products Scholarship Foundation**
13633 South Western Avenue
Gardena, CA 90249

**$ Given:** 2 grants ranging from $600-$2,300.

**Restrictions:**
Hispanic CA residents.

---

**San Mateo County Farm Scholarship Bureau**
765 Main Street
Half Moon Bay, CA 94019 (415)726-4485

**Contact:** Betty Stone.
**Deadline:** April 1.

**Restrictions:**
Members or dependents of San Mateo CA Farm Bureau.

---

**Santa Barbara Foundation**
15 East Carrillo Street
Santa Barbara, CA 93101 (805)963-1873

**Contact:** Edward R. Spaulding, Executive Director.
**Deadline:** February 18.

**Restrictions:**
Loans for residents of Santa Barbara, CA.

---

**Bay District Joint Council of the Service Employees International Union Charles Hardy Memorial Scholarship Awards**
240 Golden Gate Avenue
San Francisco, CA 94102 (415)885-5479

**$ Given:** $750, renewable. 3 scholarships of $750 per year for four years.

**Restrictions:**
Students with a "B" average in high school or college freshmen whose parents have been members in good standing with any local union affiliated with the California State Council of Service Employees for at least one year prior to application.

## 14·FREE MONEY

**Anna and Charles Stockwitz Fund for Education of Jewish Children**
c/o Crocker National Bank
111 Sutter Street, 11th Floor
San Francisco, CA 94104

**$ Given:** 39 grants totaling $27,408, ranging from $400-$750.

**Restrictions:**
Jewish residents of the San Francisco Bay area, graduates from area high schools.

---

**Swiss Relief Society of San Francisco**
235 Montgomery, Suite 1035
San Francisco, CA 94104 (415)641-8528

**Deadline:** May 15.

**Restrictions:**
Swiss nationals or descendents living within a 150 mile radius of San Francisco City for 4 years prior to application.

---

**Perry S. and Stella H. Tracy Scholarship Fund**
c/o The Bank of America, Trust Department
900 8th Street
Sacramento, CA 95814 (916)622-3634

**$ Given:** 123 grants, totaling $49,830, ranging from $350-$700.
**Contact:** Bart Tamblyn, Paula Sanderson, El Dorado High School, 561 Canal St., Placerville, CA 95667
**Deadline:** April 30.

**Restrictions:**
Graduates of Eldorado County CA high schools.

---

**Grace Vehmeyer Trust**
c/o Wells Fargo National Bank,
Trust Tax Division
P.O. Box 38002
San Francisco, CA 94138 (415)396-4970

**$ Given:** 45 scholarships, ranging from $500-$5,000.

**Restrictions:**
CA residents.

---

**Charles A. Winans Memorial Trust**
c/o Trust Department
P.O. Box 1359
Carlsbad, NM 88220

**$ Given:** 8 grants totaling $4,000, ranging from $400-$800.
**Contact:** Student Counseling Office-Beaumont H.S.
**Deadline:** January 15.

**Restrictions:**
Beaumont CA high school graduates.

---

**Edna Yelland Memorial Scholarship Fund**
California Library Association
717 K Street, Suite 300
Sacramento, CA 95814 (916)447-8541

**$ Given:** 1-2 grants of generally $2,500.
**Deadline:** April.

**Restrictions:**
Ethnic students accepted to graduate library school in CA.

# COLORADO

**Boettcher Foundation**
800 Boston Building
828 Seventeenth St., Suite 800
Denver, CO 80202

**$ Given:** Total amount given $1,227,080.
**Contact:** John C. Mitchell II, President.

**Restrictions:**
CO residents attending CO colleges. (Must have been CO resident for at least two years prior to graduation.)

---

**Lucille R. Brown Foundation, Inc.**
2301 Ridge Drive
Bloomfield, CO 80020 (303)773-7594

**$ Given:** 5 grants totaling $22,644, average grant $1,000-$3,000.
**Contact:** Carol Ashley, Secretary.

**Restrictions:**
CO residents.

---

**The Colorado Masons Benevolent Fund Association**
306 Masonic Temple Building
1614 Welton Street
Denver, CO 80202

**$ Given:** Grants totaling $397,610.
**Contact:** Scholarship Correspondent, P.O. Box 7729, Colorado Springs, CO 80904.
**Deadline:** February 15.

**Restrictions:**
Residents attending CO schools.

---

**Colorado Commission on Higher Education**
1550 Lincoln Street
Denver, CO 80203 (303)866-2723

**$ Given:** Unspecified number of full tuition scholarships & grants to $1,500.
**Contact:** Financial Aid Officer at Institution of choice.

**Restrictions:**
Enrolled in eligible program at public institution, resident; financial need.

---

**Colorado Commission on Higher Education**
**Colorado Veterans Tuition Assistance Program**
1300 Broadway, Second Floor
Denver, CO 80203 (303)866-2723

**$ Given:** Full tuition.
**Contact:** Mary Leisring.

**Restrictions:**
CO residents enrolled in CO institutions who served in the military between August 5, 1964 and May 12, 1975 and who were CO residents at time of induction.

## 16•FREE MONEY

| | | |
|---|---|---|
| **Colorado Commission on Higher Education**<br>**Colorado Graduate Fellowship Program**<br>1550 Lincoln Street<br>Denver, CO 80203 (303)866-2723 | **$ Given:** Unspecified number of $4,000 (max.) fellowships plus tuition per year.<br>**Contact:** Financial aid officer at institution of choice. | **Restrictions:**<br>Graduate students attending CO institutions. |
| **Colorado Commission on Higher Education**<br>1550 Lincoln Street<br>Denver, CO 80203 (303)866-2723 | **$ Given:** Unspecified number of full tuition scholarships and grants to $1,500.<br>**Contact:** Financial aid officer at institution of choice. | **Restrictions:**<br>Enrolled in eligible program at public institution, resident, financial need. |
| **Viola Vestal Coulter Foundation, Inc.**<br>c/o United Bank of Denver<br>P.O. Box 5247<br>Denver, CO 80274 | **$ Given:** 21 grants totaling $33,750; high $5,000, low $1,250.<br>**Contact:** Charles H. Meyers, Trust Officer. | **Restrictions:**<br>CO, ID, WA students. |
| **Thomas and Jennie Hiebler Memorial Scholarship Fund Trust**<br>c/o California First Bank<br>P.O. Box 109<br>San Diego, CA 92112 (714)294-4686 | **Contact:** High School Scholarship Committee-Mancos or Montrose. | **Restrictions:**<br>Graduates from Mancos H.S. District or Montrose H.S. District in CO who are attending colleges or universities in the state of CA. |
| **The Piton Foundation**<br>511 16th St., Suite 700<br>Denver, CO 80202 (303)825-6246 | **$ Given:** 54 grants totaling $79,992. | **Restrictions:**<br>Given in CO, primarily the Denver area. |
| **Sachs Foundation**<br>418 First National Bank Building<br>Colorado Springs, CO 80903 (303)633-2353 | **$ Given:** Grants average $1,200-$3,000.<br>**Deadline:** March 15. | **Restrictions:**<br>Black undergraduate and graduate CO students. |

**The Thatcher Foundation**
P.O. Box 1401
Pueblo, CO 81002

**$ Given:** 46 grants totaling $33,360
**Deadline:** Prior to beginning of school year.

**Restrictions:**
Resident of Pueblo County for attendance at CO institution.

---

**Von Trotha Educational Trust**
c/o United Bank of Greeley
P.O. Box 1057
Greeley, CO 80631 (303)356-1000, ext. 204

**$ Given:** 14 grants of $300.
**Contact:** Natalie Kanuh
**Deadline:** April 1.

**Restrictions:**
Graduating seniors from Weld County and Wiggins high school, Wiggins County, CO.

---

**Cora W. Wood Scholarship Fund**
c/o First National Bank Trust Department
P.O. Box 1699
Colorado Springs, CO 80942 (303)471-5131

**$ Given:** 5 grants totaling $8,000, each grant $1,600.
**Contact:** Trustees.
**Deadline:** April 30.

**Restrictions:**
Graduating high school seniors in Pike's Peak region who will attend state supported schools.

# CONNECTICUT

**The Balso Foundation**
c/o The Ball & Socket Manufacturing Company
493 West Main Street
Cheshire, CT 06410 (203)272-5381

**$ Given:** Grants totaling $13,000, ranging from $500-$1,500.
**Contact:** Neil J. Longobard, South Main Street, Cheshire, CT 06410.
**Deadline:** April 10.

**Restrictions:**
Cheshire, CT and surrounding area high school students and college undergraduates.

---

**William H. Chapman Foundation**
c/o William W. Miner
P.O. Box 1321
New London, CT 06320

**Contact:** Caroline K. Driscoll, Secretary to Awards Committee.
**Deadline:** April 1.

**Restrictions:**
Residents of New London County, CT.

---

**Connecticut Board of Higher Education**
**Connecticut Aid to Dependents of Deceased/Disabled Veterans**
61 Woodland Street
Hartford, CT 06105 (203)566-2618

**$ Given:** Unspecified number of $400 (max) grants per academic year.
**Contact:** Above address, Hartford, CT 06101.

**Restrictions:**
Ages 16-23. Children of veterans who were residents of CT at time of induction, must show need.

## 18 • FREE MONEY

**Connecticut Board of Higher Education Connecticut Scholastic Achievement Grants**
61 Woodland Street
Hartford, CT 06105 (203)566-2618

**$ Given:** Awards ranging from $100-$1,000. Renewable for three successive years.
**Deadline:** February 1.

**Restrictions:**
High school senior or graduate in top 15% of class who has not yet attended college.

---

**Connecticut Board of Higher Education Grants for Connecticut Students in Private Colleges and Universities**
61 Woodland Street
Hartford, CT 06105 (203)566-2618

**Contact:** Financial aid officer at private institution.

**Restrictions:**
CT residents.

---

**Connecticut State Supplemental Grant Program**
61 Woodland Street
Hartford, CT 06105 (203)566-2618

**$ Given:** Unspecified number of $1,500 grants per year. Renewable.
**Contact:** Financial Aid Office at college or university.

**Restrictions:**
Residents enrolled in CT college or university at least as ½ time student. Submit FAF or FFS to show financial need.

---

**Maud Glover Folsom Foundation, Inc.**
P.O. Box 151
Harwinton, CT 06791 (203)485-0405

**$ Given:** 52 grants at $2,000.

**Restrictions:**
CT males ages 14-20 of English and German descent on both sides whose ancestors came to North America prior to the American Revolution.

---

**Jacob L. and Lewis Fox Foundation Trust**
c/o Connecticut National Bank and Trust Co.
777 Main Street
Hartford, CT 06115 (203)728-2316

**$ Given:** 107 grants totaling $84,623.
**Contact:** Guidance counselors at Hartford public schools.

**Restrictions:**
Hartford, CT, public school graduates.

---

**The Horbach Fund**
c/o National Community Bank of New Jersey
113 West Essex Street
Maywood, NJ 07607

**$ Given:** 5 grants totaling $4,500; high $1,000, low $500.
**Contact:** 40 Glen Road, Mountain Lakes, NJ 07041.

**Restrictions:**
CT, MA, NJ, NY, RI gifted students under the age of 20; financial need.

# Connecticut·19

**ITT Rayonier Foundation**
1177 Summer Street
Stamford, CT 06904 (203)348-7000

**$ Given:** 47 awards totaling $62,300.
**Contact:** Jerome O. Gregoire, VI
**Deadline:** November 30.

**Restrictions:** Stamford, CT residents.

---

**Elisha Leavenworth Foundation**
35 Park Place
Waterbury, CT 06702 (203)758-1042

**$ Given:** 10 grants totaling $7,500.
**Contact:** Mrs. E. Donald Rogers, Three Mile Hill, Middlebury, CT 06762.
**Deadline:** June.

**Restrictions:** Female college residents of Waterbury, CT.

---

**The MacCurdy-Salisbury Educational Foundation, Inc.**
Old Lyme, CT 06371 (203)434-7983

**$ Given:** 98 grants totaling $92,050
**Contact:** Secretary-Treasurer
**Deadline:** April 30 for 1st semester, November 15 for 2nd semester.

**Restrictions:** Residents of Lyme & Old Lyme.

---

**John B. McLean Scholarship Fund**
Simsbury Bank & Trust
740 Hopmeadow Street
Simsbury, CT 06070 (203)658-7641

**$ Given:** 12 awards of $780.

**Restrictions:** Simsbury, CT residents.

---

**William T. Morris Foundation, Inc.**
P.O. Box 5786
New York, NY 10017 (212)986-8036

**$ Given:** 4 grants totaling $8,000.
**Contact:** Arthur C. Laske, President.

**Restrictions:** NY, CT residents.

---

**James Z. Naurison Scholarship Fund**
c/o New England-West
P.O. Box 9006
Springfield, MA 01102-9006 (413)787-8745

**$ Given:** 573 grants totaling $349,600.
**Contact:** Phyllis M. Farrell, Administrator.
**Deadline:** May 1.

**Restrictions:** Students from Hampden, Hampshire, Franklin, Berkshire counties, MA; and Enfield, Suffield counties, CT.

---

**Record Journal Foundation**
11 Crown Street
Meriden, CT 06450 (203)235-1661

**$ Given:** 16 awards of $500-$1,000.
**Contact:** Mr. Eliot White.

**Restrictions:** Residents within Meridian Record circulation area.

## 20·FREE MONEY

**Sassp Scholarship Fund**
c/o Home Bank & Trust Company
P.O. Box 912, 400 E. Main Street
Meriden, CT 06450 (203)237-8411

**$ Given:** $400-$900.

**Restrictions:**
Meriden, CT residents.

---

**The Vera H. & William R. Todd Foundation**
c/o Connecticut National Bank
777 Main Street
Bridgeport, CT 06115 (203)579-3534

**$ Given:** 14 grants totaling $9,350, ranging from $350-$750.
**Contact:** Sandra Porr.
**Deadline:** March 15.

**Restrictions:**
Derby-Sheldon CT school system high school graduates.

---

**Vitramon Foundations, Inc.**
P.O. Box 544
Bridgeport, CT 06601 (203)268-6261

**$ Given:** 17 grants totaling $6,575 (high $1,250, low $50).
**Contact:** Patricia A. Dake, Vice-Chairman.

**Restrictions:**
Students from Newton, Monroe, Trumbull, Shelton, Easton-Redding, CT.

---

**The Westport-Weston Foundation**
P.O. Box 5177
Westport, CT 06881 (203)227-1201

**Restrictions:**
Residents of Westport and Weston, CT. Financial need.

## DELAWARE

**Avon Products Foundation, Inc.**
9 West Fifty-seventh Street
New York, NY 10019 (212)546-6729

**$ Given:** $3,000 max. per year. Renewable for 3 years.
**Deadline:** November 2.
**Contact:** Personnel Manager.

**Restrictions:**
Attended Newark School District in DE; since junior year. Top ⅓ of class.

---

**Delaware Postsecondary Education Commission**
820 North French Street
Wilmington, DE 19801 (302)571-3240

**$ Given:** 850 scholarships of $200-$1,000.
**Deadline:** April 30.

**Restrictions:**
Residents attending schools outside DE; financial need.

---

**Delaware Postsecondary Scholarship Fund**
820 North French Street
Wilmington, DE 19801 (302)571-3240

**$ Given:** 850 grants of $200-$1,000.
**Deadline:** April 30.

**Restrictions:**
DE students of architecture, dentistry, law, medicine, social work, veterinary medicine.

# Florida•21

**John B. Lynch Scholarship Foundation**
P.O. Box 4248
Wilmington, DE 19807-0248 (302)654-3444

**$ Given:** 294 grants totaling $151,983.
**Deadline:** March 15.

**Restrictions:**
DE residents, undergraduate only.

---

**The Pickard Scholarship**
Del-Mar-Va Council
Eighth & Washington Streets
Wilmington, DE 19801 (302)652-3741

**Restrictions:**
Members of Explorer and Boy Scouts' Councils of DE, MD, VA.

---

**Joseph P. Pyle Trust/Will**
c/o Bank of Delaware
300 Delaware Avenue
Wilmington, DE 19899 (302)429-1460

**Contact:** James Morris.

**Restrictions:**
DE residents.

---

**Sico Foundation**
15 Mount Joy Street
Mount Joy, PA 17552 (717)653-1411

**$ Given:** 90 awards of $1,000-$4,000.
**Contact:** High School guidance counselor.
**Deadline:** February 15.

**Restrictions:**
DE, MD, PA students who attend designated schools; financial need.

# FLORIDA

**The Children's Foundation of Lake Wales, Florida, Inc.**
c/o Albert E. McCormick
11705 Yarnell Avenue
Lake Wales, FL 33853

**$ Given:** 14 grants totaling $5,400, ranging from $300-$400.
**Contact:** David Rockness, Chairman.
**Deadline:** May 15.

**Restrictions:**
Residents of Lake Wales, FL.

---

**Leroy E. Dettman Foundation, Inc.**
108 Southeast Eighth Avenue
Fort Lauderdale, FL 33301 (305)525-6102

**$ Given:** 48 grants totaling $93,500.

**Restrictions:**
FL residents.

---

**Alfred I. Dupont Foundation**
803 Edward Ball Building
P.O. Box 1380
Jacksonville, FL 32201 (904)356-8311

**$ Given:** 214 grants totaling $329,280.

**Restrictions:**
Given primarily in the Southeast.

## 22·FREE MONEY

**Florida Scholarships for Children of Deceased or Disabled Veterans**
Knott Building
Tallahassee, FL 32304 (904)488-4347

**$ Given:** Unspecified.

**Restrictions:**
FL resident for 5 years between the ages of 16-22. Enrolled in FL institution. Parent must be deceased or disabled veteran or official POW or MIA.

---

**Florida Student Financial Assistance Commission**
**Confederate Memorial Scholarships**
Knott Building
Tallahassee, FL 32304 (904)488-4347

**$ Given:** Unspecified number of $150 grants. Renewable.
**Deadline:** March 1.
**Contact:** Administrator at above address.

**Restrictions:**
Citizen of U.S., resident of FL. Must be lineal descendant of Confederate soldier or sailor. (Lineage must be certified by a chapter of United Daughters of the Confederacy.) Must enroll full-time in Florida public community college or university.

---

**Florida Student Finance Assistance Commission**
**Florida Seminole-Miccosukee Indian Scholarship Program**
Knott Building
Tallahassee, FL 32304 (904)488-4347

**$ Given:** 8 awards of $600, 4 to men, 4 to women. Renewable to $2,400.
**Contact:** Administrator.
**Deadline:** March 1.

**Restrictions:**
Members of Seminole or Miccosukee Indian tribes who are residents of FL, citizen of U.S.; financial need.

---

**Florida Student Finance Assistance Commission**
**Florida Student Assistance Grants**
Knott Building
Tallahassee, FL 32304 (904)488-4347

**$ Given:** 3,600 awards of $200-$1,200. Renewable.
**Contact:** Administrator.
**Deadline:** April 30.

**Restrictions:**
Students who have been residents of FL for at least 24 months immediately prior to beginning of academic year for which application is made and have enrolled in or been accepted by eligible FL institutions.

---

**Gore Family Memorial Foundation Trust**
501 East Las Olas Boulevard
Fort Lauderdale, FL 33302

**$ Given:** 106 grants totaling $139,485.

**Restrictions:**
Given in FL, particularly Broward County.

| | | |
|---|---|---|
| **Rinker Companies Foundation, Inc.**<br>1501 Belvedere Road<br>West Palm Beach, FL 33406 (305)833-5555 | **$ Given:** 47 grants totaling $82,273.<br>**Deadline:** May, November. | **Restrictions:**<br>FL residents with business or construction industry related majors |
| **The Southwest Florida Community Foundation, Inc.**<br>Drawer LL<br>Fort Myers, FL 33902 (813)936-1645, 232-3315 | **$ Given:** Various grants.<br>**Deadline:** February 1; May 1. | **Restrictions:**<br>Residents of Southwest FL. |
| **Ethel H. & George W. Tweed Scholarship Endowment Trust**<br>c/o First Florida Bank, N.A.<br>7500 Gulf Boulevard<br>St. Petersburg, FL 33706 (813)367-2786 | **$ Given:** 5 Grants totaling $5,000, ranging from $750-$1,125.<br>**Contact:** Robert L. Baker, Vice-President.<br>**Deadline:** April 30. | **Restrictions:**<br>High school seniors located within the corporate confines of St. Petersburg, FL. |
| **Winter Park Community Trust Fund**<br>c/o Barnett Bank Trust Company<br>P.O. Box 1000<br>Winter Park, FL 32790 (305)646-3290 | **$ Given:** 16 grants totaling $22,160.<br>**Contact:** Mrs. Kelly Pflug, 1430 Alabama Drive Winter Park, FL 32789. | **Restrictions:**<br>Given in Central FL area. |

# GEORGIA

| | | |
|---|---|---|
| **Avon Products, Inc.**<br>2200 Cotillion Drive<br>Atlanta, GA 30338 | **$ Given:** $3,000 per year. Renewable for 3 years.<br>**Deadline:** November 1.<br>**Contact:** Manager, Human Resources. | **Restrictions:**<br>Attended school in Dekalb County, GA since junior year. Top 1/3 of class. High school completed by August 31 prior to fall term. Financial need. |
| **Clark and Ruby Baker Foundation**<br>c/o Bank South, Financial Services Division<br>P.O. Box 4956<br>Atlanta, GA 30302 (404)529-4625, 27 | **$ Given:** 10 grants totaling $18,000.<br>**Contact:** Secretary, above address. | **Restrictions:**<br>Given in GA. |

## 24•FREE MONEY

**Callaway (Fuller E.) Foundation**
209 Broome Street
La Grange, GA 30240 (404)884-7348

**$ Given:** 10 awards of $2,100 (max.) per year. Renewable to $8,400.
**Contact:** Fuller E. Callaway Foundation Hatton Lovejoy Scholarship Plan Committee P.O. Box 790 La Grange, GA 30240
**Deadline:** February 15.

**Restrictions:** Resident of Troup County, GA for 2 years. Top 25% of class. Must maintain standing in upper ½ of college class.

---

**Cape Foundation, Inc.**
550 Pharr Road, N.E. Suite 605
Atlanta, GA 30305

**$ Given:** 11 grants totaling $18,434, ranging from $270-$3,700, average of $1,800.

**Restrictions:** Undergraduate students attending Atlanta area institutions.

---

**Ty Cobb Educational Foundation**
P.O. Box 725
Forest Park, GA 30051 (404)588-8449

**$ Given:** Various awards.
**Deadline:** May 1.

**Restrictions:** College sophomores with "B" average, residents of GA.

---

**Ty Cobb Educational Foundation**
P.O. Box 725
Forest Park, GA 30051 (404)588-8449

**$ Given:** 318 grants totaling $176,994.
**Deadline:** May 31.

**Restrictions:** GA residents who have completed one year in institute of higher learning. Graduate scholarship for law, medical & dental students.

---

**Fieldcrest Foundation**
c/o Fieldcrest Cannon, Inc.
326 Stadium Road
Eden, NC 27288 (919)627-3000

**$ Given:** Grants totaling $33,000.

**Restrictions:** Children of employees of Fieldcrest Cannon, Inc.

---

**Georgia Student Finance Authority**
**Georgia Law Enforcement Personnel Dependents Grant**
2187 Northlake Parkway
Tucker, GA 30084 (404)393-7253

**$ Given:** Unspecified number of $2,000 grants. Renewable to maximum of $8,000 over a four year period.
**Deadline:** August 1 or 30 days prior to beginning of school term.

**Restrictions:** Citizen of U.S., Resident of GA. Child of GA Law Enforcement officers, firemen or prison guards killed or disabled in line of duty. Must stay in GA while receiving funds.

# Georgia·25

**Georgia Student Finance Authority**
**Georgia Student Incentive Grant**
2187 Northlake Parkway,
9 LaVista Perimeter Park, Suite 1110
Tucker, GA 30084 (404)393-7253

**$ Given:** Unspecified number of $150-$450 grants per year. Renewable.
**Deadline:** June 1.
**Contact:** Georgia Student Finance Authority
9 La Vista Perimeter Park, Suite 1110
2187 Northlake Parkway
Tucker, GA 30084

**Restrictions:**
Citizen of U.S. & Resident of GA for 12 months prior to registration in full-time GA institution. Must show financial need.

---

**Georgia-Pacific Foundation, Inc.**
133 Peachtree Street, Northeast
Atlanta, GA 30303 (404)521-5228

**$ Given:** Grants totaling $535,714.

**Restrictions:**
Residents in areas of company operations.

---

**Private College Tuition Equalization Grant**
2187 Northlake Parkway
Tucker, GA 30084 (404)393-7253

**$ Given:** Unspecified number of grants $600/per year.
**Deadline:** Beginning of school term.
**Contact:** Financial Aid Officer at Institution of Choice.

**Restrictions:**
Citizen of U.S., resident of GA 12 months prior to registration. Full-time student in GA institution. No degrees in theology, divinity or religious education.

---

**The Daniel Ashley & Irene Houston Jewell Memorial Foundation**
c/o American National Bank and Trust Company
P.O. Box 1638
Chattanooga, TN 37401 (615)757-3204

**$ Given:** 4 grants totaling $4,000.
**Contact:** Peter T. Cooper, Trust Officer.

**Restrictions:**
TN, GA residents.

---

**Sapelo Island Research Foundation Inc.**
1425 21st Street N.W.
Washington, DC 20036 (202)822-9193

**$ Given:** Various grants.
**Deadline:** March 15; September 15.

**Restrictions:**
Residents of GA.

---

**Harold & Sara Wetherbee Foundation**
c/o First State Bank & Trust Company
P.O. Box 8
Albany, GA 31702

**$ Given:** $500-$1,000 (11 grants totaling $10,000).
**Deadline:** April 15.

**Restrictions:**
Residents of Dougherty County, GA.

# HAWAII

**California Masonic Foundation**
1111 California Street
San Francisco, CA 94108

**$ Given:** Grants averaging $400.

**Restrictions:**
Undergraduates of CA & HI.

---

**Fukunaga Scholarship Foundation**
900 Fort Street Mall, Suite 500
Honolulu, HI 96813 (808)521-6511

**$ Given:** 27 grants totaling $13,100; average grant is $500
**Contact:** George J. Fukunaga, Trustee.
**Deadline:** March 15.

**Restrictions:**
HI business students who are attending the University of HI or any other university in the West.

---

**Hawaii Postsecondary Education Commission**
University of Hawaii, Bachman Hall 209
2444 Dole Street
Honolulu, HI 96822 (808)948-8213

**Contact:** Carl Makino.

**Restrictions:**
None.

---

**The Hawaiian Foundation**
111 South King Street
P.O. Box 3170
Honolulu, HI 96802 (808)525-8548

**$ Given:** 75 grants totaling $28,686.
**Deadline:** First day of December, March, June, September.

**Restrictions:**
Given in HI.

---

**Hawaiian Trust Company Limited Marion Maccarrell Scott Scholarship**
Financial Plaza of the Pacific
P.O. Box 3170
Honolulu, HI 96802 (808)525-8511

**$ Given:** Unspecified.
**Deadline:** March 1.

**Restrictions:**
Must be graduate of HI public high school. Must plan to attend college or university on Mainland and major in field of study that contributes to promotion of international understanding, cooperation & world peace. Demonstrate financial need.

---

**Hawaiian Veterans Memorial Fund**
Hawaiian Trust Company, Ltd.
P.O. Box 3170
Honolulu, HI 96802 (808)525-8511

**Deadline:** March 1.

**Restrictions:**
HI high school graduates attending HI institutions; financial need.

# Hawaii·27

| | | |
|---|---|---|
| **Health & Community Services Council of Hawaii**<br>200 North Vineyard Boulevard, Room 602<br>Honolulu, HI 96817 (808)521-3861 | **$ Given:** $2,000.<br>**Deadline:** February 1. | **Restrictions:**<br>HI residents; financial need; send self-addressed stamped envelope. |
| **Kaiulani Home for Girls Trust**<br>Hawaiian Trust Company<br>Financial Plaza of the Pacific<br>P.O. Box 3170<br>Honolulu, HI 96802 (808)525-8511 | **$ Given:** Unspecified.<br>**Deadline:** March 1. | **Restrictions:**<br>Female students attending Hawaiian institutions. Resident; financial need. |
| **Kaiulani Scholarship Fund**<br>Hawaiian Trust Company, Ltd.<br>P.O. Box 3170<br>Honolulu, HI 96802 (808)525-8511 | **Deadline:** March 1. | **Restrictions:**<br>Female HI residents; financial need. |
| **The Kamehameha Schools**<br>**Na Hookama A Pauahi Scholarship Program**<br>Department of Financial Aid<br>Kapalama Heights, Honolulu, HI 96817<br>(808)842-8216 | **$ Given:** $100-$1,000.<br>**Contact:** Dexter K. Soares, Coordinator or Herman H. Libarios, Counselor. | **Restrictions:**<br>HI residents who graduated from HI high schools; financial need. |
| **Ida M. Pope Memorial Scholarship Fund**<br>c/o Hawaiian Trust Company, Ltd<br>P.O. Box 3170<br>Honolulu, HI 96802 (808)842-8612 | **$ Given:** 29 grants totaling $17,300. Grants ranging from $400-$800.<br>**Contact:** Mrs. G. Johnson c/o The Kamehameha Schools Counseling Office, Kapalama Heights, Honolulu, HI 96817<br>**Deadline:** May 1. | **Restrictions:**<br>HI females who are of Hawaiian or past Hawaiian descent attending colleges and universities preferably in HI. Undergraduate and graduate scholarships. |
| **John M. Ross Foundation**<br>c/o Bishop Trust Company Ltd.<br>Box 2390<br>Honolulu, HI 96804 (808)935-3737 | **$ Given:** 77 grants of $12,150 (high $250, low $150). | **Restrictions:**<br>HI residents of the Big Island. |

**Gertrude S. Straub Trust Estate**
c/o Hawaiian Trust Company, Ltd.
P.O. Box 3170
Honolulu, HI 96802 (808)525-8511

**$ Given:** 156 grants totaling $138,925.
**Deadline:** March 1.

**Restrictions:** Given in HI.

---

**Vi Bohnett Memorial Foundation**
315 Uluniu Street, Room 208A
P.O. Box 1361
Kailua, HI 96734

**$ Given:** 35 grants totaling $68,250.

**Restrictions:** HI residents.

## IDAHO

**Viola Vestal Coulter Foundation, Inc.**
c/o United Bank of Denver
P.O. Box 5247
Denver, CO 80274

**$ Given:** 21 grants totaling $33,750, ranging from $1,250-$5,000.
**Contact:** Charles H. Meyers, Trust Officer.

**Restrictions:** CO, ID, WA students. Undergraduate & graduate awards.

---

**Idaho State Board of Education**
Len B. Jordan Building, Room 307
650 West State Street
Boise, ID 83720 (208)334-2270

**$ Given:** 25 awards of $1,500. Renewable.
**Deadline:** Apply October 1-December 31.
**Contact:** Scholarship officer at above address.

**Restrictions:** Graduate of ID high school; must attend Idaho institution.

---

**Potach Foundation for Higher Education**
c/o George C. Cheek
P.O. Box 3591
San Francisco, CA 94119 (415)981-5980

**$ Given:** 180 grants totaling $127,050.
**Deadline:** February 1 for new applications. July 1 for scholarship renewals.

**Restrictions:** AR, ID, MN students. Awards mainly in areas of company operations.

---

**A. P. & Louise Rouch Boys Foundation**
c/o Twin Falls Bank & Trust Company
P.O. Box 7
Twin Falls, ID 83301

**$ Given:** 18 grants totaling $4,154, ranging from $90-$470.

**Restrictions:** Students attending college in the Magic Valley area of ID; financial need.

# ILLINOIS

**The Clara Abbott Foundation**
14 Street and Sheridan Road
North Chicago, IL 60064 (312)937-3840

**$ Given:** 1,108 grants totaling $922,808.
**Contact:** c/o Abbott Laboratories, D-579, AP 68, North Chicago, IL 60064
**Deadline:** March 15.

**Restrictions:**
IL residents.

---

**G.J. Aigner Foundation, Inc.**
5617 Dempster Street
Morton Grove, IL 60053 (312)966-5782

**Restrictions:**
Dependents of employees of Aigner, Inc.

---

**Aileen Andrew Foundation**
10500 West 153rd Street
Orland Park, IL 60462 (312)349-3300

**$ Given:** 82 grants totaling $183,570.

**Restrictions:**
Residents of Orland Park; children of Andrew Corp. Employees & graduates of local high school.

---

**The Aurora Foundation**
32 Water Street Mall
P.O. Box 1247
Aurora, IL 60507 (312)897-4284

**$ Given:** Grants totaling $441,930.

**Restrictions:**
Aurora, IL area residents.

---

**Joseph Blazek Foundation**
8 South Michigan Avenue
Chicago, IL 60603 (312)372-3880

**$ Given:** 52 grants of $500.
**Deadline:** February 1 of high school senior year.
**Contact:** Samuel S. Brown.

**Restrictions:**
Cook County, IL high school senior students planning to major in engineering, math, chemistry, physics, or related scientific fields.

---

**Boynton Gillespie Memorial Funds**
Heritage Federal Building
Sparta, IL 62286

**$ Given:** 59 grants totaling $50,325.

**Restrictions:**
Sparta, IL residents.

## 30·FREE MONEY

**The William, Agnes, & Elizabeth Burgess Memorial Scholarship Fund**
c/o First National Bank
1515 Charleston
Mattoon, IL 61938 (217)234-7454

**$ Given:** Grants to $41,400.
**Contact:** Senior Trust Officer.
**Deadline:** March 15.

**Restrictions:**
Mattoon County, IL high school graduates.

---

**Chicago & North Western Transportation Co.**
One North Western Center
Chicago, IL 60606 (312)559-6700

**$ Given:** Two $1,000 awards. Not renewable.
**Deadline:** July 1 of preceding academic year.
**Contact:** Chicago Cook County 4-H Foundation Scholarship Committee
36 So. Wabash, Suite 1402
Chicago, IL 60606

**Restrictions:**
Member or former member of 4-H, living in Cook County, IL. Must have completed at least 1 semester at college. Show record of 4-H accomplishments and scholastic achievements. Financial need.

---

**Du Page Medical Society Foundation**
800 Roosevelt Road, Glen Hill North Bldg.,
Suite 300
Glen Ellyn, IL 60137

**$ Given:** 15 grants, average grant $1,000.
**Contact:** Mrs. Lillian S. Widmer.
**Deadline:** April 20.

**Restrictions:**
Medical and nursing students of Dupage County, IL. Financial need.

---

**Educational Communications Scholarship Foundation**
721 McKinley
Lake Forest, IL 60045 (312)295-6650

**$ Given:** Awards of $1,000.
**Deadline:** June 1.
**Contact:** High School Counselor or the foundation.

**Restrictions:**
High school seniors who plan undergraduate study. Awards based on merit.

---

**Fieldcrest Foundation**
c/o Fieldcrest Mills
324 Stadium Road
Eden, NC 27288

**$ Given:** Grants totaling $33,000.

**Restrictions:**
NC, CA, GA, IL, NJ, NY, VA residents.

---

**Furnas Foundation, Inc.**
1000 McKee Street
Batavia, IL 60510

**$ Given:** 54 grants totaling $45,153.
**Deadline:** March 1.

**Restrictions:**
Given in Batavia, IL & Clarke County, IA.

| | | |
|---|---|---|
| **Illinois Congress of Parents and Teachers**<br>**Lillian E. Glover, IL PTA Scholarship Program**<br>901 South Spring Street<br>Springfield, IL 62704 (217)528-9617 | **$ Given:** $200-$600.<br>**Deadline:** March 1. | **Restrictions:**<br>IL high school students. |
| **Illinois Department of the American Legion Scholarships**<br>P.O. Box 2910<br>Bloomington, IL 61701 (309)663-0361 | **$ Given:** 20 - $500 awards per year.<br>**Deadline:** March 15.<br>**Contact:** Department Adjutant at above address. | **Restrictions:**<br>Child of member of Illinois American Legion. |
| **Illinois Department of the American Legion Scouting Scholarship**<br>P.O. Box 2910<br>Bloomington, IL 61701 (309)663-0361 | **$ Given:** $500. (One per year.)<br>**Contact:** Legion Scout Chairman at above address. | **Restrictions:**<br>IL residents. Scout or Explorer. Must submit 500 word essay on Legion's "Americanism" and scouting program. |
| **Illinois Department of Veterans Affairs**<br>208 W. Cook Street<br>P.O. Box 5054<br>Springfield, IL 62705 (217)782-3564 | **$ Given:** Unspecified number of awards covering full tuition for 4 years at Illinois Institution.<br>**Deadline:** 2 months from end of term for which reimbursement is requested.<br>**Contact:** Financial aid office at Institute of your choice. | **Restrictions:**<br>Child or spouse of deceased or disabled veteran, POW or MIA who was resident of IL for 6 months prior to entering service. |
| **Illinois State Academy of Science**<br>Illinois State Museum<br>Springfield, IL 62701 | **$ Given:** Cash grants to $100 for research supplies.<br>**Deadline:** February 1, May 1, August 1, November 1.<br>**Contact:** Dr. Carol B. Aybell, Science Dept. St. Louis Community College at Florissant Valley 3400 Pershall Rd. St. Louis, Missouri 63135 | **Restrictions:**<br>IL high school student, college freshman or sophomores for writing scientific proposal & conducting research. Must be sponsored by a signing instructor. |

## 32·FREE MONEY

**Illinois Prisoners of War-Missing in Action Dependents Educational Benefits**
106 Wilmot Road
Deerfield, IL 60015 (312)948-8500

**$ Given:** Unspecified number of $1,550 awards per year.

**Restrictions:**
Spouse or dependent child of IL resident-POW, MIA, killed or 90% disabled since January 1, 1960.

---

**Illinois State Scholarship Commission Illinois National Guard Scholarships**
106 Wilmot Road
Deerfield, IL 60015 (312)948-8500

**$ Given:** Full tuition, 4 years at Illinois institution.
**Deadline:** October 1; March 15; July 1.
**Contact:** Above address or Financial Aid Office at Institution.

**Restrictions:**
Current member of IL Army Nat'l Guard, have served at least 1 yr.

---

**Illinois State Scholarship Commission Monetary Award Program**
106 Wilmot Road
Deerfield, IL 60015 (312)948-8500

**$ Given:** Unspecified number of $1,800 awards per year. Renewable.
**Deadline:** October 1.

**Restrictions:**
IL residents. New or continuing students with financial need.

---

**Illinois State Scholarship Commission Benefits for Survivors of Policemen and Firemen**
106 Wilmot Road
Deerfield, IL 60015 (312)948-8500

**$ Given:** Unspecified number of $1,650 awards per year. Ten semesters of full-time study.

**Restrictions:**
IL residents. Children, aged 25 and under of policemen and firemen killed in line of duty.

---

**Illinois State Scholarship Commission Scholarships for Survivors or Dependents of Correctional Workers**
106 Wilmot Road
Deerfield, IL 60015 (312)948-8500

**$ Given:** Unspecified number of $1,650 awards per year.

**Restrictions:**
IL residents. Dependents of employee of IL Department of Corrections killed in line of duty, or 90% disabled; must have been responsible for inmates after January 1, 1960.

---

**The George E. Johnson Foundation**
8522 South Lafayette Ave.
Chicago, IL 60620 (312)483-4100

**$ Given:** 123 grants from $350-$600.
**Deadline:** August 31.

**Restrictions:**
Preferably freshmen minority IL students of engineering, chemistry, physics, math, medicine, law, dentistry.

# Illinois·33

**John G. Koehler Fund**
103 North Main Street
Pontiac, IL 61764 (815)635-3134

**$ Given:** 50 grants totaling $53,330.
**Deadline:** June 1.
**Contact:** Stephen Herr, Citizens Bank Building, Chatsworth, IL.

**Restrictions:** Graduates of Chatsworth High School, Chatsworth, IL.

---

**Marcus & Theresa Levie Educational Fund**
c/o Jewish Federation of Metropolitan Chicago
1 South Franklin Street
Chicago, IL 60606 (312)346-6700

**$ Given:** $5,000 awards.
**Contact:** Scholarship Secretary.
**Deadline:** Mid-February.

**Restrictions:** Jewish Residents of Cook County, IL; financial need.

---

**McFarland Charitable Foundation**
c/o Havana National Bank
112 South Orange Street
Havana, IL 62644

**$ Given:** 30 grants totaling $124,737.
**Contact:** Kathey Tarvin, Director of Nursing Service, Macon District Hospital, 520 E. Franklin Street, Havana, IL 62644 (309)543-4431
**Deadline:** May 1.

**Restrictions:** Nursing students from Central IL.

---

**Ella G. McKee Foundation**
c/o First National Bank
First National Bank Building
Vandalia, IL 62471 (618)283-1141

**$ Given:** 56 grants totaling $66,825, ranging from $600-$1,600.

**Restrictions:** Residents of Fagette County, IL.

---

**Edward Arthur Mellinger Educational Foundation, Inc.**
1025 East Broadway
P.O. Box 278
Monmouth, IL 61462 (309)734-2419

**$ Given:** 947 grants totaling $264,813.
**Deadline:** June 1.

**Restrictions:** Students must reside or attend college in Midwest.

---

**Nesbitt Medical Student Foundation**
c/o National Bank & Trust Co. of Sycamore
230 West State Street
Sycamore, IL 60178 (815)895-2125

**$ Given:** 8 grants totaling $16,000, ranging from $1,000-$3,000.
**Contact:** James M. Kirby, Assistant Vice-President.
**Deadline:** April 1.

**Restrictions:** Preferably female medical students from DeKalb County, IL.

## 34•FREE MONEY

**Peoria Journal Star
Scholarship Program**
1 News Plaza
Peoria, IL 61643 (309)686-3027

**$ Given:** $1,000-$4,000.
**Deadline:** May 1.

**Restrictions:**
High school senior living in Journal Star area.

---

**Esper A. Petersen Foundation**
c/o Bertha Matthews
4241 Kirk Street
Skokie, IL 60076 (312)677-0049

**$ Given:** Grants totaling $25,349.
**Deadline:** January 1.

**Restrictions:**
IL, CA residents.

---

**George M. Pullman Educational Foundation**
5020 South Lake Shore Drive
Chicago, IL 60615 (312)363-6191

**$ Given:** 629 grants totaling $477,603.
**Contact:** Executive Director.

**Restrictions:**
Residents of Cook County, IL or child or grandchild of graduates of the Pullman Free School of Manual Training.

---

**Anita H. Richard Trust**
115 North 4 Street
Savanna, IL 61074 (815)273-2028

**$ Given:** One $1,000 Scholarship per year. Renewable.
**Deadline:** Spring of year scholarship is offered.
**Contact:** Manager at above address.

**Restrictions:**
Carrol County graduating seniors; financial need. Recommended by school personnel.

---

**Jacob Stump, Jr. & Clara Stump Memorial Scholarship Fund**
c/o Central National Bank of Mattoon
Broadway & Charleston at 14th Street
Mattoon, IL 61938 (217)234-6434

**$ Given:** Grants totaling $143,265.
**Deadline:** April 1.
**Contact:** Trust Officer.

**Restrictions:**
High school graduates from Coles, Cumberland, Douglas, Moultrie City who will attend college in IL (state-supported schools).

---

**The Swiss Benevolent Society of Chicago**
P.O. Box 2137
Chicago, IL 60690

**$ Given:** 34 awards, average of $750.
**Deadline:** March 31.

**Restrictions:**
Persons living within 150 miles of Chicago who are of Swiss descent.

---

**Tallman Foundation**
City National Bank Trust Department
189 East Court Street
Kankakee, IL 60901

**$ Given:** $58,000.

**Restrictions:**
Protestant boys under 21 who are residents of Kankakee County, IL.

# INDIANA

**Fred A. Bryan Collegiate Students Fund**
National Bank
112 West Jefferson Boulevard
South Bend, IN 44601 (219)237-3316

**$ Given:** One $1,000 award per year. Renewable 4 years.
**Deadline:** March 31.
**Contact:** Trustee of the Fred A. Bryan Collegiate Students Fund.

**Restrictions:**
Must be scout and student from So. Bend, IN. FAF forms.

---

**Olive B. Cole Foundation, Inc.**
3242 Mallard Cove Lane
Fort Wayne, IN 46804 (219)436-2182

**$ Given:** Grants totaling $118,018.
**Contact:** Executive Vice-President.

**Restrictions:**
Residents of the Kendallville, Noble County, IN area.

---

**The Cultural Society, Inc.**
P.O. Box 27459
Indianapolis, IN 46227

**$ Given:** 4 grants, ranging from $4,500-$6,000.
**Contact:** T. Al Suwaidan, 10242 East 34th St., Tulsa, OK 74146.

**Restrictions:**
IN Muslim students.

---

**Eisenhower Memorial Scholarship Foundation**
539 South Walnut Street
Bloomington, IN 47401 (812)332-2257

**$ Given:** Undergraduate: unspecified number of $2,500 awards per year; Graduate: unspecified number of $3,000 awards per year.

**Restrictions:**
Undergraduate: outstanding student of an Indiana high school. Must have open and inquiring mind, firm belief in Divine Being, patriotic awareness and firm belief and willingness to defend free enterprise system and American way of life. Graduate: must have already demonstrated the above & show potential of soon providing intellectual guidance & leadership.

---

**Peter G. Flinn Estate**
c/o Bank One
Marion, IN 46952 (317)662-6611

**$ Given:** 21 grants totaling $15,360, ranging from $500-$1,000.

**Restrictions:**
Grant County, IN high school seniors.

## 36 • FREE MONEY

**Habig Foundation, Inc.**
1549 Royal Street
Jasper, IN 47546 (812)482-8268

**$ Given:** 32 grants totaling $45,000.

**Restrictions:**
Children of employees.

---

**George M. Hillenbrand Scholarship Gift Fund**
c/o First Bank and Trust Company
Batesville, IN 47006 (812)934-2808

**$ Given:** 2 scholarships.

**Restrictions:**
Graduating seniors of Batesville High School, Batesville, IN.

---

**Indiana State Student Assistance Commission**
Second Floor, EDP Building
219 North Senate Avenue
Indianapolis, IN 46202 (317)633-5445

**$ Given:** Unspecified number of $100-$1,400 awards. Renewable.
**Deadline:** December 1-March 1.
**Contact:** Executive Secretary at above address.

**Restrictions:**
U.S. citizen by September 1 of year of application, 6 month resident of Indiana prior to enrollment, age 24 or less. Must show financial need and have no felony convictions.

---

**E.H. Kilbourne Residuary Charitable Trust**
c/o Lincoln National Bank Trust Department
116 East Berry Street
Fort Wayne, IN 46802 (219)423-6419

**$ Given:** Grants totaling $131,078.
**Deadline:** April 15.
**Contact:** Trust Officer.

**Restrictions:**
Residents of Allen County.

---

**Lincoln National Life Foundation, Inc.**
P.O. Box 1110, 1300 South Clinton Street
Fort Wayne, IN 46801 (219)427-3172

**Contact:** Dorothy Rapp.

**Restrictions:**
Fort Wayne, IN minority students.

---

**Edward Arthur Mellinger Educational Foundation, Inc.**
1025 East Broadway
P.O. Box 278
Monmouth, IL 61462 (309)734-2419

**$ Given:** 947 grants totaling $264,813; average grant $450.
**Deadline:** June 1.
**Contact:** Shirley J. Neill, Administrative Assistant.

**Restrictions:**
Students must reside or attend college in the Midwest.

---

**Meredith Corporation**
**Edwin T. Meredith Foundation 4-H Scholarship**
1767 Locust Street
Des Moines, IA 50336 (515)284-2545

**Contact:** State 4-H leader.

**Restrictions:**
IL, IN, IA, KS, MI, MO, MN, NE, NY, ND, OH, OK, PA, SD, WI residents, present or former 4-H Club members.

# Indiana·37

**Miles Laboratories Foundation**
1127 Myrtle Street, P.O. Box 40
Elkhart, IN 46514 (219)264-8225

**$ Given:** 8 grants totaling $2,400.
**Contact:** Lehman F. Beardsley, Chairman.

**Restrictions:** Students attending the Goshen College School of Nursing in Goshen, IN or high school students from Illinois or Indiana.

---

**Ruth M. Minear Educational Trust**
c/o First National Bank in Wabash
202 S. Wabash Street
Wabash, IN 46992 (219)563-1116

**$ Given:** Grants totaling $114,200.
**Deadline:** Mid-February.
**Contact:** Vice-President.

**Restrictions:** Graduates of Wabash High School attending school in IN.

---

**James Moorman Orphans Home**
c/o James M. Mock
526 West North Street
Winchester, IN 47394

**$ Given:** 4 grants totaling $4,100; average grant $1,200.
**Contact:** James M. Mock.

**Restrictions:** Randolph County IN residents.

---

**Murphy College Fund**
c/o First National Bank of Warsaw Trust Department
P.O. Box 1447
Warsaw, IN 46580

**$ Given:** 11 grants from $350-$750.
**Deadline:** April 15.

**Restrictions:** Kosciusko County, IN students of music, medicine, computer science, theology, education, nursing, language, engineering.

---

**Niccum Educational Trust Foundation**
c/o Midwest Commerce Banking Company
P.O. Box 27
Goshen, IN 46526 (219)533-2175

**$ Given:** 5 grants totaling $5,000; average grant $1,000.
**Contact:** James A. McClellan, Jr., Vice-President.
**Deadline:** March 1.

**Restrictions:** Graduates of public schools in Goshen, IN area.

---

**George and Marie G. Spencer Educational Foundation and Trust**
c/o Citizens National Bank
102 North Main Street
Tipton, IN 46072 (317)675-7431 or 963-2560

**$ Given:** 50 grants totaling $50,000; each grant $1,000.
**Deadline:** September 1.
**Contact:** Tipton Community High School, Tipton, IN 46072 or Tri-Central High School, R.R. #2, Sharpsville, IN 46068.

**Restrictions:** Residents of Tipton County, IN.

## 38•FREE MONEY

| | | |
|---|---|---|
| State Student Assistance Commission<br>Freedom of Choice Grant<br>964 North Pennsylvania<br>Indianapolis, IN 46204 (317)232-2350 | **$ Given:** $100-$1,450.<br>**Deadline:** March 1. | **Restrictions:**<br>IN residents studying at private institutions. |
| State Student Assistance Commission of Indiana<br>Hoosier Scholarships and Higher Education Awards<br>964 North Pennsylvania<br>Indianapolis, IN 46204 (317)232-2350 | **$ Given:** Grants of $150-$500, plus one $500 Hoosier Award.<br>**Deadline:** March 1. | **Restrictions:**<br>IN high school graduates attending an eligible IN institution; financial need. |

## IOWA

| | | |
|---|---|---|
| Easter Seal Society<br>Scholarship Program<br>P.O. Box 4002<br>Des Moines, IA 50333 (515)289-1933 | **$ Given:** 10 awards of $350-$500.<br>**Deadline:** April 15. | **Restrictions:**<br>IA resident in financial need. Sophomore through graduate studies; above average scholarship; minimum load of 14 credit hours each term. |
| Easter Seal Society of Iowa Inc.<br>Scholarships and Awards/El Peterson Memorial Scholarship<br>P.O. Box 4002<br>Des Moines, IA 50333 (515)289-1933 | **$ Given:** $350-$500.<br>**Deadline:** April 15. | **Restrictions:**<br>IA sophomore pre-med students and graduate medical students for study in rehabilitation related fields. |
| Easter Seal Society of Iowa, Inc.<br>James L. and Lovon Mallory Annual Disability Scholarship<br>P.O. Box 4002<br>Des Moines, IA 50333 (515)289-1933 | **$ Given:** 1 scholarship of $1,000.<br>**Deadline:** April 15. | **Restrictions:**<br>IA residents who have a permanent disability; financial need; above average academic record. |
| Fahrney Education Foundation<br>c/o Union Bank, Trust Department<br>123 East Third Street<br>Ottumwa, IA 52501 (515)683-1641 | **$ Given:** 78 grants totaling $101,874.<br>**Deadline:** February 15. | **Restrictions:**<br>Residents of Wapello County. |

# Iowa·39

**Forestner Scholarship Foundation**
P.O. Box 101
Amana, IA 52203 (319)622-5511

**$ Given:** $2,000 average.

**Restrictions:**
Children of Amana employees.

---

**Furnas Foundation, Inc.**
1000 McKee Street
Batavia, IL 60510

**$ Given:** 54 grants totaling $45,153.
**Deadline:** March 1.

**Restrictions:**
Given in Batavia, IL and Clarke County, IA.

---

**William L. & Ethel Gund Memorial Fund**
Cherokee State Bank
Cherokee, IA 51012 (712)225-5131

**Restrictions:**
Marcus Community School high school seniors.

---

**Mary Catherine Hagedorn Trust**
c/o Thomas L. McCullough
701 West Main Street
Sac City, IA 50583 (712)662-4721

**$ Given:** $1,350-$1,500.

**Restrictions:**
IA high school students.

---

**Lee A. & Mabel H. Horn Educational Trust**
Seventh & Walnut Streets
Des Moines, IA 50309 (515)245-3222

**Contact:** Des Moines National Bank, Trust Department
666 Walnut Street, Des Moines, IA 50309.

**Restrictions:**
Students of Ida Grove high school.

---

**Iowa College Aid Commission**
201 Jewett Building
Ninth and Grand
Des Moines, IA 50309 (515)281-3501

**$ Given:** More than 10,140-$2,250 grants; 1,270-$600 scholarships.
**Contact:** Director, Student Aid Program at above address or Guidance Counselor.
**Deadline:** January 1-March 1.

**Restrictions:**
IA residents planning to attend private IA institutions; financial need.

---

**Iowa Department of Veterans Affairs**
State Capital
Des Moines, IA 50319 (515)278-9331

**$ Given:** Unspecified number of $400 awards per year. Renewable.

**Restrictions:**
Iowa resident 2 years prior to application, child of parent deceased in military service. Must attend IA institution approved by IA Department of Veteran Affairs.

## 40·FREE MONEY

**The Maytag Company Foundation, Inc.**
c/o Maytag Company, Inc.
403 West Fourth Street, North
Newton, IA 50208 (515)792-7000

**$ Given:** 175 grants totaling $125,331.

**Restrictions:** Newton, IA high school graduates, as well as children of company employees.

---

**Edward Arthur Mellinger Educational Foundation, Inc.**
1025 East Broadway
P.O. Box 278
Monmouth, IL 61462 (309)734-2419

**$ Given:** 947 grants totaling $264,813; average grant $450.
**Contact:** Shirley J. Neill, Administrative Assistant.
**Deadline:** June 1.

**Restrictions:** Students must reside or attend college in the Midwest.

---

**Meredith Corporation**
**Edwin Meredith Foundation 4-H Scholarship**
1716 Locust Street
Des Moines, IA 50336 (515)274-2545

**Contact:** State 4-H leader.

**Restrictions:** Present or former 4-H club member residing in IL, IN, IA, KN, MI, MN, MO, NE, NY, ND, OH, OK, PA, SD, or WI.

---

**NIACC Foundation**
William F. Muse Scholarship Fund
500 College Drive
Mason City, IA 50401 (515)421-4399

**Contact:** Dr. David L. Buettner, Chairperson, Nominating Committee.
**Deadline:** March 2.

**Restrictions:** Mason City graduates and undergraduates and Cerro Gordo County, IA residents; financial need.

---

**Elmer O. & Ida Preston Educational Trust**
11 Floor Des Moines Building
Des Moines, IA 50307 (515)243-4191

**$ Given:** $500-$1,350.
**Contact:** Beverly Graves, Administrative Assistant.

**Restrictions:** Male Protestant theology students attending an IA college.

---

**Reifel-Ellwood Education Trust**
c/o H. Deemer Houghton
212 Coolbaugh Street
Red Oak, IA 51566 (712)623-2151

**$ Given:** 18 grants totaling $6,000; average grant $200-$400.
**Contact:** H. Deemer Houghton.

**Restrictions:** Residents who are high school seniors of Montgomery County, IA.

---

**Teresa Treat Stearns Trust**
c/o L. Richard Anderson, V.P. & Trust Officer
P.O. Box 370
Webster City, IA 50595 (515)832-1133

**Deadline:** June 1.

**Restrictions:** Webster City, IA high school graduates.

**Sidney A. Swensrund Scholarship Fund**
c/o Superintendent of Schools
P.O. Box 164
Northwood, IA 50459 (515)324-2021

**$ Given:** Grants averaging $1,200-$1,500.
**Contact:** Perry H. Uhl.

**Restrictions:**
Students of North Kensett high school.

---

**The Van Buren Foundation, Inc.**
c/o Farmers State Bank
Keosauqua, IA 52565 (319)293-3794

**$ Given:** Grants totaling $10,292.
**Contact:** Treasurer.

**Restrictions:**
Van Buren County, IA residents.

---

**Vierhus Educational Trust**
Avoca State Bank
Avoca, IA 51521 (712)343-6308

**$ Given:** 10 grants of $250-$5,300.
**Contact:** Milton Hanson.

**Restrictions:**
Avoca, IA area students.

---

**Lyman & Kathryn A. Wood Trust**
c/o Norwest Bank, Trust Division
666 Walnut
Des Moines, IA 50304 (515)245-3222

**$ Given:** Grants of $750.

**Restrictions:**
IA students.

# KANSAS

**Jennie G. and Pearl Abell Education Trust**
723 ½ Main Street, P.O. Box 487
Ashland, KS 67831

**$ Given:** 91 grants totaling $138,365.
**Contact:** Sarah D. Shattuck, Manager.
**Deadline:** June 15, December 15.

**Restrictions:**
Graduates of Clark County, KS high schools.

---

**Baughman Foundation**
P.O. Box 1356
Liberal, KS 67901 (316)624-1371

**Contact:** Eugene W. Slaymaker, President.
**Deadline:** Second Wednesday of each month.

**Restrictions:**
KS residents.

---

**James A. and Juliet L. Davis Foundation, Inc.**
P.O. Box 2027
Hutchinson, KS 67501-2027 (316)663-5021

**$ Given:** 23 grants totaling $31,500.
**Contact:** Secretary-Treasurer.
**Deadline:** March 15.

**Restrictions:**
Hutchinson high school graduates.

## 42•FREE MONEY

**R. L. and Elsa Helvering Trust**
c/o Ira Shrock
307 South Thirteenth Street
Marysville, KS 66508 (913)562-3437

**Deadline:** May 1.

**Restrictions:**
Marshall county high school seniors planning to attend KS colleges.

---

**Walter S. and Evan C. Jones Foundation**
Citizens National Bank Building
Emporia, KS 66801 (316)342-1714

**$ Given:** Grants totaling $1,256,342.
**Contact:** General Manager.
**Deadline:** July 1.

**Restrictions:**
Students from Osage, Coffey and Lyon counties.

---

**Jordaan Foundation Trust**
c/o First State Bank and Trust Company
111 East 84th Street, P.O. Box 360
Larned, KS 67550 (316)285-3157

**$ Given:** 20 grants totaling $30,000.
**Contact:** Chairman.
**Deadline:** First Tuesday of every month.

**Restrictions:**
Pawnee County residents.

---

**Kansas Board of Regents**
Suite 609 Capital Tower
400 Southwest Eighth Street
Topeka, KS 66603 (913)296-3517

**$ Given:** Unspecified number of $500 scholarships, renewable.
**Deadline:** April 1.
**Contact:** Above address.

**Restrictions:**
High school graduate, enrolled in KS institution. Financial need, state scholar.

---

**Ivy A. Monk Scholarship Trust**
National Bank of America
P.O. Box 560
Salina, KS 67402-050 (913)825-0511

**$ Given:** 19 awards totaling $9,500.

**Restrictions:**
Salina, Dickenson and Ottawa country residents; must contact your high school.

---

# KENTUCKY

**Blanche and Thomas Hope Fund**
P.O. Box 1270
Ashland, KY 41101

**$ Given:** 216 grants totaling $115,850.
**Deadline:** March 1.

**Restrictions:**
KY students.

---

**Kentucky Center for Veterans Affairs**
600 Federal Plaza, Room 1365
Louisville, KY 40202 (502)584-2231

**$ Given:** Unspecified number of awards.

**Restrictions:**
Children or spouses under age 23, of veteran of armed forces or KY National Guard - deceased, POW, MIA or totally disabled.

| | | |
|---|---|---|
| **Kentucky Higher Education Assistance Authority (KHEAA)**<br>1050 US 127 South<br>Frankford, KY 40601 (502)564-7990 | **$ Given:** Grants of $200-$1,400. Renewable.<br>**Deadline:** No deadline, but best to apply as soon after January 1 of year one plans to enter school. | **Restrictions:** KY residents; financial need. Enrolled full time in non-religious degree program. |
| **The Louisville Community Foundation, Inc**<br>Three Riverfront Plaza<br>Louisville, KY 40202 (502)585-4649 | **$ Given:** Grants averaging $4,000-$6,000.<br>**Deadline:** May 1; November 1.<br>**Contact:** Executive Director. | **Restrictions:** Greater Louisville area. |
| **The Edward C. and Hazel L. Stephenson Foundation**<br>505 Hampton Road<br>Grosse Pointe Woods, MI 48236<br>(313)886-2659 | **Contact:** Ludger A. Beauvais, Vice-President.<br>**Deadline:** November 15. | **Restrictions:** MI, IN, KY, OH students; financial need. |

# LOUISIANA

| | | |
|---|---|---|
| **Joe W. and Dorothy Dorsett Brown Foundation**<br>1801 Pere Marquette Building<br>New Orleans, LA 70112 | **$ Given:** 9 grants totaling $28,682. | **Restrictions:** Given in LA. |
| **The William T. and Ethel Lewis Burton Foundation**<br>101 North Hunt<br>Sulphur, LA 70663 | **$ Given:** 71 grants totaling $16,776, ranging from $494-$1,000. | **Restrictions:** Residents of southwest, LA, preferably Sulphur H.S. graduates. |
| **Louisiana Governor's Special Commission on Education Services**<br>P.O. Box 4406, Capitol Station<br>Baton Rouge, LA 70804 (504)342-5882 | **$ Given:** Unspecified number of scholarships.<br>**Deadline:** June 1; December 31.<br>**Contact:** Director, Scholarship Division at above address. | **Restrictions:** LA high school graduates with a grade point average of 3.0 or above. Plan to attend state supported school in LA. |

## 44•FREE MONEY

**Louisiana Department of Veterans Affairs**
Old State Capitol, 4th Floor
Baton Rouge, LA 70801 (504)342-5920

**$ Given:** Grants of $500. Renewable.

**Restrictions:** Children age 16-25 or widow of deceased LA veterans attending LA state institutions. Also disabled veteran who had been LA resident for two years. Full time enrollment.

---

**Masonic Education Foundation, Inc.**
1306 Masonic Temple Building
New Orleans, LA 70130

**$ Given:** 40 grants totaling $27,683, average grant $800.

**Restrictions:** LA residents.

---

**H.J. Lutcher and Nelda C. Stark Foundation**
P.O. Drawer 909
Orange TX 77630 (713)883-3513

**$ Given:** 4 grants totaling $1,670.
**Contact:** Clyde V. McKee, Jr., Secretary-Treasurer.

**Restrictions:** TX, Southwest LA residents.

---

**Fred B. and Ruth B. Zigler Foundation**
P.O. Box 986
Jennings, LA 70546 (318) 824-2413

**$ Given:** 44 grants totaling $64,987.
**Contact:** Secretary-Treasurer.
**Deadline:** March 10.

**Restrictions:** High school seniors of Jefferson Davis Parish, LA.

# MAINE

**George P. Davenport Trust Fund**
55 Front Street
Bath, ME 04530 (207)443-3431

**$ Given:** 57 grants totaling $73,800.
**Deadline:** 5th of each month.

**Restrictions:** Bath area high school graduates.

---

**Fred Forsyth Educational Trust Fund**
c/o Norstar Bank
2 State Street
Bangor, ME 04401

**$ Given:** Grants totaling $21,510.
**Contact:** Bucksport High School, Bucksport, ME 04416.

**Restrictions:** Graduates of Bucksport High School, ME.

# Maine·45

**Beulah Pack Scholarship Fund**
c/o Casco Northern Bank,
NA Trust Department
P.O. Box 678
Portland, ME 04104 (207)774-8221, ext. 457

**$ Given:** 9 grants totaling $3,300, ranging from $200-$500.
**Contact:** Jeanne Heikkinen.

**Restrictions:**
Union, ME high school students.

---

**Maine Bureau of Veteran Services**
Camp Keyes, Station 33
Augusta, ME 04333 (207)622-9331

**$ Given:** Grants of $300. Renewable.

**Restrictions:**
Wife or child of deceased or disabled veteran, who was resident of ME at time of entry. Student must be 5 yr. resident prior to application, between ages 16-21.

---

**Maine State Department of Educational and Cultural Services**
**Division of Higher Education Services**
State House Station 123
Augusta, ME 04333 (207)289-2183

**Restrictions:**
None.

---

**William Searles Scholarship Fund**
c/o First National Bank of Bar Harbor
102 Main Street
Bar Harbor, ME 04609 (207)288-3341

**$ Given:** 29 grants totaling $3,325, averaging $100-$200.

**Restrictions:**
Mt. Desert high school graduates; contact your school.

---

**Tibbetts Industries Foundation**
P.O. Box 1096
Camden, ME 04843 (207)236-3301

**$ Given:** 13 grants of $300-$700.
**Contact:** W. Kent Stanley.

**Restrictions:**
Graduates of certain high schools or colleges in ME.

---

**Marion W. Warman Irrevocable Scholarship Fund**
c/o Gordon W. H. Buzza, Jr.
P.O. Box 1029
Presque Isle, ME 04769 (207)769-2211

**$ Given:** 21 grants totaling $24,852, ranging from $250-$2,000.

**Restrictions:**
Aroostook County, ME high school graduates.

# MARYLAND

**Abell Foundation**
210 North Charles
1116 Fidelity Building
Baltimore, MD 21201 (301)547-1300

**$ Given:** Grants totaling $24,160.
**Contact:** Cita Culman.

**Restrictions:**
MD organizations.

---

**Lavinia Eagle Scholarship Fund, Inc.**
c/o B. Steckel
1312 Banbury Place
Silver Springs, MD 20904

**Restrictions:**
Montgomery County, MD residents, attend MD school, political science, public administration.

---

**Loats Foundation**
P.O. Box 240
Frederick, MD 21701 (301)662-2191

**$ Given:** 92 grants totaling $83,792.
**Contact:** c/o Evangelical Lutheran Church, E. Church St., Frederick, MD 21701 (301)663-6361.

**Restrictions:**
Residents of Frederick County, MD. Financial need.

---

**Maryland State Scholarship Board**
**Maryland House of Delegates Scholarships**
2100 Guilford Avenue
Baltimore, MD 21218 (301)659-6420

**$ Given:** 2 to 4 year scholarships, from each member of House of Delegates during his 4 yr. term in office.
**Contact:** Maryland House of Delegates member.
**Deadline:** February 15.

**Restrictions:**
Students living in a delegate's district.

---

**Maryland State Scholarship Board**
**Maryland General State Scholarships**
2100 Guilford Avenue
Baltimore, MD 21218 (301)659-6420

**$ Given:** Grants of $200-$2,000. Renewable.
**Contact:** College Scholarship Services, Princeton, NJ 08540.
**Deadline:** March 1.

**Restrictions:**
Graduates of MD high schools; financial need. Legal resident of legislative district from which award is expected.

# Maryland·47

**Maryland State Scholarship Board**
**Maryland Distinguished Scholar Program**
2100 Guilford Avenue
Baltimore, MD 21218 (301)659-6420

**$ Given:** Grants of $300-$800. Renewable.
**Contact:** High school guidance counselor.
**Deadline:** July 15.

**Restrictions:**
MD residents with high academic record (3.7-4.0 average through first 3 years of high school or National Merit finalist) attending MD colleges. Must maintain a "B" average.

---

**Maryland State Scholarship Board**
**Maryland Professional School Scholarships**
2100 Guilford Avenue
Baltimore, MD 21218 (301)659-6420

**$ Given:** Grants of $200-$1,000.
**Deadline:** February 15.

**Restrictions:**
Students of medicine, dentistry, law, nursing, pharmacy; MD residents for one year.

---

**Maryland State Scholarship Board**
**Maryland Scholarships for Children of Deceased Firemen, Law Enforcement Officers, Rescue Squad Members and National Guardsmen**
2100 Guilford Avenue
Baltimore, MD 21218 (301)659-6420

**$ Given:** Grants of $1,000.
**Deadline:** February 15.

**Restrictions:**
Children of MD firefighters, law enforcement officers, rescue squad members or national guardsmen killed in the line of duty. Ages 16-23. Demonstrate financial need.

---

**Maryland State Scholarship Board**
**Maryland Senatorial Scholarships**
2100 Guilford Avenue
Baltimore, MD 21218 (301)659-6420

*NEED BASED*

**$ Given:** Grants of $200-$1,500. Renewable.
**Deadline:** February 15.

**Restrictions:**
MD high school graduates or seniors. Must be resident of legislative district from which award is sought.

---

**Maryland State Scholarship Board**
**Maryland Veterans Grants**
2100 Guilford Avenue
Baltimore, MD 21218 (301)659-6420

**$ Given:** unspecified.
**Deadline:** February 15.

**Restrictions:**
MD Vietnam veterans.

---

**Maryland State Scholarship Board**
**Maryland War Orphan Grants**
2100 Guilford Avenue
Baltimore, MD 21218 (301)659-6420

**$ Given:** Grants of $500.
**Contact:** Above address.
**Deadline:** February 15.

**Restrictions:**
MD children, between ages 16 and 23, whose parent was MD resident prior to entering service and was killed or disabled after 12/7/41 or was a POW or MIA in Southeast Asia after 1/1/60.

## 48•FREE MONEY

**The Pickard Scholarship**
Del-Mar-Va Council
Eighth & Washington Streets
Wilmington, DE 19801 (302)652-3741

**Restrictions:**
Explorer and Boy Scouts from DE, MD, VA.

---

**Sico Foundation**
15 Mount Joy Street
Mount Joy, PA 17552 (717)653-1411

**$ Given:** 90 awards of $1,000-$4,000.
**Contact:** See high school guidance counselor.
**Deadline:** February 15.

**Restrictions:**
DE, MD, PA students attending certain schools; financial need.

---

# MASSACHUSSETTS

**The Bailey Foundation**
c/o State Street Bank & Trust Company
P.O. Box 351
Boston, MA 02101

**$ Given:** 1 scholarship covering tuition, books, supplies and laboratory fees for 4 years. 4 grants totaling $5,000; each grant is $1,250.

**Restrictions:**
Students or graduates of Amesbury, MA high school; residents of Amesbury, MA.

---

**Albert B. and Evelyn H. Black Scholarship Fund**
c/o Bank of New England, N.A.
28 State Street
Boston, MA 02107

**$ Given:** 43 grants totaling $23,100, ranging from $400-$850.
**Contact:** George S. Ames, Trust Officer.
**Deadline:** April 1.

**Restrictions:**
Concord, MA public school students.

---

**Charles H. Bond Trust**
c/o First National Bank of Boston
P.O. Box 1890
Boston, MA 02105

**$ Given:** 15 grants totaling $9,750; high $750, low $500.
**Contact:** Augusta K. Haydock, Assistant Trust Officer.
**Deadline:** April 15.

**Restrictions:**
MA high school seniors.

---

**Charles W. Caldwell Scholarship Fund**
c/o State Street Bank and Trust Company
P.O. Box 351
Boston, MA 02101 (617)654-3361

**$ Given:** 2 grants totaling $6,000, each grant $3,000.
**Contact:** Sharon Doherty-Clancy.

**Restrictions:**
Male seniors at Princeton University for post-graduate study.

# Massachussetts·49

**Isaac Harris Cary Educational Fund**
c/o Lexington Savings Bank
1776 Massachusetts Avenue
Lexington, MA 02173 (617)861-0650

**$ Given:** 27 grants totaling $22,450; average grant $500-$1,000.
**Contact:** F. David Wells, Jr., 1775 Massachusetts Ave., Lexington, MA 02173.

**Restrictions:**
Graduating seniors from Lexington, MA.

---

**Grover Cronin Memorial Foundation**
223 Moody Street
Waltham, MA 02154 (617)894-1000

**Contact:** Lawrence D. Chappell, Trustee.

**Restrictions:**
Waltham county residents.

---

**The Deloura Family Trust**
c/o Shawmut Bank of Boston
P.O. Box 4276
Boston, MA 02106 (617)292-3509

**Contact:** Alan Flanders.

**Restrictions:**
Martha's Vineyard, MA residents.

---

**Diocese of Western Massachusetts**
37 Chestnut Street
Springfield, MA 01103 (413)737-4787

**$ Given:** $500 awards.
**Contact:** Bement Educational Grants Committee at above address.
**Deadline:** February 1.

**Restrictions:**
Unmarried student with financial need, active in Episcopal Churches in the Diocese.

---

**District of Columbia Public Schools**
Division of Student Services
Boston Area Black Alumni Association
415 12th Street, NW
Washington, DC 20004

**Restrictions:**
Black high school senior of the District of Columbia enrolling at a college in the Boston, MA metropolitan area. See guidance counselor.

---

**Duxbury Yacht Club Charitable Foundation**
c/o State Street Bank and Trust Company
P.O. Box 351
Boston, MA 02101

**$ Given:** 5 grants of $500.

**Restrictions:**
Duxbury, MA high school graduates.

---

**Friendship Fund, Inc.**
c/o Boston Safe Deposit and Trust Co.
1 Boston Place, OBP-2
Boston, MA 02106 (617)722-7538

**$ Given:** 5 grants totaling $7,100; average grant $1,500.
**Contact:** Mrs. Bruce C. Fisher, President.
**Deadline:** May 31.

**Restrictions:**
MA residents.

## 50•FREE MONEY

**The General Charitable Society of Newburyport**
8 Roosevelt Place
Newburyport, MA 01950 (617)465-0920

**Contact:** Mrs. Leroy Hiller.

**Restrictions:**
Newburyport, MA residents.

---

**Cynthia E. and Clara H. Hollins Foundation**
100 Summer Street
Boston, MA 02110 (617)426-5720

**$ Given:** 12-20 grants of $100-$1,200.
**Contact:** Ms. Alette E. Reed, Trustee.
**Deadline:** April 1.

**Restrictions:**
Graduate students residing in Boston, MA and studying medicine, nursing, social work, psychology, etc.

---

**Terri Ann Holovak and Joseph P. Logan Memorial Scholarship Fund**
P.O. Box 201
Arlington, MA 02174 (617)648-7000

**$ Given:** $200-$1,000.
**Deadline:** June 1.

**Restrictions:**
Freshmen students commuting from eastern MA.

---

**Charles H. Hood Fund**
500 Rutherford Avenue
Boston, MA 02129 (617)242-0600

**$ Given:** 6 grants of $3,000.

**Restrictions:**
CT, MA, ME, NH, RI, VT students of employees.

---

**The Horbach Fund**
c/o National Community Bank of New Jersey
113 West Essex Street
Maywood, NJ 07607

**$ Given:** 5 grants totaling $4,500, ranging from $500-$1,000.
**Contact:** 40 Glen Road, Mountain Lakes, NJ 07041.

**Restrictions:**
CT, MA, NJ, NY, RI gifted students under the age of 20; financial need.

---

**Edward Bangs and Eliza Kelley Foundation, Inc.**
243 South Street, P.O. Drawer M
Hyannis, MA 02601 (617)775-3117

**$ Given:** 35 grants totaling $35,000.
**Contact:** Administrative Manager.
**Deadline:** April 30.

**Restrictions:**
Barnstable County, MA residents.

---

**Charles H. Kohlrausch, Jr. Trust Fund**
Box 341
Billerica, MA 01821

**$ Given:** 10-20 grants per year.
**Deadline:** July 15.

**Restrictions:**
Billerica, MA residents who have successfully completed one semester of undergraduate study.

# Massachusetts・51

| | | |
|---|---|---|
| **Massachusetts Board of Higher Education**<br>Massachusetts War Orphan Scholarships<br>330 Stuart Street<br>Boston, MA 02116 | **$ Given:** $750. Unspecified number of awards. Renewable.<br>**Contact:** War Orphans Unit given address. | **Restrictions:**<br>Student aged 16-24, of parents killed serving in World War I, World War II, Vietnam or Korea. Born in or lived 1 yr. in MA. |
| **Massachusetts Board of Higher Education**<br>Massachusetts Scholarships for Children of Deceased Members of Fire, Police, Corrections Departments, State Police, State Capitol Police or Metropolitan District Police<br>330 Stuart Street<br>Boston, MA 02116 | **$ Given:** Unspecified number of awards. | **Restrictions:**<br>MA high school graduates; children of fire, corrections, police departments; state police, capitol police, or metropolitan police department members killed in the line of duty. Must attend MA state-supported school. |
| **Massachusetts Board of Higher Education**<br>Massachusetts Honor Scholarships<br>330 Stuart Street<br>Boston, MA 02116 | **$ Given:** 4 scholarships per state senatorial district. Renewable.<br>**Contact:** High school guidance counselor.<br>**Deadline:** January 24. | **Restrictions:**<br>MA residents planning to attend a 4-year, state-supported college. Must have highest total verbal and math score on SAT. |
| **Massachusetts State Federation of Women's Clubs**<br>148 President's Lane<br>Quincy, MA 02169 (617)471-3212 | **$ Given:** Two $2,000 scholarships.<br>**Contact:** Memorial Education Chairman at above address.<br>**Deadline:** February 15. | **Restrictions:**<br>Woman graduate student residing in MA at least 5 years. Must be sponsored by local women's club in MA. |
| **Microwave Associates Charitable Foundation**<br>60 South Avenue<br>Burlington, MA 01803 (617)272-3000, ext. 1206 | **Deadline:** September 30. | **Restrictions:**<br>Burlington, Boston and Merrimac Valley, MA residents. |

## 52•FREE MONEY

**James Z. Naurison Scholarship Fund**
c/o Bank of New England-West
P.O. Box 9006
Springfield, MA 01102 (413)787-8745

**$ Given:** Grants averaging $500-$700.
**Contact:** Administrator.
**Deadline:** May 1.

**Restrictions:**
Students from Hampden, Hampshire, Franklin, Berkshire counties, MA and Enfield, Suffield counties, CT.

---

**The Pilgrim Foundation**
8 Perkins Avenue
Brockton, MA 02401 (617)586-6100

**$ Given:** 185 grants totaling $137,177.
**Contact:** Executive Director.
**Deadline:** April 1 for high school graduates, May 1 for returning college students.

**Restrictions:**
Residents of Brockton, MA.

---

**Mary T. and William A. Richardson Fund Corp.**
c/o Malden Trust Co.
94 Pleasant Street
Malden, MA 02148 (617)321-1111

**$ Given:** $400-$1,000.
**Contact:** Robert M. Wallask, Trust Officer.
**Deadline:** June 1.

**Restrictions:**
MA high school seniors.

---

**Wilmot Roby Evans Corporation**
1 Beacon Street, Room 2200
Boston, MA 02108 (617)227-4400, ext. 285

**$ Given:** Awards of $350-$1,500.
**Deadline:** May 1.

**Restrictions:**
Students from Newburyport, MA area (high school senior or college student).

---

**Horace Smith Fund**
Box 3034
Springfield, MA 01101 (413)739-4222

**$ Given:** Unspecified number of $1,000 fellowships. Renewable for 2 years.
**Contact:** Executive Secretary, above address.
**Deadline:** February 1.

**Restrictions:**
Resident of Hampden County, MA. Submit GRE Aptitude scores. Must be working towards a career in politics, scientific research, the ministry, or the learned professions. Demonstrate financial need.

---

**Albert H. & Reuben S. Stone Fund**
c/o Nichols & Stone
232 Sherman Street
Gardner, MA 01440

**$ Given:** 188 grants totaling $127,460.
**Contact:** Carlton Nichols or Carlton Nichols Jr., Trustees.
**Deadline:** Early in 2nd semester.

**Restrictions:**
Residents of Gardner, MA

**Urann Foundation**
P.O. Box 1788
Brockton, MA 02403 (617)588-7744

**$ Given:** 14 grants totaling $29,800.
**Contact:** High school guidance office.
**Deadline:** April 15.

**Restrictions:**
MA residents who are engaged in the production of cranberries.

---

**Fred G. Wells Trust Fund**
Bank of New England-Franklin, Trust Department
1 Federal Street
Greenfield, MA 01301 (413)772-0281

**$ Given:** 125 grants totaling $64,914.
**Contact:** Trust Officer.
**Deadline:** May 1.

**Restrictions:**
Residents of towns in Franklin County, MA.

---

**Arthur Ashley Williams Foundation**
345 Union Avenue, P.O. Box 665
Framingham, MA 01701 (617)429-1149

**$ Given:** 44 grants totaling $54,250.
**Contact:** Chairman.
**Deadline:** One week prior to board meetings in January, April, July, & October.

**Restrictions:**
Residents of Framingham, MA.

# MICHIGAN

**Alvin M. Bentley Foundation**
312 W. Main Street
P.O. Box 458
Owosso, MI 48867 (517)723-5114

**$ Given:** Grants totaling $24,808.
**Contact:** Secretary-Treasurer.
**Deadline:** March 1.

**Restrictions:**
Students attending MI colleges or universities.

---

**Joe W. and Dorothy Dorsett Brown Foundation**
1801 Pere Marquette Building
New Orleans, LA 70112

**$ Given:** 9 grants available ranging from $1,200-$5,000.

**Restrictions:**
LA, MI residents.

---

**H. T. Ewald Foundation**
15175 East Jefferson Avenue
Grosse Pointe, MI 48230 (313)821-2000

**$ Given:** 54 grants totaling $58,000, ranging from $500-$2,000.
**Contact:** Henry T. Ewald, President.
**Deadline:** May 1.

**Restrictions:**
Metropolitan Detroit high school seniors; financial need.

## 54•FREE MONEY

**Fabri-Kal Foundation**
3303 East Cork Street
Kalamazoo, MI 49001 (616)385-5050

**Contact:** Charles Wright III, Secretary.

**Restrictions:** Employee's children.

---

**Foster Foundation Scholarship Program**
3128 Higgins Southwest
Grandville, MI 49418 (616)534-8486

**$ Given:** Scholarships of $300-$750. Could be renewable after 4 years.
**Deadline:** February 1. Call to see if it can be extended.

**Restrictions:** Residents of Grand Rapids and Kent County, MI; financial need.

---

**The Fremont Area Foundation**
108 South Stewart
Fremont, MI 49412 (616)924-5350

**$ Given:** 43 grants totaling $24,369.
**Contact:** Executive Director.
**Deadline:** October 15.

**Restrictions:** Residents of Newaygo County.

---

**Louis Glick Memorial and Charitable Trust**
701 Lewis Street, P.O. Box 1166
Jackson, MI 49204 (517)787-4940

**Contact:** Carlton Glick, Trustee.
**Deadline:** May 15.

**Restrictions:** Must be Jackson County high school graduate, intending to enroll in a state college, private college, or trade school within the state of MI.

---

**The Grand Rapids Foundation**
300 East Waters Building,
161 Ottawa Northwest
Grand Rapids, MI 49503 (616)454-1751

**$ Given:** Grants totaling $51,904.
**Contact:** Executive Director.

**Restrictions:** Residents of Kent County.

---

**Corwill and Margie Jackson Foundation**
c/o Comerica Bank-Detroit
211 West Fort Street
Detroit, MI 48231

**$ Given:** 32 grants totaling $21,500, ranging from $250-$3,250.

**Restrictions:** Freshmen from Ludington, MI area.

---

**Kent Medical Foundation**
1155 Front Avenue Northwest
Grand Rapids, MI 49504 (616)458-4157

**$ Given:** 17 grants of $350-$400.

**Restrictions:** Residents of Kent, MI and bordering counties, for education in medicine, nursing and related health fields.

# Michigan•55

**McCurdy Memorial Scholarship Foundation**
134 West Van Buren Street
Battle Creek, MI 49014 (616)962-9591

**$ Given:** Grants of $100-$1,000 per year. Renewable.
**Deadline:** March 31.

**Restrictions:** Calhoun County, MI residents.

---

**Edward Arthur Mellinger Educational Foundation, Inc.**
1025 East Broadway
P.O. Box 278
Monmouth, IL 61462 (309)734-2419

**$ Given:** 947 grants totaling $264,813; average grant $450.
**Contact:** Shirley J. Neill, Administrative Assistant.
**Deadline:** June 1.

**Restrictions:** OH, IN, IL, MI, WI, MN, IA, MO residents or students.

---

**Meredith Corporation Edwin T. Meredith Foundation 4-H Scholarship**
1767 Locust Street
Des Moines, IA 50336 (515)284-2545

**Contact:** State 4-H leader.

**Restrictions:** IL, IN, IA, KS, MI, MO, MN, NE, NY, ND, OH, OK, PA, SD, WI residents, present or former 4-H Club members.

---

**Allen H. Meyers Foundation**
P.O. Box 100
Tecumseh, MI 49286 (517)423-7629

**$ Given:** 27 grants totaling $6,925, average grant is $250.
**Contact:** Mrs. Allen H. Meyers.
**Deadline:** March 15.

**Restrictions:** Lenawee County, MI high school seniors planning studies in the sciences and allied fields.

---

**Michigan Department of Education Student Financial Assistance Service**
P.O. Box 30008
Lansing, MI 48909 (517)373-3394

**$ Given:** Grants of $100-$1,300. Renewable.
**Contact:** High school guidance counselor or college financial aid office.

**Restrictions:** MI residents for 12 months planning to attend MI colleges. Some grants require financial need.

---

**Michigan Indian Awards**
Michigan Commission on Indian Affairs
Department of Management and Budget
P.O. Box 30026
Lansing, MI 48909 (517)373-0654

**$ Given:** Full tuition.

**Restrictions:** MI resident attending MI state school; one-fourth Indian heritage.

## 56•FREE MONEY

**Michigan Veterans Trust Fund**
Board of Trustees
P.O. Box 30026
No. Ottawa Building, Third floor
Lansing, MI 48909 (517)373-3130

**$ Given:** Unspecified number of tuition grants.

**Restrictions:** 12 month resident of MI, 16-22 years of age. Child of MI veteran killed or disabled. Must be admitted to MI State tax-supported institution.

---

**McCurdy Memorial Scholarship Foundation**
134 West Van Buren Street
Battle Creek, MI 49014 (616)962-9591

**$ Given:** Grants of $100-$1,000 per year. Renewable.
**Deadline:** March 31.

**Restrictions:** Calhoun County, MI residents.

---

**Allen H. Meyers Foundation**
P.O. Box 100
Tecumseh, MI 49286 (517)423-7629

**$ Given:** 27 grants totaling $6,925. Average grant is $250.
**Deadline:** March 15.
**Contact:** Mrs. Allen H. Meyers.

**Restrictions:** Lenawee County, MI high school seniors, planning studies in the sciences and allied fields.

---

**Midland Foundation**
117 McDonald Street
P.O. Box 289
Midland, MI 48640 (517)839-9661

**$ Given:** 35 grants totaling $21,210.
**Deadline:** January 1, April 1, November 1.

**Restrictions:** Residents of Midland County.

---

**Muskegon County Community Foundation, Inc.**
Frauenthal Center, Suite 304
407 West Western Avenue
Muskegon, MI 49440 (616)722-4538

**$ Given:** 192 grants totaling $163,259.
**Contact:** Executive Director.
**Deadline:** January, April, July, October.

**Restrictions:** Muskegon County, MI residents.

---

**Plym Foundation**
Star Building
Niles, MI 49120 (616)683-8300

**$ Given:** 2 grants totaling $2,160.
**Contact:** Murray C. Campbell, Secretary.

**Restrictions:** Residents of the Niles, MI area.

---

**Emily Scofield Scholarship Fund**
134 West Van Buren Street
Battle Creek, MI 49017 (616)962-9591

**$ Given:** $100-$500.
**Deadline:** June 1.

**Restrictions:** Residents of Calhoun County, MI.

**Student Aid Foundation Of Michigan**
8146 Macomb Road
Grosse Ile, MI 48138

**$ Given:** 63 grants totaling $165,212.
**Contact:** President.
**Deadline:** February.

**Restrictions:**
Graduating seniors from Wayne, Oakland, Macomb, Monroe & Washtenaw counties.

---

**The Vomberg Foundation**
1023 Reynolds Road
Charlotte, MI 48813 (517)543-0430

**$ Given:** Grants totaling $55,417.
**Contact:** Carlene Price.
**Deadline:** December 1.

**Restrictions:**
Eaton County, MI residents.

---

**Winship Memorial Scholarship Foundation**
c/o Comerica Bank-Battle Creek, Trust Division
25 West Michigan Mall
Battle Creek, MI 49017 (616)966-6340

**$ Given:** 92 grants totaling $109,060.
**Deadline:** November 15.

**Restrictions:**
Residents of Battle Creek.

# MINNESOTA

**Marshall H. and Nellie Alworth Memorial Fund**
604 Alworth Building
Duluth, MN 55802 (218)722-9366

**$ Given:** Varies.
**Deadline:** March 1.

**Restrictions:**
Graduate of a No. MN high school; show financial need.

---

**Charles K. Blandin Foundation**
100 Pokegama Avenue North
Grand Rapids, MN 55744 (218)326-0523

**$ Given:** 302 grants totaling $225,292; ranging from $500-$1,500.
**Contact:** Paul M. Olson, Executive Director
**Deadline:** May 15.

**Restrictions:**
Primarily Itasca County & Northeastern MN.

---

**Cenex Foundation**
5600 Cenex Drive
Inver Grove Heights, MN 55075
(612)451-5105

**$ Given:** 43 grants totaling $124,537

**Restrictions:**
Residents of MN, ND, SD, WI, WA, ID, WY, MT, OR.

---

**Eddy Foundation**
c/o Trust Department
Northwest Bank Duluth
P.O. Box 488
Duluth, MN 55802 (218)723-2773

**$ Given:** 21 grants totaling $29,268.

**Restrictions:**
Duluth residents studying in field of communication disorders; non-residents attending University of Minnesota at Duluth.

## 58 • FREE MONEY

| | | |
|---|---|---|
| **Orson A. and Minnie E. Hull Educational Fund**<br>1610 Pioneer Building<br>Saint Paul, MN 55101 (612)228-9004 | **$ Given:** Unspecified.<br>**Deadline:** Apply January 1-March 31. | **Restrictions:**<br>Residents of St. Paul, MN. |
| **The Jostens Foundation Inc.**<br>5501 Norman Center Drive, P.O. Box 20367<br>Minneapolis, MN 55437 (612)830-8429 | **$ Given:** 220 grants totaling $110,000.<br>**Contact:** Citizens Scholarship Foundation of America, Inc., Box 112A, Londonberry Turnpike, RFD number 7, Manchester, NH 03104 (603)627-3870. | **Restrictions:**<br>MN residents, especially Twin Cities residents. |
| **Kelber, Abrahamson, Weinstein & Hatch**<br>Shelard Plaza, Suite 460<br>Minneapolis, MN 55426 (612)544-1521 | **$ Given:** Varies. | **Restrictions:**<br>Must have attended private or parochial school in Delano, MN school District or currently reside within 7 miles of the city. |
| **Edward Arthur Mellinger Educational Foundation, Inc.**<br>1025 East Broadway<br>P.O. Box 278<br>Monmouth, IL 61462 (309)734-2419 | **$ Given:** 947 grants totaling $264,813; average grant $450.<br>**Contact:** Shirley J. Neill, Administrative Assistant.<br>**Deadline:** June 1. | **Restrictions:**<br>OH, IN, IL, MI, WI, MN, IA, MO residents or students. |
| **Meredith Corporation**<br>**Edwin T. Meredith Foundation 4-H Scholarship**<br>1767 Locust Street<br>Des Moines, IA 50336 (515)284-2545 | **Contact:** State 4-H leader. | **Restrictions:**<br>IL, IN, IA, KS, MI, MO, MN, NE, NY, ND, OH, OK, PA, SD, WI residents, present or former 4-H Club members. |
| **Minnesota Higher Education Coordinating Board**<br>550 Cedar Street, Suite 400<br>St. Paul, MN 55101 (612)296-5715 | | **Restrictions:**<br>None. |

# Minnesota·59

**Minnesota State Grants**
Minnesota Higher Education Coordinating Board
550 Cedar Street, Suite 400
St. Paul, MN 55101 (612)296-5715

**$ Given:** 65,000 $100-$3,406 scholarships and grants. Renewable. Amount based on need.
**Contact:** Manager, Minnesota Scholarship and Grant Programs.
**Deadline:** May 31 of present academic year.

**Restrictions:**
MN residents.

---

**Minnesota State Department of Veterans Affairs**
**Minnesota Educational Assistance for Veterans**
Veterans Services Building
St. Paul, MN 55155 (612)296-2562

**$ Given:** Grants of $350. Not renewable.
**Contact:** Veterans Benefits Division.

**Restrictions:**
Resident of MN at time of entry into Armed Forces. Must attend school in MN. Must have exhausted all other VA entitlement benefits.

---

**Minnesota State Department of Veterans Affairs**
**Minnesota War Orphans Educational Assistance**
Veterans Services Building
St. Paul, MN 55155 (612)296-2562

**$ Given:** Unspecified number of $350 scholarships.
**Contact:** Veterans Benefits Division.

**Restrictions:**
Child, with 2 years residence in MN, whose veteran parent was killed in or died as a result of service. Parent must have been MN resident. Demonstrate financial need.

---

**Potach Foundation for Higher Education**
c/o George C. Cheek
P.O. Box 3591
San Francisco, CA 94119 (415)981-5980

**$ Given:** 180 scholarships totaling $127,050.
**Deadline:** February 1 for new applications. July 1 for scholarship renewals.

**Restrictions:**
AR, ID, MN students. Awards mainly in areas of company operations.

---

**Rochester Area Foundation**
436 First Bank Building
Rochester, MN 55901 (507)282-0203

**Contact:** Isabel Huizenga, Chairperson.

**Restrictions:**
Olmstead County, MN students.

---

**Tozer Foundation, Inc.**
c/o Lawson, Ranum, & Raleigh
104 North Main Street
Stillwater, MN 55082

**$ Given:** 635 grants totaling $49,595.

**Restrictions:**
MN residents.

## 60•FREE MONEY

**Wedum Foundation**
P.O. Box 644
Alexandria, MN 56308 (612)473-0974

**Contact:** Mayo Johnson, President and Treasurer.

**Restrictions:**
Alexandria area high school seniors. See guidance counselor.

---

**Robert B. and Sophia Whiteside Scholarship Foundation**
c/o First Bank of Duluth
306 West Superior Street
Duluth, MN 55801

**$ Given:** 294 grants totaling $810,547.
**Contact:** Local high school counselor.

**Restrictions:**
MN residents. Top 5% of graduating classes.

---

# MISSISSIPPI

---

**Robert M. and Lenore W. Carrier Foundation**
c/o Union Planters National Bank, Trust Department
P.O. Box 387
Memphis, TN 38147 (901)685-2053

**$ Given:** 73 grants totaling $68,850.
**Contact:** Charlotte C. Gahagan, Assistant Vice-President and Trust Officer.

**Restrictions:**
Mississippi residents who plan to attend the University of Mississippi at Oxford, MS.

---

**Joe W. and Dorothy Dorsett Brown Foundation**
1801 Pere-Marquette Building
New Orleans, LA 70112

**$ Given:** Grants totaling $28,682, ranging from $1,200-$5,000.
**Contact:** Mrs. Joe W. Brown.

**Restrictions:**
LA, MS residents.

---

**Mississippi Board of Trustees, Institutions of Higher Learning Mississippi Law Enforcement and Firemen Scholarship Program**
P.O. Box 2336
Jackson, MS 39225-2336 (601)982-6611

**$ Given:** 8 semesters of full tuition at any Mississippi state-supported school.

**Restrictions:**
MS children under 23 years of age of police officers or firefighters killed or totally disabled in the line of duty; students at MS sponsored colleges.

---

**Mississippi Board of Trustees, Institutions of Higher Learning Mississippi Vietnam POW/MIA Dependents Program**
P.O. Box 2336
Jackson, MS 39225-2336 (601)982-6611

**$ Given:** 8 semesters of full tuition.
**Contact:** School of your choice.

**Restrictions:**
MS children under 23 years of age of MS Vietnam veterans officially reported as prisoners of war or missing in action; students at MS sponsored colleges.

Missouri•61

**Mississippi Post-Secondary Education Financial Assistance Board**
P.O. Box 2336
Jackson, MS 39205 (601)982-6168

**Restrictions:**
None.

---

**W.E. Walker Foundation**
3800 I-55 North, Box 9407
Jackson, MS 39206 (601)981-7171

**$ Given:** 7 grants totaling $21,200, ranging from $1,000-$9,200.
**Contact:** Jo C. Prichard, Director.

**Restrictions:**
Local residents.

---

# MISSOURI

**Avon Products Foundation**
83rd & College
Kansas City, MO 64141 (816)361-8480

**$ Given:** One $2,000 award (max). Renewable for 3 years.
**Deadline:** November 1.

**Restrictions:**
Students from Kansas City, MO school district or Center school district since junior year, top ⅓ of class.

---

**William Bradley Scholarship Foundation, Inc.**
811 Mississippi Avenue
Crystal City, MO 63019 (314)937-6270

**$ Given:** One $1,400 award, one $750 award per year. Renewable.
**Contact:** Secretary-Treasurer.
**Deadline:** April 1.

**Restrictions:**
Graduate of Crystal City High School, Festus High School or St. Pius X High School in Jefferson County, MO. Top 10% of class.

---

**James A. and Juliet L. Davis Foundation, Inc.**
P.O. Box 2027
Hutchinson, KS 67501-2027 (316)663-5021

**$ Given:** 23 grants totaling $31,500.
**Contact:** W.Y. Chalfant, Secretary-Treasurer.

**Restrictions:**
Hutchinson school system students who will attend college in KS or MO.

---

**Hallmark Educational Foundations**
Charitable and Crown Investment-323
P.O. Box 580
Kansas City, MO 64141 (816)274-5615

**$ Given:** 93 grants totaling $93,125.
**Contact:** Sarah V. Hutchison, Program Officer.

**Restrictions:**
College students who are relatives of Hallmark employees.

---

**May H. Ilgenfritz Testamentary Trust**
P.O. Box 311
Sedalia, MO 65301 (816)826-3310

**$ Given:** 100 grants totaling $62,179.

**Restrictions:**
Sedalia, MO residents.

## 62 • FREE MONEY

**Joe W. Ingram Trust**
Centerre Bank of Kansas City
900 Walnut, P.O. Box 666
Kansas City, MO 64141

**$ Given:** 9 grants totaling $900.
**Contact:** Joe W. Ingram Trust Office, 111 West Third Street, Salisbury, MO 65281 (816)388-5555.

**Restrictions:**
Residents of Chariton County.

---

**Charles Lyons Memorial Foundation, Inc.**
P.O. Box 236
Lexington, MO 64067

**$ Given:** 85 grants totaling $38,000, ranging from $300-$500.
**Contact:** Hon. H. Townsend Hader, President.
**Deadline:** April 1.

**Restrictions:**
Residents of Lafayette County, MO.

---

**Edwin T. Meredith Foundation 4-H Scholarship**
Meredith Corporation
1767 Locust Street
Des Moines, IA 50336 (515)284-2545

**Contact:** State 4-H leader.

**Restrictions:**
IL, IN, IA, KS, MI, MO, MN, NE, NY, ND, OH, OK, PA, SD, WI residents, present or former 4-H Club members.

---

**MFA Foundation**
201 South Seventh Street
Columbia, MO 65201 (314)876-5395

**$ Given:** 213 grants totaling $224,859.
**Contact:** President.
**Deadline:** April 15.

**Restrictions:**
Given in MO, in area of company's operation.

---

**Missouri Coordinating Board of Higher Education**
P.O. Box 1438
Jefferson City, MO 65102 (314)751-3940

**$ Given:** Unspecified number of $700 grants. Renewable.
**Deadline:** April 30.

**Restrictions:**
Citizen or permanent resident of U.S. Resident of Missouri. Demonstrate financial need. No Theology or Divinity degrees.

---

**Mother Joseph Rogan Marymount Foundation**
c/o Joseph E. Lynch
2217 Clayville Court
St. Louis, MO 63017 (314)391-6248

**Deadline:** April and November

**Restrictions:**
Loans for college students and grants for high school graduates in metropolitan St. Louis, MO.

Montana·63

**Edward Arthur Mellinger Educational Foundation, Inc.**
1025 East Broadway, P.O. Box 278
Monmouth, IL 61462 (309)734-2419

**$ Given:** 947 grants totaling $264,813; average grant $450.
**Contact:** Shirley J. Neill, Administrative Assistant.
**Deadline:** June 1.

**Restrictions:**
OH, IN, IL, MI, WI, MN, IA, MO students or residents.

---

**Orscheln Industries Foundation, Inc.**
339 North Williams
Moberly, MO 65270 (816)263-6693.

**$ Given:** 18 grants totaling $8,716.
**Contact:** William E. Clark, Orscheln Industries Foundation Scholarship Committee, P.O. Box 266, Moberly, MO 65270
**Deadline:** April 1.

**Restrictions:**
Graduates of Cairo, Higbee, Moberly & Weshan high schools.

---

**The Sunshine Trust**
3154 Reid Drive
Corpus Christi, TX 78404 (512)851-2813

**$ Given:** 11 grants totaling $14,010, ranging from $250-$1,500.

**Restrictions:**
NY, VA, TX, MO, CA, OH, DC residents; financial need.

---

**Rosalie Tilles Nonsectarian Charity Fund**
705 Olive St., Suite 906
St. Louis, MO 63101

**$ Given:** 197 grants totaling $234,799.

**Restrictions:**
Students attending St. Louis University, University of Missouri's Columbia, Rolla & St. Louis campuses; Washington University.

---

**James L. & Nellie M. Westlake Scholarship Fund**
c/o Mercantile Trust Co.
P.O. Box 387
St. Louis, MO 63166

**$ Given:** 265 grants totaling $145,150.

**Restrictions:**
Residents of MO.

# MONTANA

**Charles M. Bair Memorial Trust**
c/o First Trust Company of Montana
P.O. Box 30678
Billings, MT 59115 (406)657-8124

**$ Given:** 36 grants totaling $98,719.

**Restrictions:**
Graduates of Meagher & Wheatland counties.

**64•FREE MONEY**

| | | |
|---|---|---|
| **Thomas and Dorothy Leavey Foundation**<br>4680 Wilshire Boulevard<br>Los Angeles, CA 90036 (213)436-5875 | **$ Given:** 72 grants of $1,200-$2,500. | **Restrictions:**<br>AZ, CA, CO, MT, NM, NV, OR, WY, ID, UT students. |
| **Lloyd D. Sweet Foundation**<br>c/o Chinook Public High School<br>528 Ohio Street<br>Chinook, MT 59523 | **$ Given:** 168 grants totaling $166,380.<br>**Deadline:** March 1. | **Restrictions:**<br>Chinook, MT high school graduates. |

## NEBRASKA

| | | |
|---|---|---|
| **Christian Record Braille Foundation, Inc.**<br>4444 South 52nd Street<br>Lincoln, NE 68506 (402)488-0981 | **$ Given:** Limited number of $300-$1,000 awards. Renewable.<br>**Contact:** Treasurer above address. | **Restrictions:**<br>Legally blind, high school graduate. |
| **Edward Arthur Mellinger Educational Foundation, Inc.**<br>1025 East Broadway<br>P.O. Box 278<br>Monmouth, IL 61462 (309)734-2419 | **$ Given:** 947 grants totaling $264,813; average grant $450.<br>**Contact:** Shirley J. Neill, Administrative Assistant.<br>**Deadline:** June 1. | **Restrictions:**<br>IL, IA, KY, MI, MN, NE, SD, WI students. |
| **Meredith Corporation**<br>**Edwin T. Meredith Foundation, 4-H Scholarship**<br>1767 Locust Street<br>Des Moines, IA 50336 (515)284-2545 | **Contact:** State 4-H leader. | **Restrictions:**<br>IL, IN, IA, KS, MI, MO, MN, NE, NY, ND, OH, OK, PA, SD, WI residents, present or former 4-H Club members. |
| **Nebraska Coordinating Commission for Postsecondary Education**<br>301 Centennial Mall South<br>P.O. Box 95005<br>Lincoln, NE 68509 (402)471-2847 | **Contact:** See financial aid officer. | **Restrictions:**<br>None. |

## Nevada·65

**Nebraska Department of Veterans Affairs**
301 Centennial Mall South
Lincoln, NE 68509 (402)471-2458

**$ Given:** Unspecified number of tuition waivers.
**Contact:** Service Officer in county of residence or above address.
**Deadline:** Beginning of term.

**Restrictions:**
Child or spouse of Nebraska resident who, due to military service, died, was disabled, is a POW or MIA. Under 26 years of age. Attend Nebraska institution.

---

**Peter Kiewit Foundation**
Woodmen Tower, Suite 900
Farnham at Seventeenth
Omaha, NE 68102 (402)344-7890

**$ Given:** Grants totaling $6,353,912.
**Contact:** Executive Director.
**Deadline:** June 30, September 30, December 31, March 3.

**Restrictions:**
Students in Omaha, NE; Council Bluffs, IA.

---

**Phelps County Community Foundation, Inc.**
c/o Tim Anderson
P.O. Box 466
Holdrege, NE 68949 (308)995-6191

**$ Given:** 6 grants totaling $199,272.

**Restrictions:**
Given primarily in NE, particularly Phelps County.

---

# NEVADA

**Golden Nugget Scholarship Fund, Inc.**
P.O. Box 610
129 East Fremont Street
Las Vegas, NV 89125 (702)385-7111

**$ Given:** 122 grants totaling $179,800.
**Contact:** Vice-Chairperson.
**Deadline:** March 10.

**Restrictions:**
Graduates of high schools in NV or NJ.

---

**Thomas & Dorothy Leavey Foundation**
4680 Wilshire Boulevard
Los Angeles, CA 90036 (213)436-5875

**$ Given:** 72 grants of $1,250-$2,500.

**Restrictions:**
AZ, CA, CO, MT, NM, NV, OR, WY, ID, UT residents.

---

**Nevada Scholarships**
University of Nevada System
405 March Avenue
Reno, NV 89509 (702)784-4666

**Restrictions:**
High school graduates with 3.0 or better, interested in attending the University of Nevada, Reno.

# NEW HAMPSHIRE

**Cogswell Benevolent Trust**
875 Elm Street
Manchester, NH 03101 (603)622-4013

**Restrictions:**
NH students.

---

**Charles and Caroline Greenfield Fund**
c/o Bank East Trust Co.
P.O. Box 1
Rochester, NH 03867 (603)332-4242

**$ Given:** Awards up to $1,000.
**Contact:** Trust Administrator.

**Restrictions:**
Residents of Stafford County, NH.

---

**Abbie M. Griffin Educational Fund**
c/o S. Robert Winer
111 Concord Street
Nashua, NH 03060 (603)882-5157

**$ Given:** 18 grants totaling $18,400, ranging from $1,000-$1,650.

**Restrictions:**
Residents of Merrimack, NH.

---

**Charles H. Hood Fund**
500 Rutherford Lane
Boston, MA 02129 (617)242-0600

**$ Given:** 6 grants of $3,000.

**Restrictions:**
ME, NH, MA, RI, CT students.

---

**Henry C. Lord Scholarship Fund Trust**
c/o Amoskeag National Bank and Trust Company
P.O. Box 150
Manchester, NH 03105

**$ Given:** 420 grants totaling $271,772.
**Deadline:** April 30.

**Restrictions:**
Residents of Petersborough, NH and contiguous towns.

---

**New Hampshire Charitable Fund**
**Grace Blanchard and Frances Abbott Student Fund**
1 South Street, P.O. Box 1335
Concord, NH 03301

**$ Given:** Unspecified number of $500 grants per year.
**Contact:** Director, Student Aid Program.
**Deadline:** May 28.

**Restrictions:**
Women, resident of Concord NH, graduate of a Concord high school.

---

**The New Hampshire Charitable Fund**
One South Street
P.O. Box 1335
Concord, NH 03301 (603)225-6641

**$ Given:** 205 grants totaling $187,428.
**Contact:** Associate Director.
**Deadline:** February 1, May 1, August 1, November 1.

**Restrictions:**
Given in NH.

# New Hampshire·67

**New Hampshire Charitable Fund**
**Nellie E. Hall and Alice C. Racine Trust**
1 South Street, P.O. Box 1335
Concord, NH 03301

**$ Given:** Unspecified number of $500 grants. Renewable.
**Contact:** Director, Student Aid Program.
**Deadline:** May 28.

**Restrictions:** Graduates of these NH high schools: Merrimack Valley, Bishop Brady, Hopkinton and Concord. Employees of the Bank of New Hampshire and their dependents are not eligible. Demonstrate financial need.

---

**New Hampshire Charitable Fund**
**Protestant Episcopal Fund**
1 South Street, P.O. Box 1335
Concord, NH 03301

**$ Given:** Grants of $1,200 (unspecified numbers).
**Contact:** Above address.
**Deadline:** May 30.

**Restrictions:** NH dependents of NH Episcopal ministers; financial need.

---

**New Hampshire Charitable Fund**
**Alfred Quimby Fund/Sylvania White Fund**
1 South Street, P.O. Box 1335
Concord, NH 03301

**$ Given:** Grants of $100-$1,500 (unspecified number).
**Deadline:** May 30.

**Restrictions:** Residents of Sandwich, NH; financial need.

---

**New Hampshire Charitable Fund**
**Allen Greeley Ring Fund**
1 South Street, P.O. Box 1335
Concord, NH 03301

**$ Given:** Grants of $500-$2,500 (unspecified number).
**Deadline:** May 30.

**Restrictions:** NH residents who are handicapped or are pursuing the Protestant ministry. Demonstrate financial need.

---

**New Hampshire Postsecondary Education Commission**
61 South Spring Street
Concord, NH 03301 (603)271-2555

**$ Given:** 1200 $100-$1,500 scholarships per year. Renewable.
**Contact:** College Scholarship Service, FAS, Princeton, NJ 08541.
**Deadline:** May 1.

**Restrictions:** Resident of NH, upper ⅗ of high school graduating class.

---

**Edward Wagner & George Hosser Scholarship Fund Trust**
c/o Amoskeag National Bank and Trust Company
P.O. Box 150
Manchester, NH 03105 (603)624-3608

**$ Given:** 295 grants totaling $125,301.
**Deadline:** April 30.

**Restrictions:** Male residents from Manchester, NH and vicinity.

**Sarah E. Young Trust**
c/o Bankeast Trust Company
P.O. Box 1
Rochester, NH 03867 (603)335-1527

**$ Given:** Grants totaling $21,650.
**Contact:** Brenda Harrington.

**Restrictions:** College sophomores or above, residents of Rochester or surrounding counties.

# NEW JERSEY

**Allied Foundation**
Columbia Road and Park Avenue
P.O. Box 2245R
Morristown, NJ 07960 (201)455-2671

**$ Given:** 80 grants totaling $283,600.
**Contact:** Margaret C. Petri, Contributions Administrator.

**Restrictions:** NJ residents.

**Fieldcrest Foundation**
c/o Fieldcrest Mills
326 Stadium Road
Eden, NC 27288 (919)627-3000

**$ Given:** Grants totaling $33,000.

**Restrictions:** NC, CA, GA, IL, NJ, NY, VA students.

**The Horbach Fund**
c/o National Community Bank of New Jersey
113 West Essex Street
Maywood, NJ 07607

**$ Given:** 5 grants from $500-$1,000.
**Contact:** 40 Glen Road, Mountain Lakes, NJ 07041.

**Restrictions:** CT, MA, NJ, NY, RI students; financial need. Must be under 20.

**Dorothy Van Dyke McLane Association**
c/o A. C. Reeves Hicks
6 Charlton Street
Princeton, NJ 08540 (201)924-1065

**$ Given:** 41 grants totaling $18,400 ranging from $150-$1,200.
**Contact:** J. L. Bolster, Jr., Chairman Scholarship Committee, Princeton University.

**Restrictions:** NJ high school seniors from Princeton borough and township.

**Marine Corps Scholarship Foundation Inc.**
**Marine Corps Scholarship Foundation Awards**
20 Nassau Street
Princeton, NJ 08540 (609)921-3534

**$ Given:** Grants of $250-$1,000.
**Deadline:** February 1.

**Restrictions:** Children of Marines or ex-Marines; financial need.

**New Jersey Department of Higher Education**
Office of Student Assistance, CN 540
Trenton, NJ 08625 (609)292-4435 or (800)792-8670

**$ Given:** Grants of $200-$1,500 for undergraduates, $200-$4,000 for graduate students.
**Deadline:** Varies.

**Restrictions:**
NJ residents, financial need. Some grants only for dependents of emergency service or law enforcement personnel killed in line of duty.

---

**Virginia Harkness Sawtelle Foundation**
c/o Summit and Elizabeth Trust Company
367 Springfield Avenue
Summit, NJ 07901

**$ Given:** 25 grants totaling $32,749.
**Contact:** 33 North Fullerton Ave., Montclair, NJ 07042.
**Deadline:** April 1.

**Restrictions:**
NJ residents.

---

**William A. and Mary A. Shreve Foundation, Inc.**
c/o Robert M. Wood, Esquire
200 Atlantic Avenue
P.O. Box I
Manasquan, NJ 08736

**$ Given:** 30 grants totaling $34,323, ranging from $375-$2,900.

**Restrictions:**
NJ, PA, VT students.

---

**Otto Sussman Trust**
c/o Sullivan & Cromwell
125 Broad Street
New York, NY 10004

**$ Given:** 25 grants totaling $52,114.

**Restrictions:**
Residents of NY, NJ, OK, PA.

---

# NEW MEXICO

**American Indian Scholarships, Inc.**
P.O. Box 1106
Taos, NM 87571 (505)758-8601

**Deadline:** April 30.

**Restrictions:**
American Indian members of a federally recognized tribe; NM graduate students.

---

**Thomas & Dorothy Leavey Foundation**
4680 Wilshire Boulevard
Los Angeles, CA 90036 (213)436-5875

**$ Given:** 72 grants of $1,250-$2,500.

**Restrictions:**
AZ, CA, CO, MT, NM, NV, OR, WY, ID, UT residents.

**New Mexico Veterans Service Commission**
P.O. Box 2324
Santa Fe, NM 87503 (505)827-2292

**$ Given:** Unspecified number of full tuition scholarships per year.

**Restrictions:** NM children 16-26 years of age, of NM veterans who were killed in action or died during a period of armed conflict. Demonstrate financial need; attend school in NM.

---

**Viles Foundation, Inc.**
c/o Sunwest Bank
3000 Mackland Avenue, NE
Albuquerque, NM 87106

**$ Given:** 74 grants totaling $44,056, ranging from $250-$750.
**Contact:** Viles Foundation, P.O. Box 1177, Las Vegas, NM 87701.
**Deadline:** April 1.

**Restrictions:** Students from San Miguel and Mora Counties, NM.

---

# NEW YORK

**American Occupational Therapy Foundation, Inc.**
**Carolyn W. Kohn Scholarship Fund**
1383 Piccard Dr., Suite 203
Rockville, MD 20850-4375 (301)948-9626

**$ Given:** 2 awards of $500 for assistant students. 15 awards of $1,000 for undergraduates. 2 awards of $1,000 for graduate students.
**Deadline:** December 15.

**Restrictions:** NY undergraduate and graduate students.

---

**Arthur R. Atwood Scholarship Fund**
Key Trust Company
60 State Street
Albany, NY 12207

**$ Given:** 21 grants totaling $4,400, average grant $200.
**Contact:** Superintendent of schools, Northeast Clinton County School District, Champlain, NY 12919.
**Deadline:** April 15.

**Restrictions:** Students from Clinton and Champlain counties, NY, who are seven-year residents.

# New York·71

**Avon Products, Inc.**
**Scholarship Program**
Suffern, NY 10901

**$ Given:** $2,000 max per yr. Renew 3 yrs.
**Contact:** Personnel Manager.
**Deadline:** November 2.

**Restrictions:**
Resident of Ramapo Central School District in Suffern, NY area since junior year. Complete high school by August 31 prior to fall term. Top 10% of class. Financial need.

---

**Baird Memorial Trust**
c/o Marcella Pambrun
The Domestic and Foreign Missionary Society
of The Episcopal Church
815 Second Avenue
New York, NY 10017

**$ Given:** 30 grants totaling $15,500.

**Restrictions:**
Children of NY Episcopal and Protestant clergy and missionaries.

---

**The Theodore H. Barth Foundation, Inc.**
530 Fifth Avenue
New York, NY 10036

**$ Given:** 19 grants totaling $15,331.
**Contact:** Irving P. Berelson, Vice-President.

**Restrictions:**
NY residents.

---

**James Gordon Bennett Memorial Corporation**
200 Park Avenue, Sixth floor
New York, NY 10166 (212)692-3988

**$ Given:** 83 grants totaling $84,850, ranging from $250-$2,000.
**Contact:** Eleanor H. Keil, Associate Director for Graduate Processing, Office of Financial Aid, N.Y.U., c/o P.O. Box 908; Madison Square Station, NY, NY 10159 (212)481-5905 or 481-5906.
**Deadline:** March 1.

**Restrictions:**
NY children of journalists who have worked 10 years for a New York City daily newspaper.

---

**James J. Bloomer Charitable Trust**
P.O. Box 1522
Elmira, NY 14902

**$ Given:** 14 grants totaling $10,000, ranging from $500-$1,000.

**Restrictions:**
Residents of Elmira, NY who attend Catholic schools and are members of the Catholic Church.

## 72·FREE MONEY

**Boy Scouts of America
Greater New York City Scholarships**
345 Hudson Street
New York, NY 10014 (212)242-1100

**$ Given:** Grants of $2,500.
**Contact:** Dr. Harry Britenstool, Scholarship Committee.
**Deadline:** June 1.

**Restrictions:**
NY Boy Scouts; financial need.

---

**Branch-Wilbur Fund Inc.**
65 Broad Street
Rochester, NY 14614

**$ Given:** $500-$5,000.
**Contact:** President.

**Restrictions:**
Students from or planning to study in the Rochester, NY area. Demonstrate financial need.

---

**The Buffalo Foundation**
237 Main Street
Buffalo, NY 14203 (716)852-2857

**$ Given:** 421 grants totaling $245,263.
**Contact:** W.L. Van Schoonhoven, Director.
**Deadline:** May 25.

**Restrictions:**
Buffalo and Erie City, NY residents; financial need.

---

**Chautauqua Region Community Foundation, Inc.**
812 Hotel Jamestown Building
Jamestown, NY 14701

**$ Given:** 43 grants totaling $18,687.
**Deadline:** April 30.

**Restrictions:**
Residents of the Chautauqua area.

---

**Chautauqua Region Community Scholarship, Inc.**
812 Hotel Jamestown Office Building
Jamestown, NY 14701 (716)488-0387

**$ Given:** Many different scholarship programs.
**Contact:** Francis F. Grow.

**Restrictions:**
Residents of Jamestown, NY.

---

**Clark Foundation Scholarship Program**
P.O. Box 427
Cooperstown, NY 13326 (212)269-1833

**$ Given:** 56 awards of $500-$5,000. Renewable. 15 fellowships of $500-$3,500. Renewable.

**Restrictions:**
U.S. citizen. Restricted to residents of 11 central districts in and around Cooperstown, NY Upper ⅓ of class, GPA 3.0.

---

**Bruce L. Crary Foundation Inc.**
Hand House, River Street
P.O. Box 396
Elizabethtown, NY 12932 (518)873-6496

**$ Given:** 297 grants totaling $108,137.
**Deadline:** March.

**Restrictions:**
Residents of Clinton, Essex, Franklin, Hamilton and Warren counties.

## New York · 73

**Daughters of the Cincinnati**
122 East 58th Street
New York, NY 10022 (212)319-6915

**$ Given:** 59 grants totaling $32,674; general range $250-$750.
**Contact:** Scholarship Administrator.
**Deadline:** April 15.

**Restrictions:** High school seniors who are daughters of regular commissioned officers.

---

**Deke Foundation**
16 East 64th Street
New York, NY 10021 (212)759-0660

**$ Given:** 9 grants of $1,000.

**Restrictions:** Undergraduate members of the Delta Kappa Epsilon fraternity.

---

**Eagleton War Memorial Scholarship Fund, Inc.**
c/o Bridgehampton National Bank
Bridgehampton, NY 11932

**$ Given:** 7 grants from $500-$3,500

**Restrictions:** Graduates of Bridgehampton High School.

---

**Enrico Fermi Educational Fund of Yonkers, Inc.**
65 Pondfield Road
Bronxville, NY 10708 (914)337-4168

**$ Given:** 25 grants of $600.
**Deadline:** March.

**Restrictions:** Italian-American students from Yonkers, NY high schools.

---

**Federation of Jewish Women's Organizations**
Alexander Graham Bell Association for the Deaf, Inc.
3417 Volta Place, NW
Washington, DC 20007 (202)337-5220

**$ Given:** 1 grant of $300 and 1 grant of $200.
**Deadline:** April 15.

**Restrictions:** Deaf students in greater New York City area.

---

**Fieldcrest Foundation**
c/o Fieldcrest Mills
326 Stadium Road
Eden, NC 27288 (919)627-3000

**$ Given:** Grants totaling $33,000.

**Restrictions:** NC, CA, GA, IL, NJ, NY, VA residents.

---

**The Glens Falls Foundation**
237 Glen Street
P.O. Box 311
Glens Falls, NY 12801 (518)792-1151

**$ Given:** 27 grants totaling $7,500.
**Contact:** G. Nelson Lowe, Secretary.
**Deadline:** January 1, April 1, July 1, October 1.

**Restrictions:** Residents of Warren, Washington, & Saratoga counties.

# 74•FREE MONEY

**The Golub Foundation**
501 Duanesburg Rd.
Schenectady, NY 12306

**$ Given:** Grants totaling $217,302.
**Deadline:** April 1.

**Restrictions:** High school graduates in area served by the Price Chopper Supermarket marketing area.

---

**The Horbach Fund**
c/o National Community Bank of New Jersey
113 West Essex Street
Maywood, NJ 07607

**$ Given:** 5 grants totaling $4,500; high $1,000, low $500.
**Contact:** 40 Glen Road, Mountain Lakes, NJ 07041.

**Restrictions:** CT, MA, NJ, NY, RI gifted students under the age of 20; financial need.

---

**Howard Memorial Fund**
500 East 62nd Street
New York, NY 10021

**$ Given:** 45 grants totaling $15,290, ranging from $180-$600.
**Contact:** Gertrude N. Thomas, 199 Lawrence Ave., Inwood, N.Y. 11696 (516)CE 9-2592.

**Restrictions:** NY residents; financial need.

---

**Jewish Foundation for the Education of Women**
330 West 58th Street
New York, NY 10019 (212)265-2565

**$ Given:** Awards of $750-$1,000.
**Deadline:** October 15-January 31.

**Restrictions:** Female NY metropolitan area residents.

---

**Charles P. and Pauline M. Kautz Foundation**
United National Bank
Callicoon, NY 12723

**$ Given:** Awards of $500-$3,000.
**Deadline:** May 15.

**Restrictions:** Graduates of Delaware Valley High School.

---

**Grace Legendre Fellowships**
**Business and Professional Women's Foundation**
212 Mayro Building, 239 Genesee Street
Utica, NY 13501

**$ Given:** Grants of $1,000.
**Deadline:** February 28.

**Restrictions:** NY female graduate students.

---

**Ludwig Vogelstein Foundation Inc.**
P.O. Box 537
New York, NY 10013

**$ Given:** Up to $5,000.
**Contact:** Douglas B. Turnbaugh, Treasurer.

**Restrictions:** For individuals who have no other sources of support.

# New York • 75

**Meredith Corporation**
**Edwin T. Meredith Foundation 4-H Scholarship**
1767 Locust Street
Des Moines, IA 50336 (515)284-2545

**Contact:** State 4-H leader.

**Restrictions:**
IL, IN, IA, KS, MI, MO, MN, NE, NY, ND, OH, OK, PA, SD, WI residents, present or former 4-H Club members.

---

**Meyers Ti-Caro Foundation, Inc.**
P.O. Box 699
Gastonia, NC 28052 (704)864-9711

**$ Given:** 32 scholarships of $250-$7,000.

**Restrictions:**
Students who are children of employees.

---

**William T. Morris Foundation, Inc.**
P.O. Box 5786
New York, NY 10163

**$ Given:** Grants vary.
**Contact:** Arthur C. Laske, President.

**Restrictions:**
NY, CT residents. (Areas of American Chain and Cable Company.)

---

**New York State Higher Education Services Corporation**
99 Washington Avenue
Albany, NY 12255 (518)474-5042

**$ Given:** Unspecified number of $200-$1,800 awards for undergraduates; unspecified $350-$5,000 awards for graduate students. Renewable.
**Contact:** Above address.
**Deadline:** March 31.

**Restrictions:**
Citizen or permanent resident of U.S. NY resident for 1 year. Full-time attendance at approved NY State institution.

---

**Arthur C. and Lucia S. Palmer Foundation, Inc.**
471 Pennsylvania Avenue
Waverly, NY 14892 (607)565-4603

**$ Given:** $250-$1,500 per semester.
**Contact:** President.
**Deadline:** May 1.

**Restrictions:**
Residents of Waverly, NY. Demonstrate financial need.

---

**Phi Kappa Theta National Foundation**
c/o Gregory Stein
111-55 77th Avenue
Forest Hills, NY 11375

**$ Given:** 6 grants totaling $4,000, average grant $666.
**Deadline:** April 30.

**Restrictions:**
Members of Phi Kappa Theta fraternity.

---

**Philip E. Potter Foundation**
6 Ford Avenue
Oneonta, NY 13820 (607)432-6720

**$ Given:** 72 grants of $150-$450 totaling $28,950.
**Contact:** Henry L. Hulbert, Secretary.

**Restrictions:**
Residents of Otsego and Delaware counties, NY.

## 76·FREE MONEY

**The Pratt-Northam Foundation**
c/o Bond, Schoeneck and King
One Lincoln Center
Syracuse, NY 13202 (315)422-0121

**$ Given:** 9 grants totaling $12,500.
**Contact:** Mrs. Mary R. Petrie, P.O. Box 104, Lowville, NY 13367.

**Restrictions:**
Residents of the Black River Valley region, NY.

---

**Edith Grace Reynolds Estate Residuary Trust**
c/o Key Trust Co.
60 State Street, P.O. Box 1965
Albany, NY 12207

**$ Given:** 311 grants totaling $103,725.
**Contact:** Trust Officer.
**Deadline:** February 15.

**Restrictions:**
Graduates of school district 1, Rensselaer County.

---

**Regents of the University of the State of New York**
**Higher Education Opportunity Program (HEOP)**
Cultural Education Center, Room 5A-55
Albany, NY 12230 (518)474-5313

**$ Given:** 5,600 awards of $100-$1,500 per year. Renewable.
**Contact:** HEOP Director, Independent college or university in NY State.

**Restrictions:**
Resident of NY, high school graduate, economically disadvantaged. SAT scores, approved NY institution.

---

**Roothbert Fund, Inc.**
360 Park Avenue South, 15th floor
New York, NY 10010 (212)679-2030

**$ Given:** Average grant $1,000, total given $59,000.
**Contact:** Secretary.
**Deadline:** March 1.

**Restrictions:**
Preference given to persons with high scholastic requirements and who are considering teaching as their vocation. Must appear in NY for interview.

---

**Scalp and Blade Scholarship Trust**
c/o Manufacturers and Trade Trust Company
One Manufacturers & Traders Plaza
Buffalo, NY 14240 (716)842-5535

**$ Given:** 12 grants of $250-$500.

**Restrictions:**
Male high school seniors from Erie County, NY, who plan to attend schools outside Erie and Niagara County.

---

**The Leopold Schepp Foundation**
15 East 26th St., Suite 1900
New York, NY 10010 (212)889-9737

**$ Given:** Grants totaling $324,450.
**Contact:** Executive Secretary.
**Deadline:** December 31.

**Restrictions:**
Undergraduates under thirty years of age, graduate students under 40.

---

**The Starr Foundation**
70 Pine Street
New York, NY 10270 (212)770-6882

**$ Given:** 219 grants totaling $417,991.
**Contact:** President.

**Restrictions:**
Brewster, NY school district high school graduates.

# New York·77

**Stony-Wold Herbert Fund, Inc.**
136 East 57th Street, Room 1705
New York, NY 10022 (212)753-6565

**$ Given:** 15 grants totaling $40,875.
**Contact:** Executive Director.

**Restrictions:**
NY students with respiratory illnesses.

---

**Otto Sussman Trust**
c/o Sullivan & Cromwell
125 Broad Street
New York, NY 10004

**$ Given:** 25 grants totaling $52,114.

**Restrictions:**
Residents of NY, NJ, OK, PA.

---

**University of the State of New York Higher Education Opportunity Program (HEOP)**
Cultural Education Center, Room 5A-55
Albany, NY 12230 (518)474-5313

**$ Given:** 5,561 awards of $100-$1,500. Renewable.
**Contact:** HEOP Director at participating institution or above address.

**Restrictions:**
Resident of NY; high school graduate or equivalency, disadvantaged academically & financially but with potential. Enroll in NY institution.

---

**Utica Foundation, Inc.**
233 Genesee Street
Utica, NY 13501 (315)797-9200

**$ Given:** 37 grants between $500-$5,000.

**Restrictions:**
Residents of Utica, Oneida, and Herkimer counties.

---

**David Wasserman Scholarship Fund, Inc.**
107 Division Street
Amsterdam, NY 12010 (518)843-2800

**$ Given:** 134 grants totaling $21,450; average grant $300.
**Contact:** Norbert J. Sherbunt, President.
**Deadline:** April 15.

**Restrictions:**
Montgomery County, NY residents.

---

**Watertown Foundation, Inc.**
216 Washington Street
Watertown, NY 13601 (315)782-7110

**$ Given:** Unspecified number of $250-$2,000 awards per year. Renewable.
**Contact:** Executive Secretary at above address.

**Restrictions:**
Residents of Jefferson County, NY High School graduate enrolled in accredited institution. Must demonstrate academic achievement and financial need.

---

**Watertown Foundation, Inc.**
216 Washington St.
Chase Lincoln First Bank Building
Watertown, NY 13601 (315)782-7110

**$ Given:** 203 grants totaling $252,000.
**Deadline:** February 1, August 1.

**Restrictions:**
Residents of Watertown and Jefferson Counties.

## 78·FREE MONEY

**Roy Wilkins Educational Scholarship Program**
144 West 125th Street
New York, NY 10027 (212)666-9740

**$ Given:** 10-12 awards of up to $1,000.

**Restrictions:**
NY minority high school seniors, college freshmen and sophomores.

---

**Youth Foundation, Inc.**
36 West 44th Street
New York, NY 10036

**$ Given:** 50 grants of $1,500.
**Contact:** Include self-addressed, stamped envelope.
**Deadline:** April 15.

**Restrictions:**
NY residents, show need as well as ability.

---

# NORTH CAROLINA

**James E. and Mary Z. Bryan Foundation, Inc.**
1307 Glenwood Avenue
Raleigh, NC 27605 (919)821-4771

**$ Given:** 22 awards—$1,500 (max) per year. Not renewable.
**Contact:** Bryan Foundation Special Scholarship Committee at local high school.
**Deadline:** April 1.

**Restrictions:**
Graduating senior at Goldsboro High School or Hobbton High School in Goldsboro, NC. Financial need. Submit Parent Confidential Statement request to College Scholarship Service by March 1.

---

**Carolina Freight Carriers Corporation**
P.O. Box 697
Cherryville, NC 28021 (704)435-6811

**$ Given:** 4 grants of $1,000.
**Contact:** Public Relations Manager at above address.
**Deadline:** April 15.

**Restrictions:**
Residents of the area served by Carolina Freight Carriers Corporation. (2 awards go to children of employees.)

---

**Elizabeth City Foundation**
P.O. Box 220
Elizabeth City, NC 27909

**$ Given:** Grants totaling $26,731.
**Deadline:** April 1.

**Restrictions:**
Residents of Camden County.

---

**Chatham Foundation, Inc.**
c/o Chatham Manufacturing Co.
Elkin, NC 28621 (919)835-2211

**$ Given:** 15 scholarships of $1,000.

**Restrictions:**
Students of Chatham employees.

# North Carolina · 79

**College Foundation, Inc.**
1307 Glenwood Avenue
Raleigh, NC 27605 (919)821-4771

**$ Given:** Unspecified number of $1,500 grants per year. Renewable.
**Contact:** Program Administrator, above address.
**Deadline:** March 15.

**Restrictions:**
NC residents. Financial need.

---

**Huffman Cornwell Foundation**
Wachovia Bank and Trust Co.
P.O. Box 3099
Winston Salem, NC 27102 (919)770-5000

**$ Given:** 14 scholarships of $200-$750.

**Restrictions:**
NC residents.

---

**Percy B. Ferebee Endowment**
c/o Wachovia Bank & Trust Co.
P.O. Box 3099
Winston Salem, NC 27102 (919)770-5000

**$ Given:** 55 grants totaling $62,000.
**Deadline:** February 15.

**Restrictions:**
Given in western NC communities.

---

**Fieldcrest Foundation**
c/o Fieldcrest Mills
326 Stadium Road
Eden, NC 27288 (919)627-3000

**$ Given:** Grants totaling $33,000.

**Restrictions:**
NC, CA, GA, IL, NJ, NY, VA residents.

---

**Foundation for the Carolinas**
301 South Brevard Street
Charlotte, NC 28202 (704)376-9541

**$ Given:** 15 grants totaling $12,398.

**Restrictions:**
Given in NC, SC.

---

**Garrison Community Foundation of Gaston County, Inc.**
P.O. Box 123
Gastonia, NC 28053 (704)864-0927

**$ Given:** 15 grants totaling $6,214.

**Restrictions:**
Residents of NC, particularly Gaston County.

---

**Meyers Ti-Caro Foundation, Inc.**
P.O. Box 699
Gastonia, NC 28052 (704)864-9711

**$ Given:** 32 scholarships of $250-$7,000.

**Restrictions:**
Children of employees.

---

**John Motley Morehead Foundation**
P.O. Box 348
Chapel Hill, NC 27514 (919)962-1201

**$ Given:** 245 awards totaling $1 million.

**Restrictions:**
Selected universities only. By nomination only. See financial aid officer.

## 80•FREE MONEY

**North Carolina Association of Educators**
P.O. Box 27347
Raleigh, NC 27611 (919)832-3000

**$ Given:** $1,000 for senior year.
**Contact:** Department Head.
**Deadline:** February 1.

**Restrictions:**
NC college juniors willing to teach at least 2 years in NC public school following graduation.

---

**North Carolina Division of Veterans Affairs**
227 East Edenton Street
Raleigh, NC 27601 (919)733-3851

**$ Given:** Unspecified number of $444-$1,200 awards per year in private N.C. institution; free tuition in state institution. Renewable.
**Contact:** Above address.
**Deadline:** Apply during senior yr. in high school.

**Restrictions:**
Son or daughter of veteran who resided in NC at time of entry to Armed Forces; died or disabled, POW or MIA. If parent is not a resident, child must have been born and lived continually in NC.

---

**The C. D. Spangler Foundation, Inc.**
1028 South Boulevard
Charlotte, NC 28203

**$ Given:** Awards totaling $3,900.

**Restrictions:**
NC residents.

---

**Sigmund Sternberger Foundation, Inc.**
P.O. Box 3111
Greensboro, NC 27402 (919)378-1791

**$ Given:** 14 grants totaling $13,878.
**Contact:** Executive Director.

**Restrictions:**
Children of members of the Revolution Masonic Lodge.

---

**Thomasville Furniture Industries Foundation**
Wachovia Bank and Trust Company
P.O. Box 3077
Winston-Salem, NC 27102 (919)770-5000

**$ Given:** 46 awards totaling $27,000.

**Restrictions:**
NC residents.

---

**The Winston-Salem Foundation**
229 First Union National Bank Building
Winston-Salem, NC 27101 (919)725-2382

**$ Given:** 253 grants totaling $2,985,596.
**Contact:** Program Manager.
**Deadline:** January 1, March 1, May 1, July 1, September 1.

**Restrictions:**
Residents of Forsyth County, NC.

# NORTH DAKOTA

**The Hatterscheidt Foundation, Inc.**
c/o First Bank-Aberdeen
320 South First Street
Aberdeen, SD 57401 (605)225-9400

**$ Given:** 100 grants totaling $100,000.
**Contact:** Kenneth P. Johnson, Vice-President and Trust Officer, First Bank-Aberdeen.
**Deadline:** March 1.

**Restrictions:**
ND, SD high school seniors in top 25% of class.

---

**Meredith Corporation**
**Edwin T. Meredith Foundation 4-H Scholarship**
1767 Locust Street
Des Moines, IA 50336 (515)284-2545

**Contact:** State 4-H leader.

**Restrictions:**
IL, IN, IA, KS, MI, MO, MN, NE, NY, ND, OH, OK, PA, SD, WI residents, present or former 4-H Club members.

---

**North Dakota State Indian Scholarship Board**
State Capitol Building
Bismarck, ND 58505 (701)224-2428

**$ Given:** 120—$2,000 scholarships per year. Renewable.
**Contact:** Secretary at above address.
**Deadline:** June 15.

**Restrictions:**
ND resident attending ND college; one-fourth Indian blood or enrolled in tribe. Financial need.

---

**North Dakota Student Financial Assistance Agency**
10th floor, Capitol Building
Bismarck, ND 58505 (701)224-2960

**$ Given:** Unspecified number of $500 awards per year.
**Contact:** Director at above address.
**Deadline:** April 15.

**Restrictions:**
Resident of ND.

# OHIO

**Avon Products, Inc.**
175 Progress Place
Springdale, OH 45246

**$ Given:** $2,000 max per year. Renew 3 years.
**Contact:** Personnel Dept.
**Deadline:** November 15.

**Restrictions:**
Resident of Princeton School District since junior year. Top 10% of class. Financial need.

## 82 • FREE MONEY

**Ernst And Whinney Foundation**
2000 National City Center
Cleveland, OH 44114 (216)861-5000

**Contact:** James Peters.

**Restrictions:**
Doctoral accounting students.

---

**Fenn Educational Fund of the Cleveland Foundation**
1400 Hanna Building
Cleveland, OH 44115 (216)861-3810

**$ Given:** 100 awards of $100-$4,800. Renewable.
**Contact:** College or university in which enrolled.

**Restrictions:**
Cooperative students who are residents of OH enrolled in colleges or graduate schools in the greater Cleveland area.

---

**The S. N. and Ada Ford Fund**
P.O. Box 849
Mansfield, OH 44901 (419)526-3493

**$ Given:** 321 grants totaling $312,228.

**Restrictions:**
Residents of Richland County, OH.

---

**The Gardener Foundation**
P.O. Box 126
Middletown, OH 45042

**$ Given:** 16 grants totaling $34,995.
**Deadline:** April 1.

**Restrictions:**
Middletown and Hamilton County seniors.

---

**Hamilton Community Foundation, Inc.**
319 North Third Street
Hamilton, OH 45011 (513)863-1389

**$ Given:** 2 grants totaling $525.
**Contact:** Cynthia V. Parrish, Executive Director.

**Restrictions:**
Residents of greater Hamilton-Fairfield, OH area.

---

**Hauss-Helms Foundation, Inc.**
Peoples National Bank Building
P.O. Box 25
Wapakoneta, OH 45895 (419)738-4911

**$ Given:** 121 grants totaling $185,470.

**Restrictions:**
Graduating seniors of Auglaize or Allen County, OH; financial need.

---

**Dr. R. S. Hosler Memorial Educational Fund**
50 Bortz Street
P.O. Box 5
Ashville, OH 43103 (614)983-2054

**$ Given:** 13 grants totaling $102,191.
**Contact:** 154 E. Main St., Ashville, OH 43103

**Restrictions:**
Graduates of Teays Valley and Amanda Clearcreek school systems.

---

**Charles Kilburger Scholarship Fund**
Equitable Building
Lancaster, OH 43130 (614)653-0461

**$ Given:** 84 grants totaling $122,361.

**Restrictions:**
Residents of Fairfield County, OH.

# Ohio·83

**Edwin L. and Louis B. McCallay Educational Trust Fund**
c/o Trust First National Bank of Southwestern Ohio
P.O. Box 220
Middletown, OH 45042 (513)425-7548

**$ Given:** 27 grants totaling $15,270, ranging from $200-$850.

**Restrictions:** Middletown, Ohio city school district graduates.

---

**John McIntire Educational Fund**
c/o Zanesville Canal and Manufacturing Co.
P.O. Box 2668
Zanesville, OH 43701 (614)452-8444

**$ Given:** 114 grants totaling $109,733, ranging from $150-$1,400.
**Contact:** R. L. Hecker, Senior Trust Officer.

**Restrictions:** Unmarried students under 21 years who live within the city limits of Zanesville, OH.

---

**Edward Arthur Mellinger Educational Foundation, Inc.**
1025 East Broadway
P.O. Box 278
Monmouth, IL 61462 (309)734-2419

**$ Given:** 947 grants totaling $264,813; average grant $450.
**Contact:** Shirley J. Neill, Administrative Assistant.
**Deadline:** June 1.

**Restrictions:** IL, IA, MI, MN, MO, OH, WI, IN students.

---

**Meredith Corporation**
**Edwin T. Meredith Foundation, 4-H Scholarships**
1716 Locust Street
Des Moines, IA 50336 (515)284-2545

**Contact:** State 4-H leader.

**Restrictions:** IL, IN, IA, KA, MI, MN, NE, NY, ND, OH, OK, PA, SD, WI residents who are present or former 4-H club members.

---

**The Mount Vernon Community Trust**
c/o First Knox National Bank
P.O. Box 871
Mount Vernon, OH 43050 (614)397-6344

**$ Given:** 5 grants totaling $9,500.
**Contact:** Frederick N. Lovey, Chairman.

**Restrictions:** Residents of Knox County, OH.

---

**National Machinery Foundation, Inc.**
161 Greenfield Street, P.O. Box 747
Tiffin, OH 44883 (419)447-5211

**$ Given:** 9 awards totaling $18,000.
**Contact:** Don Bero.

**Restrictions:** Children of employees.

---

**James R. Nicholl Memorial Foundation**
The Central Trust Co. of Northern Ohio, Trust Department
1949 Broadway
Lorain, OH 44052 (216)244-1965

**$ Given:** Varies.

**Restrictions:** Needy students; residents of Lorain county for at least 2 years.

## 84•FREE MONEY

**Ohio Board of Regents**
**Ohio Academic Scholarship Program**
3600 State Office Tower
30 East Broad Street
Columbus, OH 43215 (614)466-1190

**$ Given:** 2,000—$1,000 awards per year. Renewable.
**Contact:** Director, Student Assistance Office at above address.
**Deadline:** February 23.

**Restrictions:**
U.S. citizen, OH resident, high school graduate (some scholarships require top students of OH high schools), enrolled in OH institution.

---

**Ohio Instructional Grant**
3600 State Office Tower
30 East Broad Street
Columbus, OH 43215 (614)466-1190

**$ Given:** Unspecified number of $156-$2,478 grants per year. Renewable.
**Contact:** Above address or call (614)466-7420.
**Deadline:** August 16.

**Restrictions:**
Citizen of U.S., resident of OH. Enrolled full-time in course of study leading to degree in religion or theology, or the religious profession in an institution in OH or PA. Demonstrate financial need and good academic standing.

---

**Ohio National Guard Scholarships**
3600 State Office Tower
30 East Broad Street
Columbus, OH 43215 (614)466-1190

**$ Given:** Unspecified number of $1,000 awards per year. Renewable.
**Contact:** Director, Student Assistance Office at above address.
**Deadline:** Before 10th day of classes for term of 1st scholarship use.

**Restrictions:**
U.S. citizen, OH resident. Some require enlistment in OH National Guard on or after September 1, 1977. All must sign up for 6 year service commitment with National Guard.

---

**Ohio War Orphans Scholarship Board**
3600 State Office Tower
30 East Broad Street
Columbus, OH 43215 (614)466-1190

**$ Given:** Unspecified number, varying amounts up to $1,300 per year. Renewable.
**Contact:** Above address.
**Deadline:** July 1.

**Restrictions:**
OH resident, age 16-21. Child of veteran deceased, disabled, POW or MIA (Vietnam). Must attend institution in OH. Some residency restrictions apply.

---

**George J. Record School Foundation**
P.O. Box 581
Conneaut, OH 44030 (216)599-8283

**$ Given:** 112 grants totaling $132,097.
**Deadline:** May 20 for freshmen; June 20 for upperclassmen.

**Restrictions:**
Residents of Ashtabula County, OH. Must attend approved private college and complete 6 quarter hours of religious study.

# Ohio•85

**C. R. Schmidlapp Fund**
36 East Fourth Street, Room 1004
Cincinnati, OH 45263 (513)721-5122

**$ Given:** 300 loans totaling $453,694.
**Contact:** Janice Thompson.

**Restrictions:** Females age 16-25 in the greater Cincinnati, OH area.

---

**Scholarship Fund, Inc.**
c/o Ernest Weaver, Jr.
University of Toledo
2801 West Bancroft Street
Toledo, OH 43606 (419)537-4632

**$ Given:** 28 grants totaling $18,551, ranging from $226-$1,200.

**Restrictions:** Students in northwest OH area. Based on need and academic excellence.

---

**William M. Shinnick Educational Fund**
534 Market Street
Zanesville, OH 43701

**$ Given:** 23 grants totaling $59,600.

**Restrictions:** Residents of Muskingum County, OH.

---

**John Q. Shunk Association**
P.O. Box 625
Bucyrus, OH 44820

**$ Given:** 33 grants totaling $76,976.
**Contact:** Jane C. Peppard, 1201 Timber Lane, Marion, Ohio 43302.

**Restrictions:** Graduates of Bucyrus, Colonel Crawford, Wynford and Buckeye Central, OH high schools.

---

**Florence B. and Clyde W. Stouch Foundation Fund**
Heritage Bank, Trust Department
P.O. Box 1428
Steubenville, OH 43952 (614)282-3661

**$ Given:** One $1,500 scholarship per year. Renewable to 8 years.

**Restrictions:** Resident of Jefferson County, OH interested in pursuing academic program at Ohio State University or resident of York County, PA, interested in pursuing academic program at University of Pennsylvania. Demonstrate financial need. Must not be an anarchist or person believing in violent overthrow of U.S. government.

---

**The Van Wert County Foundation**
101 ½ East Main Street
Van Wert, OH 45891 (419)238-1743

**$ Given:** 71 grants totaling $48,650.
**Deadline:** May 25, November 25.

**Restrictions:** Van Wert County, OH residents. Scholarships in art, music, agriculture, and home economics.

**The Wagnalls Memorial**
150 East Columbus Street
Lithopolis, OH 43136 (614)837-4765

**$ Given:** 218 grants totaling $182,150.
**Deadline:** June 15.

**Restrictions:**
Graduates of Bloom Township high schools.

---

**Eleanor M. Webster Testamentary Trust**
c/o AmeriTrust
P.O. Box 5937
Cleveland, OH 44101

**Contact:** Christine Kruman, Ameritrust Co., 237 Tuscarawas St. West, Canton, OH 44702.

**Restrictions:**
Students preferably from Stark City, OH who have completed at least 1 year at an OH college or university.

# OKLAHOMA

**Edward E. Bartlett and Helen Turner Bartlett Foundation**
c/o Antwine Pryor
Sapulpa High School
1 South Mission
Sapulpa, OK 74066

**$ Given:** 16 grants totaling $113,450.

**Restrictions:**
Graduates of Sapulpa High School attending certain OK colleges and universities.

---

**The Mervin Bovaird Foundation**
800 Oneok Plaza
100 West Fifth Street
Tulsa, OK 74103

**$ Given:** 62 awards totaling $226,655.
**Contact:** Fenelon Boesche, President.

**Restrictions:**
Students attending the University of Tulsa.

---

**Cherokee Nation of Oklahoma**
P.O. Box 948
Tahlequah, OK 74465 (918)456-0671
800-722-4325

**$ Given:** Varies.
**Deadline:** March/November.

**Restrictions:**
Members of Cherokee Nation of OK. Undergraduates may major in any subject. Graduate students must major in business or the health fields. Cannot receive funding from any other source.

---

**Cheyenne-Arapaho Tribe**
**Cheyenne-Arapaho Tribal Scholarships**
P.O. Box 38
Concho, OK 73022 (405)262-0345

**$ Given:** 140 grants per semester based on student's financial needs.

**Restrictions:**
Member of Cheyenne-Arapaho tribe.

# Oregon·87

**Dexter G. Johnson Educational and Benevolent Trust**
644 Avondale Dr.
Oklahoma City, OK 73116

**$ Given:** 13 grants totaling $6,669.

**Restrictions:**
Local giving.

---

**Warren B. Hudson Scholarship Trust**
c/o D. C. Anderson
21101 East 101st Street
Broken Arrow, OK 74012 (918)455-4138

**$ Given:** 14 scholarships totaling $3,480.
**Deadline:** April 15.

**Restrictions:**
Seniors of Broken Arrow High School.

---

**Meredith Corporation**
**Edwin T. Meredith Foundation, 4-H Scholarships**
1716 Locust Street
Des Moines, IA 50336 (515)284-2545

**Contact:** State 4-H leader.
**Deadline:** December, April, July, September.

**Restrictions:**
OK residents.

---

**Oklahoma State Regents for Higher Education**
State Capitol Complex
500 Education Building
Oklahoma City, OK 73105 (405)521-2444, ext. 62

**$ Given:** Grants and loans based on individuals' needs.
**Deadline:** Varies.

**Restrictions:**
OK residents attending OK colleges and universities.

---

**F. B. Parriott Educational Fund**
First National Bank and Trust Company of Tulsa, Trust Department
P.O. Box 1
Tulsa, OK 74193 (918)586-1000

**$ Given:** 12 scholarships totaling $28,780

**Restrictions:**
Those attending OK colleges and universities.

---

**Otto Sussman Trust**
c/o Sullivan & Cromwell
125 Broad Street
New York, NY 10004

**$ Given:** 25 grants totaling $52,114

**Restrictions:**
Residents of NY, NJ, OK, PA

---

# OREGON

**Bend Foundation**
510 Baker Building
Minneapolis, MN 55403 (612)332-2454

**$ Given:** 4 grants totaling $23,120.
**Contact:** 416 Northeast Greenwood, Bend, OR 97701
**Deadline:** December.

**Restrictions:**
Residents of central OR; preference to cities in Bend and Deschutes counties.

## 88·FREE MONEY

**The Clemens Foundation**
P.O. Box 427
Philomath, OR 97370 (503)929-3541

**$ Given:** 292 grants totaling $306,907.

**Restrictions:** Residents of Philomath, Eddyville, Crane and Alsea.

---

**Bernard Daly Educational Fund**
P.O. Box 309
Lakeview, OR 97630 (503)947-2196

**$ Given:** 47 awards totaling $84,600.
**Deadline:** April 1.
**Contact:** P.O. Box 351, Lakeview, OR 97630.

**Restrictions:** Residents of Lake County, OR to study at OR schools.

---

**The S. S. Johnson Foundation**
P.O. Box 356
Redmond, OR 97756 (503)548-8104

**$ Given:** 3 grants totaling $900.
**Contact:** Elizabeth Hill Johnson, President.
**Deadline:** July 15.

**Restrictions:** OR residents attending schools primarily in the Pacific Northwest and Northern California.

---

**Ochoco Scholarship Fund**
P.O. Box 668
Prineville, OR 97754 (503)447-5661

**$ Given:** 52 awards totaling $19,440; general range $240-$540.
**Contact:** David Doty, Crook County High School, East First Street, Prineville, OR 97754

**Restrictions:** OR residents in Prineville (Crook County).

---

**Oregon PTA Teacher Education Scholarships**
531 South East 14th
Portland, OR 97214 (503)234-3928

**$ Given:** $250 per year.
**Deadline:** March 1.

**Restrictions:** OR high school and college students; majoring in Education.

---

**Oregon Public Employees Union (OPEU)**
1127 25th Street, Southeast
Salem, OR 97301 (503)581-1505

**$ Given:** Unspecified number of $660 grants per year.
Renewable.
**Deadline:** April 1.
**Contact:** Oregon State Scholarship Commission.

**Restrictions:** None.

---

**Oregon Public Employees Union Scholarship**
1445 Willamette Street
Eugene, OR 97401

**Restrictions:** Member or relative of member of OPEU.

---

**The Salem Foundation**
c/o Pioneer Trust Co.
P.O. Box 2305
Salem, OR 97308

**$ Given:** 33 grants totaling $138,808.

**Restrictions:** Giving limited to Salem area.

| | | |
|---|---|---|
| **Harley and Mertie Stevens Memorial Fund**<br>P.O. Box 3168<br>Portland, OR 97208 (503) 225-4456 | **Contact:** Linda Babcock<br>**Deadline:** May 31. | **Restrictions:**<br>Graduates of Clackamas County, OR high schools attending OR state-funded institutions or Protestant church affiliated colleges in OR. |
| **General George A. White and Maria C. Jackson Aid for Children of War Veterans**<br>c/o United States National Bank of Oregon<br>P.O. Box 3168<br>Portland, OR 97208 (503)275-4456 | **$ Given:** 16 grants totaling $14,950.<br>**Contact:** Roberta Kinohi.<br>**Deadline:** May 31. | **Restrictions:**<br>U.S. armed forces veterans or their children; OR residents. |

# PENNSYLVANIA

| | | |
|---|---|---|
| **Department Of Military Affairs Bureau of Veterans Affairs**<br>Fort Indiantown Gap<br>Annville, PA 17003-5002 (717)274-4909 | **$ Given:** unlimited $200 (max) grants per semester. Renewable to $1,600 for 4 years. | **Restrictions:**<br>5 year. PA resident between 16-21 years of age. Son or daughter of veteran who died or was totally disabled in war. Must attend PA institution. |
| **Eugene Dozzi Charitable Foundation**<br>2000 Lincoln Road<br>Pittsburgh, PA 15235 | **$ Given:** 3 grants totaling $3,320; $725-$1,595. | **Restrictions:**<br>PA residents preferably from Pittsburgh. |
| **Ruby Marsh Eldred Scholarship Trust**<br>c/o Marine Bank<br>P.O. Box 8480<br>Erie, PA 16553 | **$ Given:** $5,250.<br>**Deadline:** March 1. | **Restrictions:**<br>Students from Meadville, PA area and western Crawford County, PA area. |
| **William Goldman Foundation**<br>1700 Walnut Street, Suite 800<br>Philadelphia, PA 19103 (215)546-2779 | **$ Given:** 46 awards totaling $45,750, average grant $1,000.<br>**Contact:** Marilyn Klein, Executive Director.<br>**Deadline:** March 15. | **Restrictions:**<br>Philadelphia area residents attending graduate or medical school at specific Philadelphia institutions. |

**The Hall Foundation**
2862 Russell Road
Camp Hill, PA 17011

**$ Given:** 243 grants totaling $251,417.

**Restrictions:** Children of employees & customers.

---

**Margaret & Irwin Hesher Foundation**
c/o First Seneca Bank
Oil City, PA 16301 (814)676-8666

**$ Given:** 71 grants totaling $49,925.
**Deadline:** Submit proposals in April, August, November.

**Restrictions:** Graduates of Union High School, Clarion County.

---

**The Hoyt Foundation**
c/o First National Bank Building
P.O. Box 1488
New Castle, PA 16103

**$ Given:** 72 grants totaling $72,035.
**Deadline:** July 15; December 15

**Restrictions:** Given primarily in PA.

---

**Hunt Manufacturing Company Foundation**
1405 Locust Street
Philadelphia, PA 19102 (215)732-7700

**$ Given:** 16 grants totaling $7,450.
**Contact:** William E. Parshall, Secretary.
**Deadline:** December, February, June, September.

**Restrictions:** Children of employees of Hunt Manufacturing.

---

**A. B. Kempel Memorial Fund**
c/o Mellon Bank
P.O. Box 9
Oil City, PA 16301 (814)676-7123 ext. 414

**$ Given:** 1 grant totaling $750 for one college year.
**Contact:** Shirley J. Holowell, Assistant Trust Officer.

**Restrictions:** East Brady, PA high school students.

---

**Leidy-Rhoads Foundation Trust**
c/o Girard Trust Bank
1 Girard Plaza
Philadelphia, PA 19101 (215) 367-6031

**$ Given:** 48 grants totaling $45,538; average grant $1,000.
**Contact:** Jean Butt, Boyertown Area School District, 911 Montgomery Avenue, Boyertown, PA 19512.

**Restrictions:** Boyertown, PA residents.

# Pennsylvania·91

**Meredith Corporation**
Edwin T. Meredith Foundation,
4-H Scholarships
1716 Locust Street
Des Moines, IA 50336 (515)284-2545

**Contact:** State 4-H leader.

**Restrictions:**
IL, IN, IA, KA, MI, MN, NE, NY, ND, OH, OK, PA, SD, WI residents who are present or former 4-H club members.

---

**Negro Educational Emergency Drive (NEED)**
Two Mellon Bank Center, Room 497
Pittsburgh, PA 15219 (412)566-2760

**$ Given:** 835 awards ranging from $100-$1,000.
**Deadline:** May 15.
**Contact:** Guidance counselor or above address.

**Restrictions:**
Black students from Allegheny, Armstrong, Weaver, Butler, Washington, or Westmoreland counties. High school graduate. Renewable.

---

**Mary Margaret Nestor Foundation**
Reiff and West Streets
Lykens, PA 17048 (717)453-7113

**$ Given:** 45 grants totaling $31,700, ranging from $400-$800.
**Contact:** Robert E. Nestor

**Restrictions:**
Residents of Lykens, PA and surrounding area.

---

**Horace B. Packer Foundation, Inc.**
61 Main Street
Wellsboro, PA 16901 (717)724-1406

**$ Given:** 44 grants totaling $17,163, ranging from $300-$600.
**Contact:** Charles G. Webb, President.
**Deadline:** May 1.

**Restrictions:**
Tioga County, PA residents.

---

**Pennsylvania Higher Education Assistance Agency**
Towne House
Harrisburg, PA 17102 1-800-692-7435

**$ Given:** Unspecified number of $1,500 grants for study at PA school. Renewable. For veterans, also $800 for study at out-of-state institution. Renewable.
**Deadline:** May 1.

**Restrictions:**
PA residents; financial need. Submit SAT or ACT scores and file for PELL grant. Veterans must have served 180 days or more.

---

**Pennsylvania Higher Education Assistance Agency**
**State Grants for Veterans**
Towne House
Harrisburg, PA 17102 (717)257-2500

**$ Given:** 80% of tuition and fees, not to exceed $1,500.
**Deadline:** May.

**Restrictions:**
PA residents, veterans of U.S. armed services; financial need.

## 92·FREE MONEY

**Pennsylvania Higher Education Assistance Agency**
**POW/MIA Program**
Towne House
Harrisburg, PA 17102 (717)257-2500

**$ Given:** 80% of tuition and fees, not to exceed $1,500.
**Deadline:** May.

**Restrictions:** PA residents, dependents of members or former members of U.S. armed services who served on active duty after January 31, 1955 and are or have been POW/MIA; financial need.

---

**Quaker Chemical Foundation**
Elm and Lee Streets
Conshohocken, PA 19428 (215)828-4250

**$ Given:** Grants totaling $60,622.
**Contact:** Karl H. Spaeth, Chairman.
**Deadline:** May 13.

**Restrictions:** For children of employees.

---

**William A. and Mary A. Shreve Foundation, Inc.**
P.O. Box 1
Red Bank, NJ 07701

**$ Given:** 25 grants totaling $33,975, ranging from $500-$2,000.
**Contact:** Robert M. Wood, Esquire, Secretary-Treasurer

**Restrictions:** NJ, PA, VT students.

---

**Sico Foundation**
Mount Joy, PA 17552 (717)653-1411

**$ Given:** 75 $900 scholarships per year. Renewable to $3,000 total over 4 years.

**Restrictions:** Resident of DE or counties of Adams, Berks, Chester, Cumberland, Dauphin, Delaware, Lancaster, Lebanon, York in PA or Cecil County, MD; or student attending Shippensburg H.S., the Boyertown H.S., Spring-Ford H.S. in DE. Must be entering freshman at state college in PA.

---

**Harry E. and Florence W. Snayberger Memorial Foundation**
c/o Pennsylvania National Bank and Trust Company
1 South Centre Street
Pottsville, PA 17901 (717)622-4200

**$ Given:** 839 grants totaling $117,028.
**Deadline:** February and March.

**Restrictions:** Residents of Schuylkill County, PA.

**Sordoni Foundation, Inc.**
c/o Warren E. Myers
R.D. 5, Box 148, Elmcrest Drive
Dallas, PA 18612 (717)675-5730

**$ Given:** 48 grants totaling $43,800.
**Deadline:** May 1.

**Restrictions:**
Residents of Luzerne County.

---

**Florence B. and Clyde W. Stouch Foundation Fund**
Heritage Bank, Trust Department
P.O. Box 1428
Steubenville, OH 43952 (614)282-3661

**$ Given:** 1 award of $1,500 per year, renewable.

**Restrictions:**
Residents of Jefferson County, OH or York County, PA; financial need; must not be an anarchist.

---

**Anna M. Vincent Trust**
c/o Girard Trust Bank
One Girard Plaza
Philadelphia, PA 19101 (215)585-3208

**$ Given:** 116 Grants totaling $143,174.
**Deadline:** March 1.
**Contact:** R. McKernan, Girard Bank, Three Girard Plaza, Philadelphia, PA 19101.

**Restrictions:**
Residents of PA; giving limited to Delaware Valley area.

---

**The Warren Foundation**
P.O. Drawer 69
Warren, PA 16365

**$ Given:** 105 grants totaling $60,075.

**Restrictions:**
Limited to Warren County.

---

**Benjamin & Fedora Wolf Foundation**
Park Towne Place - North Building 1205
Philadelphia, PA 19130 (215)787-6079

**$ Given:** 108 grants totaling $94,250.
**Deadline:** June 1.
**Contact:** Administrator

**Restrictions:**
Given in Philadelphia area

# PUERTO RICO

**Harvey Foundation, Inc.**
507 First Federal Building
1519 Ponce de Leon Avenue
Santurce, PR 00909

**$ Given:** 5 grants totaling $12,039.

**Restrictions:**
Given primarily in PR.

# RHODE ISLAND

**George Abrahamian Foundation**
P.O. Box 2964, North Station
Providence, RI 02908 (401)831-0008

**$ Given:** 5 grants totaling $2,750; each grant $550.
**Contact:** Abraham G. Abraham, Treasurer.
**Deadline:** September.

**Restrictions:**
RI students of Armenian descent to attend schools primarily in RI.

---

**East Providence Citizen's Scholarship Foundation**
East Providence Senior High School
2000 Pawtucket Avenue
East Providence, RI 02914 (401)437-0750

**Contact:** Guidance counselor.

**Restrictions:**
East Providence, RI high school graduates or graduating seniors who have not already received financial aid.

---

**The Horbach Fund**
c/o National Community Bank of New Jersey
113 West Essex Street
Maywood, NJ 07607

**$ Given:** 5 grants totaling $4,500; low $500, high $1,000.
**Contact:** 40 Glen Road, Mountain Lakes, NJ 07041.

**Restrictions:**
CT, MA, NJ, NY, RI students; financial need. Must be under 20.

---

**Rhode Island Higher Education Assistance Authority**
274 Weybosset Street
Providence, RI 02903 (401)277-2050

**$ Given:** Grants ranging from $250-$1,500, renewable.
**Deadline:** March 1.
**Contact:** Consultant, State Scholarships at above address.

**Restrictions:**
Residents of RI; financial need. Submit SAT scores.

---

**The Suttell Foundation**
c/o Saint Paul's Church
50 Park Place
Pawtucket, RI 02860

**$ Given:** Grants of $500.
**Deadline:** September 1.

**Restrictions:**
Residents of RI, preference given to medical studies or work with youth.

# SOUTH CAROLINA

**Bailey Foundation**
P.O. Box 1276
Clinton, SC 29325 (803)833-6830

**$ Given:** 14 grants totaling $22,268.
**Contact:** Bill Carter.

**Restrictions:**
Children of employees of Bailey Bank or Clinton Mills; educationial and medical professionals who will locate in Lawrence County.

---

**James F. Byrnes Foundation**
P.O. Box 9596
Columbia, SC 29290 (803)776-1211

**$ Given:** Average grant is $1,500.
**Contact:** Executive Secretary.
**Deadline:** March 1.

**Restrictions:**
SC residents who have lost one or both parents by death.

---

**The Dave Cameron Educational Foundation**
P.O. Box 181
York, SC 29745 (803)684-4968

**$ Given:** 40 awards totaling $25,750; average grant $500.
**Contact:** Margaret S. Adkins.

**Restrictions:**
Undergraduate students within York, SC who maintain a minimum 2.0 grade point average.

---

**Charleston Evening Post/The News and Courier**
**Post-Courier College Scholarship Program**
P.O. Box 758
Charleston, SC 29402 (803)577-7111

**$ Given:** $1,400.
**Contact:** Circulation Promotion Manager.

**Restrictions:**
Newspaper carriers of the News and Courier and Charleston Evening Post; minimum 2 years route service.

---

**Daniel Foundation of South Carolina**
The Daniel Building
Greenville, SC 29602 (803)298-2500

**$ Given:** Grants totaling $24,500.

**Restrictions:**
Daniel employees.

---

**Dr. Edgar Clay Doyle and Mary Cherry Memorial Fund**
c/o South Carolina National Bank
101 Greystone Boulevard, Unit 9075
Columbia, SC 29226

**$ Given:** 70 awards totaling $77,000.
**Deadline:** March 15.
**Contact:** Lacy McClean, SC Foundation of Independent Colleges, Scholarship Committee, P.O. Box 6998, Greenville, SC 29606; (803)233-6894.

**Restrictions:**
Oconee County, SC high school graduates for undergraduate study at a SC college.

## 96 • FREE MONEY

**Kittie M. Fairey Educational Fund**
c/o The South Carolina National Bank
P.O. Box 168
Columbia, SC 29202 (803)765-3576

**$ Given:** 49 grants totaling $184,586.

**Restrictions:** Residents of SC planning to attend colleges in SC.

---

**C. G. Fuller Foundation**
P.O. Box 2307
Columbia, SC 29202 (803)771-2990

**$ Given:** 33 grants totaling $65,500.

**Restrictions:** SC residents attending colleges and universities in SC.

---

**Horne Foundation**
**Dick Horne Scholarship**
P.O. Box 306
Orangeburg, SC 29116 (803)534-2096

**$ Given:** Grants based on need of student.
**Contact:** Helen Williams.

**Restrictions:** Orangeburg residents attending universities or colleges.

---

**Meyer Ti-Caro Foundation, Inc.**
P.O. Box 699
Gastonia, NC 28052 (704)864-9711

**$ Given:** 32 scholarships ranging from $250-$7,000.

**Restrictions:** Children of employees.

---

**Alfred Moore Foundation**
c/o C.L Page Enterprises, Inc.
P.O. Box 18426
Spartanburg, SC 29318 (803)582-6844

**$ Given:** 15 grants totaling $16,350
**Deadline:** April 15.

**Restrictions:** Limited to Anderson and Spartanburg counties.

---

**South Carolina Department of Veterans Affairs**
1205 Pendleton Street
Columbia, SC 29201 (803)758-2607

**$ Given:** Unspecified number of tuition-only awards.

**Restrictions:** Child of SC veteran deceased in action or action related service, disabled, POW or recipient of Medal of Honor. SC state-supported institution. Usually terminates at age 26.

---

**South Carolina Higher Education Tuition Grants Program**
411 Keenan Building
P.O. Box 11638
Columbia, SC 29211 (803)758-7070

**$ Given:** 8,000—$2,000 awards per year. Renewable.
**Contact:** High school guidance counselor or participating colleges.
**Deadline:** May 1.

**Restrictions:** Residents of SC studying in one of nineteen private, post-secondary schools in SC; financial need.

**Spartanburg County Foundation**
805 Montgomery Building
Spartanburg, SC 29301 (803)582-0138

**$ Given:** Scholarships totaling $37,185.

**Restrictions:**
Residents of Spartanburg County; see high school or college counselor.

# SOUTH DAKOTA

**The Hatterscheidt Foundation, Inc.**
c/o First Bank Of Aberdeen
320 South First Street
Aberdeen, SD 57401 (605)225-9400

**$ Given:** 100 grants totaling $100,000.
**Contact:** Kenneth P. Johnson, Vice President and Trust Officer.
**Deadline:** February.

**Restrictions:**
SD high school seniors in top 25% of class. ND residents within 100 mile radius of Jamestown.

**Edward Arthur Mellinger Educational Foundation, Inc.**
1025 East Broadway
P.O. Box 278
Monmouth, IL 61462 (309)734-2419

**$ Given:** 947 grants totaling $264,813; average grant $450.
**Contact:** Shirley J. Neill, Administrative Assistant.

**Restrictions:**
IL, IA, KY, MI, MN, NE, OH, SD, WI students.

**Meredith Corporation**
**Edwin T. Meredith Foundation**
**4-H Scholarships**
1716 Locust Street
Des Moines, IA 50336 (515)284-2545

**Contact:** State 4-H leader.

**Restrictions:**
IL, IN, IA, KS, MI, MN, NE, NY, ND, OH, OK, PA, SD, WI residents who are present or former 4-H club members.

**South Dakota Department of Education & Cultural Affairs**
Kneip Office Building
Pierre, SD 57501 (605)773-3134

**$ Given:** Unspecified number of $200 scholarships per semester. Renewable.
**Deadline:** June 1.
**Contact:** Secretary at above address.

**Restrictions:**
Resident of SD 12 months prior to registration as Freshman, full-time in private accredited college in SD. Demonstrate financial need. Not for theology, religion or athletic scholarship.

**South Dakota Board of Regents**
Kneip Building
Pierre, SD 57501 (605)773-3455

**$ Given:** Unspecified number of tuition scholarships. Not renewable.
**Contact:** Campus Veterans Advisor, So. Dakota Colleges & Universities.

**Restrictions:** Resident of SD; veteran who has exhausted federal benefits.

## TENNESSEE

**Aluminum Company of America**
P.O. Box 9158
Alcoa, TN 37701 (615)977-2011

**Contact:** Public Relations Manager.

**Restrictions:** Children of employees.

---

**American National Bank and Trust Company**
736 Market Street
Chattanooga, TN 37402 (615)757-3281

**Contact:** J. Ralston Wells, Secretary.

**Restrictions:** Eastern TN residents.

---

**The Daniel Ashley and Irene Houston Jewell Memorial Foundation**
c/o American National Bank and Trust Company
P.O. Box 1638
Chattanooga, TN 37401 (615)757-3204

**$ Given:** 4 grants totaling $4,000.
**Contact:** Peter T. Cooper, Trust Officer.

**Restrictions:** TN, GA residents.

---

**Elizabeth Buford Shepherd Scholarship Committee**
c/o First American Center
First American National Bank, Trust Department
Nashville, TN 37327 (615)748-2170

**$ Given:** 74 scholarships ranging from $250-$500.
**Deadline:** March 1.
**Contact:** Edith Perry.

**Restrictions:** TN residents.

---

**Tennessee Student Assistance Corporation**
B-3 Capitol Towers
Nashville, TN 37219 (615)741-1346

**$ Given:** Unspecified number of $100-$1,098 awards.
**Deadline:** August 1.

**Restrictions:** TN residents; high school graduates; must apply for PELL grant and attend TN schools; financial need.

**Westend Foundation, Inc.**
1100 American National Bank Building,
736 Market Street
Chattanooga, TN 37401 (615)265-8881

**$ Given:** 34 grants totaling $59,871.
**Contact:** Raymond B. Witt, Jr., Secretary.

**Restrictions:**
Undergraduate and graduate students from Chattanooga, TN.

# TEXAS

**Austin Community Foundation for Capitol Area**
P.O. Box 5159
Austin, TX 78763 (512)459-8292

**Restrictions:**
High school students of Austin and Travis counties, TX.

---

**Baumberger Endowment**
7701 Broadway, Dijon Plaza
P.O. Box 6067
San Antonio, TX 78209 (512)882-8915

**$ Given:** 496 grants totaling $1,791,608.
**Deadline:** January 31 for financial forms; February 15 for high school transcripts.

**Restrictions:**
High school seniors and graduates from Bexar County, TX attending TX colleges with financial need.

---

**Clark Foundation**
6116 North Central Expressway, Suite 906
Dallas, TX 75206 (214)361-7498

**$ Given:** 125 $1,000 awards. Not renewable.
**Deadline:** May 1.
**Contact:** Walter Kerbel, Executive Secretary.

**Restrictions:**
Resident of Dallas Independent School District and/or state of TX. Must compete for awards. Must be high school graduate in year award is made; score 850 on CEEB or SAT. Must carry and pass 15 credit hours each semester.

---

**The El Paso Community Foundation**
El Paso National Bank Building, Suite 1616
El Paso, TX 79901 (915)533-4020

**$ Given:** 155 grants totaling $505,542.

**Restrictions:**
El Paso area.

---

**The Fasken Foundation**
500 West Texas Avenue, Suite 1160
Midland, TX 79701 (915)683-5401

**$ Given:** 155 grants totaling $106,661.

**Restrictions:**
Midland high school students attending schools in TX.

# 100·FREE MONEY

**Fiji Foundation of Texas**
7200 North MoPac, Suite 340
Austin, TX 78731 (512)346-3917

**$ Given:** 8 grants totaling $6,300; average grant $750.
**Contact:** L. Hutch Hubby, President.

**Restrictions:**
TX residents.

---

**Paul and Mary Haas Foundation**
P.O. Box 2928
Corpus Christi, TX 78403

**$ Given:** 34 grants totaling $16,691.

**Restrictions:**
TX students; financial need.

---

**George and Mary Josephine Hamman Foundation**
1000 Louisiana, Suite 820
Houston, TX 77002

**$ Given:** 97 grants totaling $116,250.
**Contact:** Charles D. Milby, President.
**Deadline:** April.

**Restrictions:**
Houston, TX area high school students. Undergraduate scholarships.

---

**Leola W. and Charles H. Hugg Trust**
c/o First City National Bank
P.O. Box 809
Houston, TX 77001

**$ Given:** 181 grants totaling $110,125.
**Deadline:** May 1.
**Contact:** Carroll Sunseri

**Restrictions:**
Students from Williamson attending colleges and universities in TX.

---

**Carl B. and Florence E. King Foundation**
1 Preston Centre
8222 Douglas Avenue, Suite 370
Dallas, TX 75225 (214)750-1884

**$ Given:** 74 grants totaling $73,000.

**Restrictions:**
Given primarily in the Dallas area.

---

**Luling Foundation**
523 South Mulberry Avenue
P.O. Drawer 31
Luling, TX 78648 (512)875-2438

**$ Given:** 5 loans totaling $4,500.
**Contact:** Archie Abrameit, Manager.
**Deadline:** May 15.

**Restrictions:**
Residents of Caldwell, Gonzales and Guadalupe counties, TX.

---

**Bruce McMillan Jr. Foundation, Inc.**
P.O. Box 9
Overton, TX 75684 (214)834-3148

**$ Given:** 114 grants totaling $72,948.
**Deadline:** June 5.

**Restrictions:**
Specific high schools in the immediate Overton area.

---

**The Moody Foundation**
704 Moody National Bank Building
Galveston, TX 77550 (409)763-5333

**$ Given:** 518 grants totaling $350,495.

**Restrictions:**
Galveston County freshman entering TX colleges and universities.

# Texas • 101

**Minnie Stevens Piper Foundation**
201 North St. Mary's Street, Suite 100
San Antonio, TX 78205 (512)227-8119

**$ Given:** Grants totaling $238,378.
**Deadline:** February 1 and July 1.

**Restrictions:**
Residents of TX. Must be nominated.

---

**C. L. Rowan Charitable and Educational Fund, Inc.**
1918 Commerce Building
Fort Worth, TX 76102

**$ Given:** 4 grants totaling $15,795; ranging from $1,500-$7,795.
**Contact:** Nita Gothard, Secretary-Treasurer.

**Restrictions:**
TX residents attending TX universities.

---

**San Antonio Area Foundation**
808 Travis Building
405 North St. Mary's, Suite 800
San Antonio, TX 78205 (512)225-2243

**$ Given:** 37 grants totaling $27,300.
**Deadline:** February 15.

**Restrictions:**
San Antonio area.

---

**Robert Schreck Memorial Educational Fund**
Texas Commerce Bank-El Paso
P.O. Drawer 140
El Paso, TX 79941

**$ Given:** Awards of $300-$1,500.

**Restrictions:**
Students from El Paso County, TX studying theology, medicine, veterinary medicine, physics, chemistry, engineering, architecture. Must have completed 2 years of college. U.S. citizen.

---

**The M. L. Shanor Foundation**
P.O. Box 7522
Wichita Falls, TX 76307 (817)761-2401

**$ Given:** 37 grants totaling $45,140.
**Contact:** J. B. Jarratt, President.
**Deadline:** August 1.

**Restrictions:**
Primarily local giving.

---

**Nelda C. and H. J. Lutcher Stark Foundation**
602 West Main Street
P.O. Drawer 909
Orange, TX 77630 (713)883-3513

**$ Given:** 4 grants totaling $1,670.
**Contact:** Clyde V. McKee, Jr., Secretary-Treasurer.

**Restrictions:**
TX, southwest LA residents.

**Hope Pierce Tartt Scholarship Fund**
P.O. Box 1964
Marshall, TX 75670 (214)938-6622

**$ Given:** 26 grants totaling $443,103.
**Deadline:** July 31.

**Restrictions:** Preferably students from Harrison, Gregg, Marion, Upshur, Panola counties, TX attending private institutions.

---

**Texas College & University System, Coordinating Board, Div. of Student Service Public Educational State Student Incentive Grant Program**
P.O. Box 12788, Capitol Station
Austin, TX 78711 (512)475-8169

**$ Given:** Unspecified number to $2,000 (max) awards per year.
**Contact:** Financial aid office at your institution.

**Restrictions:** TX residents who are students at TX insitutions; financial need. For some awards, athletic scholarships and religious degrees are not acceptable.

---

**The Frank and Bea Wood Foundation**
2304 Midwestern Parkway, Suite 204
Wichita Falls, TX 76308

**$ Given:** 17 grants totaling $14,000.
**Contact:** Martha Kay Hendrickson, President.

**Restrictions:** TX residents.

---

# UTAH

**Ruth Eleanor and John Ernest Bamberger Memorial Foundation**
175 South Main Street, Suite 1407
Salt Lake City, UT 84111 (801)364-2045

**$ Given:** 29 awards totaling $21,965.

**Restrictions:** Given in UT; especially undergraduate scholarships for student nurses.

---

# VERMONT

**Faught Memorial Scholarships**
c/o Bellows Falls Trust
P.O. Box 399
Bellows Falls, VT 05101 (802)463-4524

**$ Given:** 5 grants ranging from $500-$1,500.
**Deadline:** June 1.

**Restrictions:** Bellows Falls, VT students.

---

**General Educational Fund, Inc.**
c/o The Merchants Trust Co.
P.O. Box 1009
Burlington, VT 05402

**$ Given:** 352 grants totaling $232,850.
**Deadline:** May.

**Restrictions:** VT residents.

**William A. and Mary A. Shreve Foundation Inc.**
P.O. Box 1
Manasquan, NJ 08736

**$ Given:** 25 grants totaling $33,975, ranging from $250-$4,000.
**Contact:** Robert M. Wood, Esq., Secretary-Treasurer.

**Restrictions:**
NJ, PA, VT residents.

---

**Vermont Student Assistance Corporation**
Box 2000
Burlington, VT 05404 (802)655-9602

**$ Given:** Unspecified number of $100-$300 scholarships.
**Contact:** Above address or VT county senator.

**Restrictions:**
Resident of VT, attend approved VT institution. Demonstrate financial need.

---

**Eleanor White Trust**
c/o First Vermont Bank and Trust Company
89 Merchants Row
Rutland, VT 05701 (802)773-3321

**$ Given:** 25 awards totaling $53,510; general range $1,000-$3,000.
**Contact:** Richard S. Smith, P.O. Box 147, Rutland, VT 05701 (802)775-3368.

**Restrictions:**
Residents of Fair Haven, VT.

---

**The Windham Foundation**
P.O. Box 68
Grafton, VT 05146 (802)843-2211

**$ Given:** 357 grants totaling $116,590.

**Restrictions:**
Windham County, VT residents.

# VIRGINIA

**David S. Blount Educational Foundation**
c/o Colonial American National Bank
P.O. Box 13888
Roanoke, VA 24038

**$ Given:** Grants totaling: $99,181.

**Restrictions:**
VA residents attending colleges and universities in VA.

---

**Ethel N. Bowen Foundation, Inc.**
c/o First National Bank of Bluefield
500 Federal Street
Bluefield, WV 24701 (304)325-8181

**$ Given:** 75 grants totaling $141,708, ranging from $500-$6,000.
**Contact:** R. W. Wilkinson, Secretary-Treasurer.

**Restrictions:**
Students from southern WV and southwestern VA coal fields.

## 104·FREE MONEY

**Camp Foundation**
c/o Sol W. Rawls, Jr.
P.O. Box 813
Franklin, VA 23851 (804)562-3439

**$ Given:** 26 grants totaling $52,000.
**Contact:** High School principal.
**Deadline:** February 26 for filing with principals. March 15 for principals to file with the foundation.

**Restrictions:**
High school graduates from Southampton, Isle of Wight, Tidewater, VA counties and northeastern NC.

---

**Fieldcrest Foundation**
c/o Fieldcrest Mills
326 Stadium Road
Eden, NC 27288 (919)627-3000

**$ Given:** Grants totaling $33,000.

**Restrictions:**
NC, CA, GA, IL, NJ, NY, VA students.

---

**The Lincoln Lane Foundation**
1 Main Plaza East, Suite 1102
Norfolk, VA 23510 (804)622-2557

**$ Given:** 132 grants totaling $181,590.

**Restrictions:**
Tidewater, VA area residents.

---

**The Norfolk Foundation**
1410 Sovran Center
Norfolk, VA 23510 (804)622-7951

**$ Given:** 150 grants totaling: $186,271.
**Contact:** R. L. Sheetz, Executive Director.
**Deadline:** December 1 to March 1.

**Restrictions:**
Residents of Norfolk, VA and 50 mile radius area.

---

**The Pickard Scholarship**
Del-Mar-Va Council
Eighth and Washington Streets
Wilmington, DE 19801 (302)652-3741

**Restrictions:**
Explorer and Boy scouts from DE, MD, VA.

---

**The William H., John G. and Emma Scott Foundation**
c/o Davenport and Co.
Ross Building, Eighth and Main Street
Richmond, VA 23219 (804)780-2035

**$ Given:** 22 grants totaling $12,950.
**Contact:** Clinton Webb, Treasurer.
**Deadline:** January 1.

**Restrictions:**
Local VA residents.

---

**Sigma Nu Educational Foundation, Inc.**
P.O. Box 1869
Lexington, VA 24450 (703)463-2164

**$ Given:** 20 grants totaling $6,200.
**Contact:** Richard R. Fletcher, President.

**Restrictions:**
Undergraduate and graduate awards to Sigma Nu Fraternity members.

# Virginia • 105

| | | |
|---|---|---|
| **The Slemp Foundation**<br>c/o W.C. Edmonds<br>Big Stone Gap, VA 24219 | **$ Given:** 209 grants totaling $166,900.<br>**Contact:** The First National Bank of Cincinnati, P.O. Box 118, Cincinnati, OH 45201 (513)852-4585. | **Restrictions:**<br>None. |
| **Virginia Federation of Women's Clubs Dorothea Buck Latin American Fellowship**<br>The Berkshire, Suite 402-W<br>300 West Franklin Street<br>Richmond, VA 23220 | **$ Given:** 1 $3,000 fellowship. Not renewable.<br>**Deadline:** January 31.<br>**Contact:** Above address. | **Restrictions:**<br>Woman, U.S. citizen, VA resident, preferably under 35 years old. Must hold degree from VA institution, be able to read, speak and write Portuguese or Spanish. Present evidence of church membership. For one year study in Latin American country. |
| **Virginia Federation of Business & Professional Women's Clubs, Inc.**<br>300 W. Franklin Street, Suite 402-W<br>Richmond, VA 23220 (804)644-2558 | **$ Given:** $300.<br>**Deadline:** May 1. | **Restrictions:**<br>Virginia residents sponsored by a local member club of the V.F.W.C. Show financial need, academic record and goals. |
| **Virginia State Council of Higher Education**<br>101 North Fourteenth Street<br>James Monroe Building<br>Richmond, VA 23229 (804)225-2141 | **$ Given:** Grants ranging from $200-$950. Renewable.<br>**Deadline:** April 15, June 1, September 10.<br>**Contact:** Above address. | **Restrictions:**<br>Undergraduate VA residents enrolled in private or public VA schools. Financial need. |
| **Young America's Foundation**<br>11800 Sunrise Valley Drive, Suite 812<br>Reston, VA 22090 | **$ Given:** $1,000.<br>**Deadline:** April 15. | **Restrictions:**<br>Emphasis on conservative philosphy and point of view. Must show aptitude for leadership and financial need. |

# WASHINGTON, DC

**Office of Post-Secondary Education, Research & Assistance**
1331 H Street Northwest, Suite 600
Washington, DC 20005 (202)727-3688

**$ Given:** Unspecified number of $400-$1,500 awards. Renewable.
**Deadline:** Apply March 1-June 30.
**Contact:** Grant Program, above address.

**Restrictions:** Citizen or permanent resident. Resident of DC 15 months prior to application. Must show financial need.

---

**District of Columbia Public Schools**
**Elks National Foundation Most Valuable Student Awards**
Division of Student Services
415 12th Street, Northwest
Washington, DC 20004

**$ Given:** Unspecified number of $600-$3,000 awards per year.
**Contact:** Guidance Counselor or above address.

**Restrictions:** High school senior; demonstrate scholarship, leadership & financial need.

---

**District of Columbia Public Schools**
Division of Student Services
Century III Leaders NASSP
415 12th Street, Northwest
Washington, DC 20004

**$ Given:** 2—$1,000 awards (max) per year.

**Restrictions:** High school senior. Must take exam in current events. Must submit original essay and take an interview.

---

**District of Columbia Public Schools**
Division of Student Services
Sgt. Michael J. Acri Memorial Award
Fifth District
415 12th Street, Northwest
Washington, DC 20004

**$ Given:** One $750 award per year.
**Contact:** Guidance counselor or above address.

**Restrictions:** Senior; reside in and attend 5th District. Demonstrate scholarship, leadership, financial need.

---

**District of Columbia Public Schools**
Division of Student Services
Boston Area Black Alumni Association
415 12th Street, Northwest
Washington, DC 20004

**$ Given:** Unspecified number of $150 awards per year.
**Contact:** Guidance counselor or above address.

**Restrictions:** Black high school senior planning to enroll in college in Boston metropolitan area.

# Washington, DC · 107

**District of Columbia Public Schools**
Division of Student Services
C & P Telephone Co., First District of Columbia
Area Colleges' Scholarship Program
415 12th Street, Northwest
Washington, DC 20004

**$ Given:** Unspecified number of $250-$1,000 awards per year.
**Contact:** Above address.

**Restrictions:**
Must be accepted for enrollment at a Washington, DC college or university. Demonstrate financial need.

---

**District of Columbia Public Schools**
Division of Student Services
Delta Sigma Theta Sorority/Alumnae Chapter Awards
415 12th Street, Northwest
Washington, DC 20004

**$ Given:** Unspecified number of $100-$500 awards per year.

**Restrictions:**
Show outstanding scholarship, potential, and financial need.

---

**District of Columbia Public Schools**
Division of Student Services
William Randolph Hearst Foundation, Senate Youth Program
415 12th Street, Northwest
Washington, DC 20004

**$ Given:** 2—$1,500 awards per year.

**Restrictions:**
High school senior.

---

**Martha V. Johnson Memorial Scholarships**
District of Columbia Public Schools
Division of Student Services
415 12th Street, Northwest
Washington, DC 20004

**$ Given:** 4 awards of $4,000.

**Restrictions:**
Washington, DC female high school seniors with financial need and outstanding potential.

---

**Washington Teachers Union Scholarship Fund**
P.O. Box 39070
Washington, DC 20016 (202)755-6593

**$ Given:** Four $1,000 Scholarships. Not renewable.
**Deadline:** April.
**Contact:** Washington Teachers Union Scholarship Fund Committee at your high school.

**Restrictions:**
High school graduate enrolled or preparing to enroll in teacher training program at accredited institution. Limited to DC public school seniors.

# WASHINGTON

**Nellie Martin Carman Scholarship Trust**
c/o Seattle Trust and Savings Bank
P.O Box 12907
Seattle, WA 98111 (206)223-2220

**$ Given:** 86 grants totaling $84,425.
**Deadline:** Submit in April.

**Restrictions:**
King, Snohomish, Pierce County, WA high school graduates who will attend colleges in WA.

---

**Viola Vestal Coulter Foundation, Inc.**
c/o United Bank of Denver
P.O. Box 5247
Denver, CO 80274

**$ Given:** 21 grants totaling $33,750.
**Contact:** Charles H. Meyers, Trust Officer.

**Restrictions:**
Students attending certain schools in CO, ID, WA.

---

**The S. S. Johnson Foundation**
P.O. Box 356
Redmond, OR 97756 (503)548-8104

**$ Given:** 3 grants totaling $900.
**Contact:** Elizabeth Hill Johnson, President.
**Deadline:** July 15.

**Restrictions:**
OR residents for schools primarily in the Pacific Northwest and northern CA.

---

**Bernice A. B Keyes Trust**
c/o Puget Sound National Bank, Trust
P.O. Box 1258
Tacoma, WA 98401 (206)593-3832

**$ Given:** 29 grants totaling $60,666.
**Contact:** High school counselors.

**Restrictions:**
Tacoma area students.

---

**The Olympia-Tumwater Foundation**
P.O. Box 4098
Tumwater, WA 98501 (206)943-2550

**$ Given:** 5 grants totaling $10,000, ranging from $500-$3,000.
**Contact:** Don M. Lee, Vice-President.
**Deadline:** May 1.

**Restrictions:**
WA residents from Thurston County who are graduating seniors from a Thurston County high school and are planning to attend college in WA.

---

**Helen Martha Schiff Foundation**
c/o Bank of California
P.O. Box 3123
Seattle, WA 98114

**$ Given:** 4 grants totaling $8,325, ranging from $1,350-$4,200.

**Restrictions:**
WA residents.

---

**Belle Smith Scholarship Fund**
c/o Puget Sound National Bank
P.O. Box 1258
Tacoma, WA 98401

**$ Given:** 12 awards totaling $30,000; each grant $2,500.

**Restrictions:**
Purdy, WA high school graduates.

# Washington · 109

| | | |
|---|---|---|
| **Spokane Inland Empire Foundation**<br>926 Paulsen Building<br>Spokane, WA 99201 (509)624-2606 | **$ Given:** 53 grants from $350-$650<br>**Deadline:** April 1. | **Restrictions:**<br>Students living in Spokane or Lincoln counties, WA to major in agriculture, business or psychology. |
| **Spokane Inland Empire Foundation**<br>926 Paulsen Building<br>Spokane, WA 99201 (509)624-2606 | **$ Given:** 53 grants totaling $18,550.<br>**Deadline:** October 1 (Spokane, WA); November 1 (Pullman & Dayton, WA). | **Restrictions:**<br>Giving limited to inland Northwest. |
| **Washington Council for Postsecondary Education**<br>**Washington State Need Grant Program**<br>908 East Fifth<br>Olympia, WA 98504 (206)753-3571 | **$ Given:** 11,000 grants per year, according to need. Renewable.<br>**Contact:** Director of Financial Aid at the institution of your choice. | **Restrictions:**<br>Citizen or permanent resident of U.S., resident of WA. Must attend WA institution and demonstrate financial need. Not for study of theology. |
| **Washington State Aid to Blind Students**<br>908 East Fifth<br>Olympia, WA 98505 (206)753-3571 | **Contact:** Marilyn Sjolund.<br>**Deadline:** September 1. | **Restrictions:**<br>Legally blind WA students attending WA institutions. |
| **George T. Welch Testamentary Trust**<br>c/o Baker-Boyer National Bank<br>P.O. Box 1796<br>Walla Walla, WA 99362 (509)525-2000 | **$ Given:** 60 grants totaling $95,730.<br>**Contact:** Trust Officer.<br>**Deadline:** May 1. | **Restrictions:**<br>Residents of Walla Walla County. |
| **W.F. & Glanch E. West Educational Fund**<br>c/o First Interstate Bank of Washington, Trust Department<br>473 North Market Boulevard, P.O. Box 180<br>Chehalis, WA 98532 | **$ Given:** Grants totaling $89,013.<br>**Deadline:** April 15.<br>**Contact:** High school. | **Restrictions:**<br>Graduates of W.F. West High School who have been residents of Lewis County for 2 years. |

# WEST VIRGINIA

| | | |
|---|---|---|
| **Ethel N. Bowen Foundation**<br>c/o First National Bank of Bluefield<br>500 Federal Street<br>Bluefield, WV 24701 (304)325-8181 | **$ Given:** Grants averaging $2,000. | **Restrictions:**<br>VA students in southern coalfields and students in southern WV. |

# 110·FREE MONEY

**The Greater Kanawha Valley Foundation**
P.O. Box 3041
Charleston, WV 25331 (304)346-3620

**$ Given:** 200 grants totaling $200,371.
**Deadline:** April 1, July 1, October 1, December 1.

**Restrictions:** WV residents.

---

**The Berkeley Minor & Susan Fontaine Minor Foundation**
c/o John L. Ray
1210 One Valley Square
Charleston, WV 25301

**$ Given:** 18 grants totaling $68,000.

**Restrictions:** WV residents admitted to University of Charleston.

---

**Herschel C. Price Educational Foundation**
P.O. Box 412
Huntington, WV 25708 (304)525-3852

**$ Given:** Grants from $175-$1,500.
**Contact:** E. Joann Price, Trustee.
**Deadline:** October 1, April 1.

**Restrictions:** WV students or students attending WV institutions. Show financial need and scholarship standing.

---

**University of Virginia**
**Protestant Episcopal Theological Seminary of Virginia**
**Marshall University**
**West Virginia University**

**$ Given:** 19 grants totaling $39,256. Should apply directly to the Foundation.
**Contact:** The Enrico Vecellio Family Foundation, Inc. c/o Raleigh County National Bank
129 Main Street
Beckley, WV 25801
**Deadline:** August 1.

**Restrictions:** Local high school graduates attending WV universities or Marshall University.

---

**West Virginia Board of Regents**
**West Virginia Higher Education Grant Program**
P.O. Box 4007
Charleston, WV 25364 (304)347-1211

**$ Given:** 5,111—$375-$1,340 grants per year. Renewable.
**Deadline:** August 1.

**Restrictions:** WV undergraduates, WV residents 1 year prior to application; financial need. Must show academic promise.

# WISCONSIN

**The Elvord & Clara Bartz Foundation**
2040 West Wisconsin Avenue
Suite 518
Milwaukee, WI 53233 (414)933-1566

**$ Given:** $750-2,000 awards per year. Renewable to 4 years.
**Deadline:** February 15.
**Contact:** Office Manager.

**Restrictions:** Graduate of Milwaukee County High School with B average; attend WI institution, demonstrate financial need.

---

**Mabel E. DuPee Foundation**
124 West Oak Street
Sparta, WI 54656 (608)269-6737

**$ Given:** 45 grants totaling $25,250.
**Deadline:** March 1.
**Contact:** John R. Wall, President and Treasurer.

**Restrictions:** Students from Sparta, WI.

---

**Walter and Mabel Fromm Scholarship Trust**
c/o First Wisconsin Trust Company
P.O. Box 2054
Milwaukee, WI 53201 (414)765-5047

**$ Given:** 30 grants totaling $89,000; grant range $1,000-$3,500.

**Restrictions:** Graduates of Maple Grove Elementary School in Hamburg and/or Merrill Senior Public High School in Merrill.

---

**Gehl Company**
**Gehl Foundation**
143 East Water Street
West Bend, WI 53095 (414)334-9461

**$ Given:** Grants totaling $22,450.
**Contact:** Joe Ecker.

**Restrictions:** West Bend, WI area students.

---

**Janesville Foundation, Inc.**
121 North Parker Drive
Janesville, WI 53545 (608)752-1032

**$ Given:** 27 scholarships totaling $24,500.
**Contact:** P.O. Box 1492, Janesville, WI 53547
**Deadline:** March 1, June 1, September 1, December 1.

**Restrictions:** High school graduates of schools in Clinton, Beloit, Brodhead, Darien, Delevan, Edgerton, Evansville, Janesville, Milton, Oxfordville, Whitewater, WI.

---

**Steven Klezevich Trust**
161 West Wisconsin Avenue
Milwaukee, WI 53203 (414)271-6364

**$ Given:** 17 grants totaling $2,500.
**Contact:** Stanley F. Hack.
**Deadline:** November 1.

**Restrictions:** WI students of Serbian descent.

**Kohler Foundation, Inc.**
501 Highland Drive
Kohler, WI 53044 (414) 458-1972

**Contact:** Eleanor A. Jung, Executive Director.
**Deadline:** April 15.

**Restrictions:**
Sheboygan County high school seniors recommended by their schools.

---

**Edward Arthur Mellinger Educational Foundation, Inc.**
1025 East Broadway
P.O. Box 278
Monmouth, IL 61462 (309)734-2419

**$ Given:** 947 grants totaling $264,813, average grant $450.
**Contact:** Shirley J. Neill, Administrative Assistant.

**Restrictions:**
IL, IA, MI, MN, IN, OH, MO, WI students.

---

**Meredith Corporation**
**Edwin T. Meredith Foundation**
**4-H Scholarships**
1716 Locust Street
Des Moines, IA 50336 (515)284-2545

**Contact:** State 4-H leader.

**Restrictions:**
IL, IN, IA, KS, MI, MN, NE, NY, ND, OH, OK, PA, SD, WI residents who are present or former 4-H club members.

---

**Oshkosh Foundation**
c/o First Wisconsin National Bank of Oshkosh
P.O. Box 2448
Oshkosh, WI 54903 (414)424-4283

**$ Given:** grants totaling $92,000.
**Deadline:** Submit proposal in April.

**Restrictions:**
Residents of Oshkosh, WI.

---

**Fred J. Peterson Foundation, Inc.**
c/o Martha Kerley
75 Utopia Circle
Sturgeon Bay, WI 54235 (414)743-3372

**$ Given:** 11 scholarships totaling $3,150.

**Restrictions:**
WI residents.

---

**Presto Foundation**
c/o National Presto Industries, Inc.
Eau Claire, WI 54701 (715)839-2121

**$ Given:** 28 scholarships totaling $67,794.

**Restrictions:**
Children of Presto Industry employees.

---

**Racine Environmental Committee Educational Fund**
310 Fifth Street, Room 101
Racine, WI 53403 (414)631-5600

**$ Given:** 150 grants; average grant $797.
**Deadline:** June 30, October 30.

**Restrictions:**
Residents of Racine, WI area.

# Wisconsin•113

**Edward Rutledge Charity**
404 North Bridge Street, P.O. Box 369
Chippewa Falls, WI 54729 (715)723-6618

**$ Given:** 34 grants totaling $29,217.

**Restrictions:**
Chippewa County, WI residents.

---

**Wisconsin Department of Veterans Affairs**
**Scholarship Program**
P.O. Box 7843
Madison, WI 53707 (608)267-7329

**$ Given:** $3,000.

**Restrictions:**
Dependent children of deceased WI veterans; financial need.

---

**Wisconsin Department of Veterans Affairs**
**Vietnam Era Full Time Grants**
P.O. Box 7843
Madison, WI 53707 (608)266-3028

**$ Given:** Grants ranging from $200-$400. Renewable.
**Deadline:** Prior to end of academic year.
**Contact:** School financial aid office.

**Restrictions:**
Undergraduates in accredited WI institutions who were WI residents upon entry into military service; financial need. Spent a minimum of 90 days in Vietnam from 8/5/64–7/1/75. Discharged under honorable conditions. Full-time enrollment.

---

**Wisconsin Higher Education Aids Board**
**Wisconsin Indian Student Assistance Program**
150 East Gilman Street
Madison, WI 53702

**$ Given:** Unspecified number of $1,500 awards per year. Renewable.
**Contact:** Indian Agencies - Bureau of Indian Affairs at above address.

**Restrictions:**
Resident of WI. ¼ degree or more of American Indian blood of certified tribe or band. Must demonstrate financial need and be accepted or eligible WI institution.

---

**Wisconsin Higher Education Grant Program**
150 East Gilman Street
Madison, WI 53702 (608)266-1954

**$ Given:** Unspecified number of $1,500 awards per year. Renewable.
**Contact:** High school counselor or Financial Aid Officer.

**Restrictions:**
Resident of WI, enrolled at least ½ time in Univ. of WI or WI state vocational-technical and/or adult education programs. Must demonstrate financial need and satisfactory academic standing.

**Wisconsin Public Service Foundation**
700 North Adams Street
P.O. Box 700
Green Bay, WI 54305 (414)433-1465

**$ Given:** Grants totaling $54,050.
**Contact:** Wisconsin Public Service Foundation Inc. Scholarship Program College Scholarship Service/Sponsored Scholarship Program
P.O. Box 176
Princeton, NJ 08541

**Restrictions:**
Limited to WI and upper MI.

---

**Wisconsin Tuition Grant Program**
150 East Gilman Street
Madison, WI 53702 (608)266-1954

**$ Given:** Unspecified number of $1,500 awards per year. Renewable to 8 semesters.
**Deadline:** March 1.
**Contact:** Submit Wisconsin Financial Aid Form to:
College Scholarship Service
Box 2700
Princeton, NJ 08540

**Restrictions:**
Resident of WI. Full-time student enrolled in college, university or nursing school in WI which charges higher tuition than UW-Madison. Must maintain academic standing and financial need.

# WYOMING

**Shoshone Tribal Scholarship**
Community Development Office
Fort Washakie, WY 82514

**$ Given:** Unspecified number of $1,250 scholarships per year. Renewable.
**Deadline:** At least 6 weeks prior to beginning of academic year.
**Contact:** Above address.

**Restrictions:**
Enrolled member of Wind River Shoshone Tribe. Must submit letters of acceptance, proposed course of study and plans upon graduation. Also FAF. For use in WY institution.

---

**Paul Stock Foundation**
P.O. Box 2020
1130 Rumsey Avenue
Cody, WY 82414 (307)587-5275

**$ Given:** 96 grants totaling $97,179.
**Deadline:** June 30, November 30.

**Restrictions:**
Cody, WY residents.

# Wyoming•115

**Davis-Roberts Scholarship Fund, Inc.**
P.O. Box 1974
Cheyenne, WY 82003 (307)632-2948

**$ Given:** 12 grants fo $350.
**Deadline:** June 15.

**Restrictions:** Members or former members of the Order of De Molay or Jobs Daughters Bethel in WY, for full-time study.

---

**Wind River Indian Agency**
**Northern Arapahoe Tribal Scholarships**
Community Development Office
Fort Washakie, WY 82514

**$ Given:** Unspecified number of $1,700 awards per year. Renewable.
**Deadline:** At least 6 weeks prior to beginning of academic year.
**Contact:** Above address.

**Restrictions:** Enrolled member of Northern Arapahoe Tribe. High school grad, submit letter of acceptance and letter stating proposed course of study and plans upon graduation. Use at any institution in WY.

# MISCELLANEOUS

**37th Division Veterans Association**
65 South Front Street, Room 707
Columbus, OH 43215 (614)228-3788

**$ Given:** 2 awards of $500.
**Contact:** Above address. Furnish record of company or regiment of father when requesting application.
**Deadline:** April 1.

**Restrictions:**
Child of 37th Division veteran who served in WWII or in Korean conflict.

---

**Air Force Sergeants Association Scholarship Awards Program**
5211 Auth Road
Suitland, MD 20746 (301)899-3500

**Deadline:** April 1.

**Restrictions:**
Single, dependent children of AFSA member or other military personnel.

---

**Air Force ROTC (AFROTC)**
Office of Public Affairs
Maxwell Air Force Base, AL 36112

**$ Given:** Unspecified number of scholarships and monthly subsistence allowance of $100. Renewable 4 years.
**Deadline:** December 15.
**Contact:** Professor of Aerospace Studies AFROTC Dept. Name of institution offering AFROTC program or Advisory Service above address.

**Restrictions:**
U.S. citizen of sound moral character, at least 17 years of age. SAT or ACT scores, high school transcript and record of extracurricular activities. Must serve 4 years active duty in Air Force after receiving commission.

---

**Air Line Pilots Association (ALPA)**
c/o Janice Redden
1625 Massachusetts Avenue, Northwest
Washington, DC 20036 (202)797-4150

**$ Given:** $8,000 ($2,000 for four years) awarded annually.

**Restrictions:**
Children of medically retired or disabled pilot members of the ALPA.

---

**Allied Industrial Workers AFL-CIO (AIW)**
**Allied Industrial Workers AFL-CIO Scholarship**
3520 West Oklahoma Avenue
Milwaukee, WI 53215 (414)645-9500

**$ Given:** 2 $750 renewable scholarships.
**Deadline:** Apply November and December. Deadline first Friday in February.
**Contact:** Office of parent's local union.

**Restrictions:**
Parent must be affiliated with the Allied Industrial Workers AFL-CIO union.

# Miscellaneous • 117

| | | |
|---|---|---|
| **Amalgamated Clothing & Textile Workers, Local 169**<br>**Thomas Slavell Scholarship Program**<br>33 West Fourteenth Street<br>New York, NY 10003 (212)255-9655 | **$ Given:** $300 a semester for four years.<br>**Deadline:** February 28. | **Restrictions:**<br>Children of union members who are under 22. |
| **American Association of University Women Educational Foundation (AAUW)**<br>**AAUW Dissertation Fellowships**<br>2401 Virginia Avenue, Northwest<br>Washington, DC, 20037 (202)785-7700 | **$ Given:** 70 $3,500-$8,000 awards per 12 month period.<br>**Deadline:** December 15.<br>**Contact:** Educational Foundation Programs Office at above address. | **Restrictions:**<br>Female citizen or resident of U.S.A. Must intend to pursue career in U.S. Fellowship used for final year of doctoral work—must have completed everything except defense of dissertation. Expected to work full time on project. |
| **American Council for the Blind**<br>1211 Connecticut Avenue, Northwest<br>Suite 506<br>Washington, DC, 20036-2775<br>(202)833-1251, (800)424-8666 | **$ Given:** 16 awards of $1,000-$3,000.<br>**Deadline:** April 1.<br>**Contact:** Scholarship Committee at above address. | **Restrictions:**<br>Legally blind. Must be enrolled in postsecondary institution. |
| **American Indian Scholarships, Inc.**<br>335 Jefferson Street Southeast<br>Suite D<br>Albuquerque, NM 87108 (505)265-8335 | **$ Given:** 218 fellowships; amount varies.<br>**Deadline:** October 15, April 15, June 1. | **Restrictions:**<br>American Indian (1/4 Indian blood) from federally recognized tribe, graduate students, 3.0 GPA, financial need. |
| **American Legion Auxiliary National President's Scholarships**<br>777 North Meridian<br>Indianapolis, IN 46204 (317)635-6291 | **$ Given:** 10 per year.<br>**Deadline:** March 15. | **Restrictions:**<br>Veterans' dependents; get application from local chapter. |
| **American Logistics Association**<br>Headquarters New York Area Command<br>Fort Hamilton<br>Attention: AT2D-FHB<br>Brooklyn, NY 11252 (718)630-4040 | **$ Given:** $3,000 awards.<br>**Deadline:** April 22. | **Restrictions:**<br>Dependent of active or retired member, financial need; within a 100 mile radius of NY. |

# 118·FREE MONEY

**American Logistics Association
New York Chapter
Air Force Scholarships**
438-ABG/DPE
McGuire Air Force Base, NJ 08641
(609)724-2315

**$ Given:** 1 annual renewable award of $500.

**Restrictions:** Dependents of active military personnel.

---

**American Logistics Association
New York Chapter
Coast Guard Scholarship**
3rd Coast Guard District and Eastern Area
New York, NY 10004 (212)668-7144

**$ Given:** $2,000.
**Deadline:** April 1.

**Restrictions:** Coast Guard dependents, active or retired, greater New York City area residents, financial need.

---

**American Mensa Education & Research Foundation**
Ms. Charlotte Jermyn, Scholarship Chair
The Roost
6 Forty-Second Avenue
Isle of Palms, SC 29451 (803)886-4157

**$ Given:** 9 awards of $1,000, $500, $200 each; 2 awards of $1,000 and $600.
**Contact:** Ms. Jermyn, with stamped, self-addressed envelope.

**Restrictions:** Student enrolled for year following award in accredited American institution of post-secondary Education. Based on essay of 500 words describing career, vocational or academic goals.

---

**American Society of Interior Designers Educational Foundation Scholarship Programs**
1430 Broadway
New York, NY 10018 (212)944-9220

**$ Given:** Varies with program.
**Deadline:** December 1.

**Restrictions:** See school or call for information.

---

**Armenian Relief Society of North America, Inc.**
212 Stuart Avenue
Boston, MA 02116 (617)542-0528

**$ Given:** $400-$1,000.
**Contact:** Scholarship Committee.
**Deadline:** May 1. (Apply October-April.)

**Restrictions:** Armenian descent, financial need.

---

**Armstrong World Industries, Inc.**
P.O. Box 3001
Lancaster, PA 17604 (717)397-0611

**$ Given:** Awards of $500-$2,000 per year. Renewable for 4 years.

**Restrictions:** Black outstanding students named thru special program of the National Merit Scholarship Corp. PSAT/NMSQT.

# Miscellaneous • 119

**Army Emergency Relief**
200 Stovall Street
Alexandria, VA 22332-0600 (703)960-3982

**$ Given:** $1,000 max. per year.
**Deadline:** March 1.

**Restrictions:**
Unmarried, under 22, children of members of Army.

---

**Associated Universities, Inc. (AUI)**
1717 Massachusetts Avenue, Northwest
Washington, DC 20036 (202)462-1676

**$ Given:** $1,700 (max) per year.
**Deadline:** Second week in November.

**Restrictions:**
High school graduate. SAT scores and scores of 3 other achievement tests.

---

**Association of the Sons of Poland (ASP) Scholarship Program**
591 Summit Avenue, Room 702
Jersey City, NJ 07306 (201)653-1163

**$ Given:** $50-$500 awards.

**Restrictions:**
Must have been a member of ASP for 2 years prior to application, high school senior.

---

**Alexander Graham Bell Association for the Deaf, Inc.**
3417 Volta Place, Northwest
Washington, DC 20007 (202)337-5220

**$ Given:** 6 awards totaling $14,000.
**Deadline:** April 15.

**Restrictions:**
Deaf students using speech or speech reading as preferred form of communication.

---

**Beta Theta Pi General Fraternity**
208 East High Street
P.O. Box 111
Oxford, OH 45056 (513)523-7591

**$ Given:** 35 awards of $750-$1,500.
**Deadline:** April 17.
**Contact:** Chairman of Scholarship Committee.

**Restrictions:**
Undergraduate and graduate fraternity members.

---

**Boy Scouts of America**
1325 Walnut Hill Lane
Irving, TX 75062 (214)580-2000

**Restrictions:**
High school seniors, past or present Boy Scouts; see local council office.

---

**Maureen Connolly Brinker Tennis Foundation**
5419 Wateka Drive
Dallas, TX 75209 (214)357-1604

**$ Given:** 10 grants, average grant $150.

**Restrictions:**
Young tennis players, 21 years and under.

# 120·FREE MONEY

**Business & Professional Women's Foundation**
**Educational Programs Dept.**
2012 Massachusetts Avenue, Northwest
Washington, DC 20036 (202)293-1200

**$ Given:** $200-$1,000 for one year.
**Contact:** Above address, with self-addressed, stamped (44¢, business size) envelope.
**Deadline:** July 1, September 15.

**Restrictions:**
"Career Advancement Scholarship Program." Women at least 25 years of age, U.S. citizens, officially accepted for program of study for re-entry to job market or for new career. "Clairol Loving Care Scholarship." Women, 30 years or over, same qualifications as above.

---

**California Junior Miss Scholarship Foundation**
P.O. Box 1863
Santa Rosa, CA 95402 (619)232-4955

**$ Given:** 29 grants, averaging $500.
**Contact:** Don Landes, 233 A Street, Suite 1300, San Diego, CA 92101.

**Restrictions:**
Contestants and former contestants of the California Junior Miss Pageant. Must apply within 5 years of being in the Pageant.

---

**Marjorie Sells Carter Boy Scout Scholarship Fund**
c/o Cummings & Lockwood
10 Stamford Forum
Stamford, CT 06904

**$ Given:** 125 grants of $1,000.
**Deadline:** April 1.
**Contact:** Mrs. B. Joan Shaffer, P.O. Box 527, West Chatham, MA 02669.

**Restrictions:**
Boy Scouts who are residents of the New England Area.

---

**Center for the History of the American Indian**
Newberry Library
60 West Walton Street
Chicago, IL 60610 (312)943-9090

**$ Given:** Varies.
**Deadline:** February; August.

**Restrictions:**
Women college graduates of Indian heritage, enrolled in graduate school.

---

**Century III Leaders Scholarship Program**
c/o National Association of Secondary School Principals
1904 Association Drive
Reston, VA 22091 (703)860-0200

**$ Given:** $1,500 for 2 primary winners per state, $500 for 2 state alternates.
**Contact:** Information available September 1 at high school.

**Restrictions:**
None.

## Miscellaneous·121

| | | |
|---|---|---|
| **Christian Record Braille Foundation Scholarships**<br>4444 South 52 Street<br>Lincoln, NE 68506 (402)488-0981 | **$ Given:** 10 awards of $300-$900.<br>**Deadline:** April 1.<br>**Contact:** Treasurer. | **Restrictions:**<br>Blind undergraduate students. |
| **Committee on Institutional Cooperation Minorities Fellowships Program**<br>Kirkwood Hall, Room 111<br>Indiana University<br>Bloomington, IN 47405 (812)335-0822<br>(800)457-4420 | **$ Given:** Full tuition and stipend of $6,000 per year.<br>**Deadline:** January 15.<br>**Contact:** Above address. | **Restrictions:**<br>Black, Native and Mexican Americans and Puerto Ricans, U.S. citizens holding bachelors or masters degree, leading to Ph.D., especially in Agriculture, Biology, Chemistry, Engineering, Math, Physics, Physical and Geological Sciences. Only used at CIC universities. Committee on Institutional Cooperation (CIC) |
| **Committee on Institutional Cooperation Minorities Fellowships Program**<br>Kirkwood Hall, Room 111<br>Indiana University<br>Bloomington, IN 47405 (812)335-0822<br>(800)457-4420 | **$ Given:** Full-tuition fellowships; and annual stipend of $6,500.<br>**Deadline:** January 17. | **Restrictions:**<br>American Indians, Asian-Americans, Black Americans, Mexican Americans, Puerto Ricans—U.S. citizens—bachelor's degree. CIC schools are: Universities of Chicago, Illinois, Iowa, Indiana, Michigan, Wisconsin, Michigan State, Minnesota, Northwestern, Ohio State, Purdue. |
| **Danish Brotherhood in America**<br>3717 Harney Street<br>Omaha, NE 68131 (402)341-5049 | **$ Given:** $250 per semester, for 8 semesters.<br>**Deadline:** February 15.<br>**Contact:** Acting Director, Fraternal Services. | **Restrictions:**<br>Member in good standing of D.B. in A. |

## 122·FREE MONEY

**Daughters of Cincinnati**
122 East 58th Street
New York, NY 10022 (212)319-6915

**$ Given:** 10-15 awards of $200-$1,500. Renewable for 4 years.
**Contact:** Scholarship Administrator.
**Deadline:** April 15.

**Restrictions:** Women high school seniors, daughters of regular, active, or retired commissioned officers in U.S. Army, Navy, Air Force, Marine Corps or Coast Guard. Send self-addressed stamped envelope.

---

**Daughters of Penelope**
42069 Oberlin Road
Elyria, OH 44035

**$ Given:** 3 $500 awards, 1 $1,000 award. Renewable for three years.
**Deadline:** June 1.

**Restrictions:** Female students of Greek ancestry. Must be sponsored by a local chapter. Financial need; must be single.

---

**The Dedicators, Inc.**
276 Lafayette Avenue
Brooklyn, NY 11238

**$ Given:** 17 grants from $200-$1,000.
**Deadline:** May 15.
**Contact:** S. Anesta Samuel, Founder.

**Restrictions:** Financially needy students.

---

**Delta Kappa Gamma Society International**
P.O. Box 1589
Austin, TX 78767

**$ Given:** 20-$3,500 awards max. per year.
**Deadline:** February 1.
**Contact:** Scholarship Committee above address.

**Restrictions:** Woman member of DKG Society for at least 2 years.

---

**Delta Sigma Theta Sorority**
1707 New Hampshire Avenue, Northwest
Washington, DC 20009 (202)483-5460

**Deadline:** March 1.

**Restrictions:** Graduate and undergraduate student sorority members.

---

**Demolay Foundation, Inc.**
10200 North Executive Hills Boulevard
Kansas City, MO 64153 (816)891-8333

**$ Given:** 40 annual awards of $800.
**Deadline:** May 1 (Fall semester), October 1 (Spring semester).

**Restrictions:** Members or children of members, incoming freshmen or sophomores with 2.0 GPA or better.

## Miscellaneous • 123

**Disabled American Veterans (DAV)**
**Disabled American Veterans Scholarship Program**
P.O. Box 14301
Cincinnati, OH 45214 (506)441-7300

**$ Given:** 60 awards of $200-$3,000. Renewable.
**Deadline:** Apply September 1 thru November 15.
**Contact:** Disabled American Veterans Auxiliary
3715 Alexandria Pike
Cold Spring, KY 41076

**Restrictions:** High school seniors and college students whose parent is a service-connected disabled veteran whose injury was incurred in or aggravated by military service which terminated with honorable discharge. Financial need.

---

**Disney Foundation**
**Disney Foundation Scholarship**
500 South Buena Vista Street
Burbank, CA 91521 (213)845-3141

**$ Given:** Unspecified number of $1,000 scholarships plus $200 per year, for fees. Renewable to four years.
**Deadline:** March 20.

**Restrictions:** High school seniors who will be graduating before June 30 of current school year and who participate in a regular Junior Achievement Program.

---

**District of Columbia Public Schools**
**Division of Student Services**
**Century III Leaders NASSP**
415 12th Street, Northwest
Washington, DC 20004

**$ Given:** $1,000 awards (maximum) per year.

**Restrictions:** High school senior. Must take exam in current events. Must submit original essay and take an interview.

---

**District of Columbia Public Schools**
**Division of Student Services**
**Sergeant Michael J. Acri Memorial Award, Fifth District**
415 12th Street, Northwest
Washington, DC 20004

**$ Given:** 1-$750 award per year.
**Contact:** Guidance counselor or above address.

**Restrictions:** Senior; reside in and attend 5th District. Demonstrate scholarship, leadership, financial need.

---

**District of Columbia Public Schools**
**Division of Student Services**
**Boston Area Black Alumni Association**
415 12th Street, Northwest
Washington, DC 20004

**$ Given:** Unspecified number of $150 awards per year.
**Contact:** Guidance counselor or above address.

**Restrictions:** Black high school senior planning to enroll in college in Boston metropolitan area.

## 124•FREE MONEY

**District of Columbia Public Schools**
**Division of Student Services**
**C&P Telephone Company**
**First District of Columbia**
**Area Colleges' Scholarship Program**
415 12th Street, Northwest
Washington, DC 20004

**$ Given:** Unspecified number of $250-$1,000 awards per year.
**Contact:** Above address.

**Restrictions:**
Must be accepted for enrollment at a Washington, DC college or university. Demonstrate financial need.

---

**District of Columbia Public Schools**
**Division of Student Services**
**Delta Sigma Theta Sorority/Alumnae Chapter Awards**
415 12th Street, Northwest
Washington, DC 20004

**$ Given:** Unspecified number of $100-$500 awards per year.

**Restrictions:**
Show outstanding scholarship, potential, and financial need.

---

**District of Columbia Public Schools**
**Division of Student Services**
**William Randolph Hearst Foundation, Senate Youth Program**
415 12th Street, Northwest
Washington, DC 20004

**$ Given:** 2-$1,500 awards per year.

**Restrictions:**
High school senior.

---

**Charles and Anna Elenberg Foundation**
c/o Rabbi David B. Hollander
3133 Brighton 7 Street
Brooklyn, NY 11235

**$ Given:** 267 grants averaging $150-$300.
**Deadline:** November 15 (written request for information by September in start of school year).

**Restrictions:**
Hebrew faith, unmarried, financial need. Preference given to orphans.

---

**Elks National Foundation**

**$ Given:** 1,100-1,200 awards of $600-$3,000.
**Contact:** Application from local Elk house.
**Deadline:** February 10.

**Restrictions:**
High school seniors who show scholarship, leadership, financial need.

---

**First Cavalry Division Association Foundation**
302 North Main
Copperas Cove, TX 76522 (817)547-6537

**$ Given:** $600 a year for four years.

**Restrictions:**
Children of soldiers who died while serving in First Cavalry Division during or since Vietnam War or children of soldiers 100% disabled as a result of war.

# Miscellaneous • 125

| | | |
|---|---|---|
| **Fourth Marine Division Association**<br>2854 South 44th Street<br>Milwaukee, WI 53219 (414)543-3474 | **$ Given:** $1,500 max. per year. Renewable to 4 years.<br>**Contact:** Scholarship Committee, above address.<br>**Deadline:** June 1. | **Restrictions:** Children of deceased or disabled veterans of the Fourth Marine Division. |
| **Kahlil Gibran Educational Fund, Inc.**<br>Four Longfellow Place<br>Suite 3802<br>Boston, MA 02114 (617)523-4455 | **$ Given:** Unspecified number of $1,000-$2,000 awards per year.<br>**Deadline:** June 1. | **Restrictions:** Males of Lebanese ancestry with financial need. |
| **Glass, Pottery, Plastics and Allied Workers International Union**<br>608 Baltimore Pike<br>P.O. Box 607<br>Media, PA 19063 (215)565-5051 | **$ Given:** 4 annual renewable awards of $2,500 for 4 years.<br>**Deadline:** November 1. | **Restrictions:** Dependents of union members, top 25% graduating high school class. Children of International Union officers not eligible. |
| **Golf Course Superintendents**<br>1617 St. Andrews Drive<br>Laurence, Kansas 66046 (913)841-2240 | **$ Given:** $300-$1,000 scholarships.<br>**Deadline:** June 15. | **Restrictions:** Submit application through student advisor. |
| **Graphic Communications International Union (GCIU)**<br>1900 L Street, Northwest<br>Washington, DC 20036 (202)462-1400 | **$ Given:** 4 annual renewable awards of $500-$2,000.<br>**Deadline:** December 15. | **Restrictions:** Graduating senior dependents of Graphic Arts International Union members with 2.5 GPA or above. |
| **Ray Hackney Scholarship Fund**<br>1925 K Street, Northwest<br>Washington, DC 20006 (202)728-2300 | **$ Given:** 4 $2,000 renewable scholarships.<br>**Deadline:** May 1. | **Restrictions:** Members of Communications Workers of America, spouse, or children. |

# 126•FREE MONEY

| | | |
|---|---|---|
| **Harness Tracks of America**<br>35 Airport Road<br>Morristown, NJ 07960 (201)295-9090 | **$ Given:** Up to $2,500.<br>Not renewable.<br>**Deadline:** Apply March 1 thru May 1.<br>**Contact:** Chic Young, Chairman<br>HTA Scholarship Committee<br>c/o Jackson Trotting Assoc.<br>P.O. Box 881<br>Jackson, MI 49204 | **Restrictions:**<br>Parent must be affiliated with sport harness racing, licensed full-time drivers, trainers and caretakers. |
| **George Heller Memorial Scholarships**<br>**Aftra Memorial Foundation, Inc.**<br>1350 Avenue of the Americas<br>New York, NY 10019 (212)265-7700 | **Deadline:** May 1. | **Restrictions:**<br>Aftra members and their children. |
| **Hualapai Tribal Council**<br>P.O. Box 168<br>Peach Springs, AZ 86434 (602)769-2216 | **$ Given:** Varies.<br>**Contact:** Education Coordinator. | **Restrictions:**<br>Members of the Hualapai Tribe. |
| **International Alliance of Theatrical Stage Employees and Moving Picture Machine Operators**<br>**Richard F. Walsh Foundation**<br>1515 Broadway, Suite 601<br>New York, NY 10036 (212)730-1770 | **$ Given:** $750 for four years.<br>**Deadline:** December 31. | **Restrictions:**<br>Dependents of union members in good standing. |
| **International Association of Machinists and Aerospace Workers (IAM)**<br>**IAM Scholarship Competition**<br>1300 Connecticut Avenue, Northwest<br>Washington, DC 20036 (202)857-5218 | **$ Given:** $1,000-$2,000 renewable awards.<br>**Deadline:** December 1. | **Restrictions:**<br>Members or dependents of members. |
| **International Brotherhood of Teamsters**<br>1710 Broadway<br>New York, NY 10019 (212)265-7000 | **$ Given:** 10 awards of $2,500.<br>**Deadline:** December 31. | **Restrictions:**<br>Union members and dependents, high school seniors. |

# Miscellaneous • 127

**International Brotherhood of Teamsters**
25 Louisiana Avenue, Northwest
Washington, DC 20001 (202)624-8727

**$ Given:** 10 awards of $1,500. Renewable. 15 $1,000 one-time, first year awards.
**Deadline:** Apply September 1 thru November 30.

**Restrictions:** Dependents of teamster members, high school senior.

---

**International Brotherhood of Teamsters (Local 190)**
**Knit Goods Workers Union—Knit Goods Scholarship Fund and Schwartz Scholarship Award**
c/o Education Director
35 South 4th Street
Philadelphia, PA 19106 (215)351-0750

**$ Given:** $2,400.
**Deadline:** April 15.

**Restrictions:** Dependents of two year union members, high school graduates not yet attending college.

---

**International Ladies Garment Workers Union**
**Upper South Department Scholarship Fund**
One North Howard Street
Baltimore, MD 21201 (301)685-0884

**$ Given:** Two awards of $2,500 each.
**Deadline:** May 22.

**Restrictions:** Union members and dependents.

---

**International Union of Operating Engineers (IUOE)**
**Joseph J. Delaney Memorial Scholarship**
1125 17th Street, Northwest
Washington, DC 20036 (202)429-9100

**$ Given:** 2 $3000 awards renewable up to 4 years.

**Restrictions:** Juniors in high school; see guidance counselor.

---

**Italian Catholic Federation, Inc.**
1801 Van Ness Avenue, Suite 330
San Francisco, CA 94109 (415) 673-8240

**$ Given:** 190 annual awards of $300.
**Deadline:** March 1.

**Restrictions:** Graduating seniors of Italian ancestry and Catholic faith.

---

**JWB**
c/o Director of Training
15 East 26th Street
New York, NY 10010 (212)532-4949

**Deadline:** February 1 (somewhat flexible).

**Restrictions:** For graduate students in social work who would be willing to work for three years in a Jewish community center.

**Kappa Epsilon Fraternity**
Box 11
Boonville, MO 65233 (816)882-7334

**$ Given:** $500, $1,000
**Deadline:** November 1.

**Restrictions:**
Fraternity member, for undergraduate or graduate degree.

---

**Kappa Kappa Gamma**
530 East Town Street
Columbus, OH 43216 (614)228-6515

**$ Given:** 20-30 $750-$1,000 fellowships for graduate studies.
**Deadline:** February 15.
**Contact:** Graduate fellowships, above address.

**Restrictions:**
Woman. Citizen of U.S. or Canada. Bachelor's degree with "B" average, from an institution with KKG chapter or graduate degree must be taken on campus with KKG chapter. Need not be a member.

---

**Kemp Scholarship**
Lutheran Church Women
2900 Queen Lane
Philadelphia, PA 19129 (215)438-2200

**$ Given:** $1,500.
**Deadline:** February.

**Restrictions:**
Minority women undergraduate and graduate students, members of Lutheran Church in America.

---

**Steven Knezevich Trust**
Plankinton Building
161 West Wisconsin Avenue
Milwaukee, WI 53203 (414)271-6364

**$ Given:** 14 grants from $100-$300.
**Contact:** Stanley Hack, with self-addressed, stamped envelope.
**Deadline:** September 1.

**Restrictions:**
Graduates and undergraduates of Serbian descent.

---

**Knights of Columbus**
**Knights of Columbus Pro Deo and Pro Patria Scholarships**
P.O. Box 1670
New Haven, CT 06507 (203)772-2130

**$ Given:** 10 awards of $1,000.
**Deadline:** March 1.

**Restrictions:**
Members or children of members of the order who will enroll in Catholic colleges.

---

**Kosciuszko Foundation**
15 East 65th Street
New York, NY 10021 (212)734-2130

**$ Given:** Unspecified number of $500-$1,000 scholarships.
**Deadline:** January 15.
**Contact:** Scholarships and Study Programs at above address.

**Restrictions:**
Students of Polish descent.

## Miscellaneous • 129

**The Koulaieff Educational Fund**
c/o Nathan B. Siegel
3406 Geary Boulevard
San Francisco, CA 94118

**$ Given:** 62 grants totaling $57,730.

**Restrictions:** Russian immigrant students.

---

**Ladies Branch of the New Bedford Port Society**
15 Johnny Cake Hill
New Bedford, MA 02740

**$ Given:** 7 grants from $350-$500.
**Deadline:** May 1.

**Restrictions:** Scholarships, with first consideration to families of descendants of seamen with preference to residents of the New Bedford community.

---

**League of United Latin American Citizens (LULAC)**
400 First Street, Northwest, Suite 716
Washington, DC 20001 (202)347-1652

**$ Given:** Grants of $250-$1,000.
**Contact:** Local LULAC council.
**Deadline:** June.

**Restrictions:** Students of Spanish origin; outstanding academic performance and financial need.

---

**The Li Foundation, Inc.**
63 Herbill Road
Glen Cove, NY 11542

**$ Given:** 44 grants totaling $208,999.

**Restrictions:** Chinese students.

---

**Lutheran Church Women**
2900 Queen Lane
Philadelphia, PA 19129-1091 (215)438-2200

**$ Given:** $1,500 per year.
**Deadline:** February 1.

**Restrictions:** Minority women, members of Lutheran Church of America. Undergraduate and graduate students.

---

**Marine Corps Scholarship Foundation, Inc.**
James Forrestral Campus
P.O. Box 3008
Princeton, NJ 08540 (609)921-3534

**$ Given:** 250 grants $600-$1,500 per year. Renewable.
**Deadline:** February 1.

**Restrictions:** Needy children of Marines or ex-Marines.

---

**Meredith Corporation**
1716 Locust Street
Des Moines, IA 50336 (515)284-2545

**$ Given:** 2 $1,000 scholarships. Not renewable.
**Contact:** State 4-H leader.

**Restrictions:** Present or former member of 4-H club. Residents of IL, IN, IA, KS, MI, MN, MO, NE, NY, ND, OH, OK, PA, SD, WI.

## 130·FREE MONEY

**Misaburo Aibara Memorial Graduate Scholarship**
1765 Sutter Street
San Francisco, CA 94115 (415)921-5225

**$ Given:** $500.
**Deadline:** March 1.
**Contact:** Youth Director.

**Restrictions:**
Graduate Japanese-American students.

---

**Mortar Board, Inc.**
**National Office**
1250 Chambers Road, #170
Columbus, OH 43212 (614)422-3319

**$ Given:** Unspecified number of $1,000 fellowships.
**Deadline:** January 15.
**Contact:** Mortar Board National Foundation at above address.

**Restrictions:**
Current members of Mortar Board or past members. For graduate studies.

---

**The Mostazafan Foundation of New York**
24 West Fortieth Street
New York, NY 10018 (212)944-8333

**$ Given:** Grants totaling $535,200.

**Restrictions:**
Iranian students.

---

**National Association of Intercollegiate Athletics Football Coaches Association Scholarship**
1221 Baltimore Avenue
Kansas City, MO 64105 (816)842-5050

**Restrictions:**
Male football player. Graduate study at a NAIA member institution. See high school counselor.

---

**National Association of Letter Carriers (NALC)**
**William C. Doherty Scholarship Program**
100 Indiana Avenue
Washington, DC 20001 (202)393-4695

**$ Given:** 15 renewable awards of $800.
**Contact:** Scholarship Committee.
**Deadline:** December 31.

**Restrictions:**
Children of active, retired, or deceased NALC members.

---

**National Athletic Trainers Association**
1001 East Fourth Street
Greenville, NC 27834 (919)752-1725

**$ Given:** $1,000.
**Contact:** W.E. Newell.
**Deadline:** February 2.

**Restrictions:**
Undergraduate and graduate scholarships for student athletic trainers.

---

**National Bowling Council**
1919 Pennsylvania Avenue
Suite 504
Washington, DC 20006

**$ Given:** 1 $500 award per year. Not renewable.

**Restrictions:**
Applicant must combine outstanding bowling ability with demonstrated academic excellence.

# Miscellaneous • 131

| | | |
|---|---|---|
| **National Center for American Indian Alternative Education Inc.**<br>P.O. Box 18329, Capital Hill Station<br>Denver, CO 80218 (303)861-1052 | **$ Given:** $2,000 per year. Renewable.<br>**Deadline:** March 15.<br>**Contact:** President. | **Restrictions:**<br>Indians, ¼ blood. Strong academic ability and financial need. Residents of CO, AZ, NM, KA, OK, San Bernadino County, CA. High school seniors. |
| **National Federation of the Blind**<br>1800 Johnson Street<br>Baltimore, MD 21230 (301)659-9314 | **$ Given:** 26 awards, varying amounts.<br>**Deadline:** March 31.<br>**Contact:** Scholarships Committee at above address. | **Restrictions:**<br>Legally blind, accepted at accredited institution. |
| **National Hispanic Scholarship Fund**<br>P.O. Box 748<br>San Francisco, CA 94101 (415)892-9971 | **Deadline:** October 5. | **Restrictions:**<br>Graduate and undergraduate students of Hispanic descent, financial need. |
| **National Science Foundation**<br>**Minority Graduate Fellowships Program**<br>Office of Research Career Development<br>Directorate for Science and National Science Foundation<br>188 G Street, Northwest<br>Washington, DC 20550 (202)357-7536 | **$ Given:** Stipend of $11,100. | **Restrictions:**<br>Minority groups; for study or work leading to masters or doctorate in the sciences. |
| **National Women's Relief Corps (NWRC)**<br>**National Women's Relief Corps Scholarship**<br>629 South Seventh Street<br>Springfield, IL 62703 (217)522-4373 | **$ Given:** Unspecified number of $200 awards per year. Renewable.<br>**Contact:** Scholarship Chairman.<br>**Deadline:** May 1. | **Restrictions:**<br>Student with relative who is a member of NWRC or veteran of any war. |
| **Naval Military Personnel Command**<br>NMPC-121D<br>Navy Department<br>Washington, DC 20370-5121 (202)694-3126 | **$ Given:** Varying number of $200-$2,000 awards per year.<br>**Deadline:** April 15.<br>**Contact:** Above address. | **Restrictions:**<br>Not over 23, dependent child of present, retired or deceased member of Navy, Coast Guard, Marine Corps. |

## 132·FREE MONEY

---

**United Papermakers and Paperworkers International Union**
P.O. Box 1475
Nashville, TN 37202 (615)834-8590

**$ Given:** 22 $1,000 awards.
**Deadline:** March 15.

**Restrictions:**
Union members' children who are high school seniors and will take one labor course during college career.

---

**Phi Upsilon Omicron Undergraduate Scholarships**
252 Mount Hall
1050 Carmack Road
Columbus, OH 43210 (614)421-7860

**$ Given:** $500.
**Deadline:** February 1.

**Restrictions:**
Members working towards a BS in Home Economics.

---

**The Piton Foundation**
511 Sixteenth Street, Suite 700
Denver, CO 80202

**$ Given:** 69 grants ranging from $500-$1,000.
**Deadline:** June 1.

**Restrictions:**
Resident of the Rocky Mt. States.

---

**Presbyterian Church**
475 Riverside Drive, Room 430
New York, NY 10115 (212)870-2515

**$ Given:** Unspecified number of $100-$1,400 awards per year.
**Deadline:** December 1 of senior year.
**Contact:** Financial Aid for studies at above address.

**Restrictions:**
Confirmed member of P.C. (U.S.A.), entering as freshman in college related to P.C.

---

**Purolator Courier Corp.**
3333 New Hyde Park Road
New Hyde Park, NY 11042 (516)684-3442

**$ Given:** 1 $10,000 award. ($2,500 for each of 4 years).
**Deadline:** June 1.
**Contact:** Personnel Manager at above address.

**Restrictions:**
Dependent children of POW or MIA from Vietnam war. Submit SAT scores.

---

**Reserve Officer Association Henry J. Reilly Memorial Scholarship**
1 Constitution Avenue, Northeast
Washington, DC 20002 (202)479-2200

**$ Given:** 100 awards at $500.
**Deadline:** April 1.

**Restrictions:**
Undergraduates and graduates; member sponsors the contender; merit basis.

## Miscellaneous • 133

**Roothbert Fund**
360 Park Avenue South
New York, NY 10016 (212)679-2030

**$ Given:** Grants average $1,000.

**Restrictions:**
Students motivated by spiritual values, financial need.

---

**Royal Neighbors of America (RNA)**
**Royal Neighbors of America Fraternal Scholarships**
230 Sixteenth Street
Rock Island, IL 61201 (309)788-4561

**$ Given:** 17 awards of $210-$500.
**Deadline:** September 18.

**Restrictions:**
Upper ¼ graduating class or recommended by high school principal, member of RNA for 2 years prior to application.

---

**S and H Foundation, Inc.**
P.O. Box 1283
New Canaan, CT 06840

**$ Given:** 5 awards each year to cover unmet expenses of senior year and tuition and up to $4,000 and living expenses for 2 years. Graduate or professional school study.
**Deadline:** Nominated by February 15, deadline March 15.
**Contact:** Must be nominated by undergraduate school.

**Restrictions:**
Citizen of U.S.; College senior planning advanced study. Demonstrate financial need and high ability. Must be nominated by institution where currently enrolled.

---

**Sante Fe Southern Pacific Foundation**
224 South Michigan Avenue
Chicago, IL 60604 (312)427-4900

**$ Given:** Varies.
**Contact:** LULAC
National Educational Service Center
400 First Street Northwest
Washington, DC 20001

**Restrictions:**
High School graduates of Spanish origin. U.S. citizen of permanent resident accepted or enrolled in college. First consideration given to students residing in states in which Santa Fe Southern Pacific Corp and subsidiaries operate.

## 134·FREE MONEY

**Scholastic Awards**
Scholastic Inc.
730 Broadway
New York, NY 10003

**$ Given:** Various awards and scholarships.
**Deadline:** Write for rules book between October and January.

**Restrictions:**
High school seniors demonstrating outstanding creative ability in writing, art, photography.

---

**Screen Actors Guild**
**John L. Dales Scholarship Fund**
7065 Hollywood Boulevard
Los Angeles, CA 90028 (213)465-4600

**Deadline:** March 20.
**Contact:** Joan Hanson, Administrator.

**Restrictions:**
Members of SAG for 3 years or children and grandchildren of members.

---

**Second Marine Division Association**
P.O. Box 158
Denver, PA 17517

**$ Given:** Unspecified number of $600 awards per year. Renewable to 2 years.
**Deadline:** April 1.

**Restrictions:**
High school senior who is 1) child of individual who lost his life serving in 2nd Marine Division or unit attached thereto; 2) child of individual serving in 2nd Marine Division.

---

**Shaw Fund for Mariner's Children**
23 Craigie Street
Cambridge, MA 02138 (617)547-1346

**$ Given:** $300 average.
**Contact:** Olivia Constable.

**Restrictions:**
Mariners and their families.

---

**Society of Daughters of Holland Dames**
200 East 66 Street, Apartment 707E
New York, NY 10021 (212)371-5995

**$ Given:** $500.
**Deadline:** April 1.
**Contact:** Mrs. Daniel Adams, Scholarship Chairman at above address.

**Restrictions:**
College juniors of Dutch descent who may prove parent or grandparent was born in the Netherlands, financial need, high scholastic standing; may extend to senior year.

---

**Society of Daughters of the United States Army (DUSA)**
7919 Falstaff Road
McLean, VA 22102 (703)538-5540

**$ Given:** Renewable $500 awards, (unspecified number).
**Deadline:** March 31.
**Contact:** Scholarship Chairman, above address. Give officer's name, rank, serial and social security number with inquiry.

**Restrictions:**
Daughters or granddaughters of retired or deceased, commissioned, or warrant officers, of Army Reserve. Financial need. Demonstrate scholastic ability.

## Miscellaneous • 135

**Soroptimist Foundations**
**Soroptimist International of America, Inc.**
1616 Walnut Street
Philadelphia, PA 19103 (215)732-0512

**$ Given:** 43 $1,250 awards. Not renewable. 1 $2,000 additional award for finalist.
**Deadline:** December 15.
**Contact:** Executive Director, above address.

**Restrictions:** High School senior, graduating during current year from school in territorial limits of Soroptimist International of the Americas. Must not be 21 prior to July 21 of that year. Must provide evidence of student, community and leadership activities.

---

**Third Marine Division Association, Inc.**
P.O. Box 634
Inverness, FL 32651

**$ Given:** Unspecified number of $400-$2,000 scholarships. Renewable.
**Deadline:** April 15.
**Contact:** Secretary, Scholarship Fund at above address.

**Restrictions:** Dependent children of deceased Third Marine Division member who was in Vietnam 3/8/65–11/27/69; 17-26 years of age, financial need.

---

**Transport Workers Union of America**
**Michael J. Quill Scholarship Fund**
80 West End Avenue
New York, NY 10023 (212)873-6000

**$ Given:** $1,200.
**Deadline:** May 1.

**Restrictions:** Dependents of union members.

---

**UNICO National, Inc.**
72 Burroughs Place
Bloomfield, NJ 07003 (201)748-9144

**$ Given:** 3 annual renewable awards of $500.
**Deadline:** April 15.
**Contact:** National Director of Scholarships at above address.

**Restrictions:** Italian-Americans residing in community with a UNICO chapter, financial need. Must submit SAT or ACT scores.

## 136·FREE MONEY

**United Daughters of the Confederacy**
602 Canal Street Northeast
Decatur, AL 35601

**$ Given:** Varying number of $400-$500 awards per year. Renewable.
**Deadline:** February 15.
**Contact:** Divisional President or 2nd Vice President at above address.

**Restrictions:**
Must be lineal descendant of worthy Confederate or of collateral descendants who are members of the Children of the United Daughters of the Confederacy. Must be endorsed by their Divisional President and Divisional Dir. of Education and 2 members of the United Daughters of the Confederacy.

---

**United Methodist Church, Board of Higher Education and Ministry**
**United Methodist Ethnic Minority Scholarships**
P.O. Box 871
Nashville, TN 37202 (615)327-2700

**$ Given:** Unspecified.
**Deadline:** May 1.
**Contact:** Office of Loans and Scholarships at above address.

**Restrictions:**
U.S. citizen or permanent resident, member of ethnic minority group (Native Americans, Asian, Black, Hispanic) and of United Methodist Church; active in Church program. Must demonstrate financial need.

---

**United Presbyterian Church in the USA**
**United Presbyterian Student Opportunity Grants**
475 Riverside Drive, Room 430
New York, NY 10115 (212)870-2515

**$ Given:** Unspecified number of $100-$1,400 grants per year.
**Deadline:** March 15.

**Restrictions:**
Young person in financial need, member of ethnic minority group, related to the United Presbyterian Church. Must be entering college as freshman and apply to college for financial aid.

---

**United Scholarship Service, Inc.**
P.O. Box 8285, Capital Hill Station
941 East Seventeenth Avenue
Denver, CO 80218

**Contact:** Roger Buffalohead.

**Restrictions:**
American Indian students with ¼ or more Indian blood, financial need.

## Miscellaneous • 137

**United States Bureau of Indian Affairs**
Eighteenth and C Streets, Northwest
Washington, DC 20245 (202)343-7387

**$ Given:** 17,000 $200-$7,000 scholarships. Renewable.
**Deadline:** June 1, October 15, April 15.
**Contact:** Office of Indian Education Programs at above address.

**Restrictions:**
U.S. citizen with ¼ or more degree American Indian, Eskimo or Aleut tribe served by Bureau of Indian Affairs. Demonstrate financial need.

---

**United States Jaycees**
4 West Twenty-first Street
P.O. Box 7
Tulsa, OK 74121 (918)584-2481

**$ Given:** 6 $1,000 awards. Not renewable.
**Deadline:** March 1 to State Jaycee Presidents.
**Contact:** Secretary-Treasurer at above address.

**Restrictions:**
High school senior accepted at college. Must show financial need, evidence of academic success, leadership traits and family service to community and country.

---

**United States Navy**
Naval Military Personnel Command
Washington, DC 20370

**$ Given:** Unspecified number of $200-$2,000 awards.
**Deadline:** March 15.
**Contact:** Commander, Naval Military Personnel Command (N641C/PES-7311) Navy Dept. Washington, DC 20370

**Restrictions:**
Dependent child of Naval personnel, unmarried, under 23. Must be admitted to college, submit SAT or ACT scores.

---

**United States Office of Education**
**Bureau of Continuing and Higher Education**
**Graduate Training Branch**
Seventh and D Streets
Washington, DC 20202 (202)245-2347

**$ Given:** 15 $4,500 awards per year. Not renewable.
**Contact:** Institution of choice.

**Restrictions:**
Citizen, native or permanent resident of U.S. Must be accepted at institution for advanced degree. Preference given to women and minority groups, but not limited to those categories.

## 138·FREE MONEY

**United States Office of Education
Bureau of Student Financial Assistance**
Washington, DC 20202 (202)245-9720

**$ Given:** Unspecified number of $200-$2,000 awards. Renewable.
**Contact:** Financial Aids Officer at institution.

**Restrictions:** Citizen or permanent resident of U.S. Already accepted or enrolled at eligible institution. Must maintain good academic standing and demonstrate financial need.

---

**United States Office of Education
Department of Health, Education and Welfare**
Washington, DC 20202 (202)472-4300

**$ Given:** unspecified number of awards. $200-$1,800 awards per year. Renewable.
**Deadline:** March 15.
**Contact:** Director of Student Financial Aid at institution.

**Restrictions:** Must be enrolled in eligible institution. Demonstrate financial need.

---

**United States Veterans Administration
Department of Veterans Benefits
Veterans Education Assistance Program**
Washington, DC 20420 (202)393-4120

**$ Given:** $327-$342 per month, to maximum of 45 months.
**Contact:** Local Veterans Administration Office or Campus Veterans Advisor.

**Restrictions:** Spouses and children (ages 18-26) of veterans who died in service, were permanently disabled, POW or MIA.

---

**United Steelworkers of America
District 7
Hugh Carcella Scholarship Program**
200 Goddard Boulevard
King of Prussia, PA 19406 (215)265-7577

**$ Given:** 8 annual renewable awards of $600-$2,400.
**Deadline:** March 15.

**Restrictions:** Union members in good standing or dependents entering college as freshmen.

---

**United Transportation Union
Scholarship Program**
14600 Detroit Avenue
Cleveland, OH 44107 (216)228-9400

**$ Given:** $500.
**Deadline:** March 31.

**Restrictions:** Union members, children, grandchildren, high school graduates under 25 years of age.

---

**Unto These Hills Educational Fund
Scholarship Program**
P.O. Box 398
Cherokee, NC 28719 (704)497-2111

**$ Given:** 10 awards of $500.
**Deadline:** May 1.

**Restrictions:** Students enrolled in the eastern band of Cherokee Indians.

## Miscellaneous・139

| | | |
|---|---|---|
| **Upward Bound**<br>**United States Department of Education**<br>Washington, DC 20202 (202)245-6664 | **$ Given:** Unspecified.<br>**Contact:** Above address or financial aid officer of qualifying institution. | **Restrictions:**<br>Deprived or under-achiever students, established income criteria and potential first generation college education. |
| **The Vatia's Educational Foundation**<br>c/o First National Bank of Boston<br>P.O. Box 1861<br>Boston, MA 02105 | **$ Given:** Varies. | **Restrictions:**<br>Students of Albanian lineage or descent. |
| **Francis S. Viele Scholarship Trust**<br>626 Wilshire Boulevard, Suite 804<br>Los Angeles, CA 90017 (213)629-3571 | **$ Given:** 21 grants of $1,500-$3,000.<br>**Contact:** Apply through local fraternity chapter. | **Restrictions:**<br>Member Sigma Phi Fraternity. |
| **Western Golf Association**<br>**Evans Scholars Program**<br>1 Briar Road<br>Golf, IL 60029 (312)724-4600 | **$ Given:** Tuition plus $200. | **Restrictions:**<br>High school seniors, top 25% of class, financial need, caddies for at least 2 years. |

# AEROSPACE SYSTEMS

**American Institute of Aeronautics and Astronautics Scholarship Program**
1633 Broadway
New York, NY 10019 (212)581-4300

**$ Given:** $1,000.
**Deadline:** February 1.

**Restrictions:**
First year student planning a career in aerospace engineering.

---

**The AOPA Air Safety Foundation**
421 Aviation Way
Frederick, MD 21701

**$ Given:** $1,000 awards.
**Deadline:** March 15.

**Restrictions:**
College sophomore enrolled in curriculum leading to degree in aviation. Must submit 250 word paper on why he/she wishes to pursue career in aviation. Show financial need.

---

**McAllister Scholarship**
c/o AOPA Air Safety Foundation Scholarship
421 Aviation Way
Frederick, MD 21701 (301)695-2170

**$ Given:** Varies.
**Deadline:** April 1.

**Restrictions:**
College junior or senior enrolled in aviation degree program with 2.5 GPA or better.

---

**Civil Air Patrol (CAP)**
National Headquarters
Maxwell AFB, AL 36112 (205)293-5332

**$ Given:** 2 $500 awards per year.
**Deadline:** April 1.
**Contact:** Squadron or Wing Commander at above address.

**Restrictions:**
CAP member who has completed requirements for senior rating in Level 11 of Senior Training Program, holds baccalaureate degree or cadet who has completed Billy Mitchell award requirements.

---

**Hughes Aircraft Company Corporate Fellowship and Rotation Programs**
Technical Education Center
Building C/B 168
200 North Sepulveda Boulevard
El Segundo, CA 90245

**$ Given:** Fellowships of $25,000-$50,000. Work-study basis.
**Deadline:** Eng. and Doctoral - February 1; Master - March 15.

**Restrictions:**
U.S. citizen for master's or Ph.D. in electrical, aerospace systems and mechanical engineering, computer science, physics and applied math.

## 142•FREE MONEY

**National Aeronautics and Space Administration**
"Graduate Student Researchers Program: NASA Centers"
Office of External Relations
Educational Affairs Division
University Programs Branch
Code LE
Washington, DC 20546 (202)453-8344

**Deadline:** February 1.
**Contact:** Above address for brochure entitled "Graduate Student Researchers Program 1986," listing NASA centers, their research activities and contact persons.

**Restrictions:**
Full-time graduate student, U.S. citizen.

---

**The Amelia Earhart Scholarship**
c/o Zonta International
35 East Wacker Drive
Chicago, IL 60601 (312)346-1445

**$ Given:** Approximately 32 awards of $6,000 each.
**Deadline:** January 1.

**Restrictions:**
Female graduate student studying aerospace, science.

---

**NASA**
"Graduate Student Researchers Program in Space Science"
Office of Space Science and Applications
Assistant Associate Administrator
Washington, DC 20546 (202)453-1410

**$ Given:** Stipend of $12,000 and subsistence allowance of $3,000.
**Deadline:** February 1.

**Restrictions:**
For study or research in space science at home institution.

---

**Radio Technical Commission for Aeronautics**
One McPherson Square
1425 K Street, Northwest, Suite 500
Washington, DC 20005 (202)682-0266

**$ Given:** $1,000 award.
**Deadline:** June 30.
**Contact:** William E. Jackson Award Committee at above address.

**Restrictions:**
Graduate or undergraduate earning degree in field or aviation electronics, or telecommunications. Submit thesis, project report or paper in technical journal.

---

**Vertical Flight Foundation**
217 North Washington Street
Alexandria, VA 22314 (703)684-6777

**$ Given:** Scholarships of $1,000-$2,000 per year.
**Deadline:** February 1.

**Restrictions:**
Undergraduate or graduate interested in pursuing career in some aspect of helicopter or vertical flight business.

---

**Zonta International**
35 East Wacker Drive
Chicago, IL 60601 (312)346-1445

**$ Given:** 32 $6,000 fellowships.
**Deadline:** January 1.

**Restrictions:**
Bachelor's degree for graduate work in aerospace or engineering.

# AGRICULTURE

**Allied Mills, Inc.**
10 South Riverside Plaza
Chicago, IL 60606 (312)930-1050

**$ Given:** 2 $1,000 scholarships. Not renewable.
**Contact:** State 4-H leader.

**Restrictions:**
Former or present 4-H member, with 1 year of 4-H work. Plan to enroll for junior year with major in Animal Science.

---

**Alpha Gamma Rho Educational Foundation**
**Future Farmers of America Scholarship**
960 Rand Road, Suite 220
Des Plaines, IL 60016 (312)824-0556

**$ Given:** 1 $1,000 scholarship.
**Contact:** Executive Director, National Vocational Agricultural Teachers Association, Inc., 5600 Mount Vernon Memorial Highway, P.O. Box 15051, Alexandria, VA 22309.
**Deadline:** July 1.

**Restrictions:**
Male student nominated for membership in Future Farmers of America by state supervisor of agricultural education.

---

**American Society for Enology and Viticulture**
P.O. Box 1855
Davis, CA 95617 (916)753-3142

**Deadline:** March 15.
**Contact:** Secretary-Treasurer at above address.

**Restrictions:**
Undergraduate or graduate science students studying wine and grape business; financial need.

---

**Bedding Plants, Inc.**
P.O. Box 286
Okemos, MI 48864 (517)349-3924

**$ Given:** $1,000 scholarship.
**Deadline:** May 1.
**Contact:** Executive Secretary.

**Restrictions:**
Student-undergraduate or graduate-attending 4 year university, majoring in horticulture with an emphasis on bedding plants.

---

**California Farm Bureau Federation**
1601 Exposition Boulevard
Sacramento, CA 95815 (916)924-4049

**$ Given:** Unspecified number of awards of $500 per year. Renewable.
**Deadline:** March 1.
**Contact:** Staff coordinator.

**Restrictions:**
Residents of CA who meet requirements of 4-year colleges and universities in CA.

## 144·FREE MONEY

**Chicago and North Western Transportation Company**
One North Western Center
Chicago, IL 60606 (312)559-6700

**$ Given:** 5 $1,000 awards per year. Not renewable.
**Contact:** State 4-H leader.

**Restrictions:** Present or former 4-H member with 1 year 4-H work. Good scholastic standing. Junior or Senior year of college or graduate school with major or minor in Agricultural Business or Economics. Must submit typed, self-prepared research paper on some phase of marketing, transportation or agricultural commodities. Top 5 candidates from IL, IA, MI, MN, MO, NE, SD, WI, WY.

---

**Continental Grain Company**
**Wayne Feed Division Scholarship Program**
277 Park Avenue
New York, NY 10172 (212)207-5578

**$ Given:** $1,000 for 2 years.
**Contact:** Local or state 4-H organizations.

**Restrictions:** Present or former members of 4-H with at least 1 year 4-H work.

---

**The Corti Family Agricultural Fund**
c/o Bank of America
1011 Van Ness Avenue, P.O. Box 1672
Fresno, CA 93721 (805)395-0880

**Deadline:** February 20.

**Restrictions:** Kern County, CA high school graduates planning study in agriculture.

---

**Dekalb Research**
**4-H Agricultural Careers Scholarship**
Sycamore Road
Dekalb, IL 60115 (815)758-3461

**$ Given:** 4 $800 scholarships. Not renewable.

**Restrictions:** Agriculture students with good academic standings and at least 1 year work as 4-H members.

---

**The Garden Club of America**
598 Madison Avenue
New York, NY 10022 (212)753-8287

**$ Given:** $2,000 annually.
**Deadline:** April 15.
**Contact:** Horticulture Chairman.

**Restrictions:** Qualified students, specializing in horticulture, recommended by director of horticultural studies. Students from Western PA, Eastern OH and Northern WV.

# Agriculture・145

**Fred C. Gloeckner Foundation Fellowships**
15 East Twenty-sixth Street
New York, NY 10010 (212)481-0943

**$ Given:** Grants ranging from $277-$6,500.

**Restrictions:**
Graduate students studying floriculture.

---

**International Society for Arboriculture**
5 Lincoln Square
P.O. Box 71
Urbana, IL 61801

**$ Given:** $1,000-$2,000 grants.
**Deadline:** December 1.
**Contact:** Executive Director.

**Restrictions:**
BS degree, planning graduate study. Request must be initialed by major professor.

---

**John W. Landis Scholarship Trust**
c/o D. Williams Evans, Jr.
1670 Christmas Run
Wooster, OH 44691 (216)262-6713

**Contact:** Wayne Company Supervisor of Schools, 2534 Burbank Road, Wooster, OH.
**Deadline:** March 15.

**Restrictions:**
Wayne County, OH residents studying agriculture.

---

**Moorman Manufacturing Company Agriculture Scholarships**
1000 North Thirtieth Street
Quincy, IL 62301 (217)222-7100

**$ Given:** 4 awards of $700.
**Contact:** University advisor at your school.

**Restrictions:**
College student majoring in some branch of agriculture.

---

**National Consortium for Black Professional Development Agricultural Sciences and Business Administration Graduate Program**
2307 Taylorsville Road
Louisville, KY 40205 (502)451-8199

**$ Given:** From $4,800-$7,200
**Deadline:** February, October.

**Restrictions:**
Black college graduates with 3.0 GPA or better planning graduate study in agriculture, business.

---

**North Dakota Community Foundation**
2900 East Broadway
Bismarck, ND 58501 (701)222-8349

**$ Given:** 19 grants from $100-$2,000.

**Restrictions:**
Primarily ND residents for study of medicine, dentistry, agriculture.

---

**Professional Grounds Management Society**
7 Church Lane
Pikesville, MD 21208 (301)653-2742

**$ Given:** Up to $1,000.
**Deadline:** May 1.

**Restrictions:**
Students preparing for career in grounds management, horticulture or related fields.

## 146•FREE MONEY

**Purina Mills**
**Ralston Purina Scholarship Program**
Checkerboard Square
St. Louis, MO 63188 (314)982-3593

**$ Given:** 69 awards of $650.
**Deadline:** Beginning of spring term, junior year.
**Contact:** Local respective scholarship committee.

**Restrictions:** Undergraduate students of agriculture. Upper ¼ of high school junior class. Show evidence of unusual growth potential and financial need.

---

**Ralston Purina Company**
Checkerboard Square
St. Louis, MO 63188 (314)982-3219

**$ Given:** 6 grants of $5,600.
**Contact:** Fellowship committee at above address.

**Restrictions:** Students qualified for graduate study at agricultural college.

---

**Safe Scholarship Program Endowment**
37 Camelot Drive
Edwardsville, IL 62025 (618)692-0045

**$ Given:** $500.

**Restrictions:** Undergraduate agriculture student engaged in 10-16 hours work/study per week and planning a career in agriculture.

---

**San Mateo County Farm Scholarship Bureau**
765 Main Street
Half Moon Bay, CA 94019 (415)726-4485

**Contact:** Betty Stone.
**Deadline:** April 1.

**Restrictions:** Agriculture students who are members or dependent children of members of San Mateo farm bureau.

---

**Abbie Sargent Memorial Scholarship, Inc.**
RFD #4, Box 3440
Concord, NH 03301 (603)224-1934

**$ Given:** 2 grants of $200. Renewable.
**Deadline:** March 15.
**Contact:** Chairman, above address.

**Restrictions:** Residents of NH and graduates of NH high schools with good academic backgrounds planning undergraduate study in agriculture, veterinary medicine.

---

**Soil Conservation Society of America (SCSA)**
7515 Northeast Ankeny Road
Ankeny, IA 50021 (515)289-2331

**$ Given:** 20 awards of $500. Not renewable.
**Deadline:** May 1.

**Restrictions:** College sophomores majoring in conservation-related subjects.

Biology • 147

**Van Wert County Foundation**
101 ½ East Main Street
Van Wert, OH 45891 (419)238-1743

**$ Given:** 63 grants totaling $33,000.
**Contact:** Robert W. Games, Executive Secretary.
**Deadline:** June 1.

**Restrictions:**
Residents of Van Wert County, OH.

---

**Women's National Farm and Garden Association, Inc.**
Chairman of the Committee
13 Davis Drive
Saginaw, MI 48602

**$ Given:** $500.
**Deadline:** April 15.

**Restrictions:**
Women graduate students in agriculture, floriculture, etc.

---

# BIOLOGY

**ADAMHA - National Institute on Drug Abuse**
**Drug Abuse NRSA - Predoctoral Fellowships**
Parklawn Building, 5600 Fishers Lane
Rockville, MD 20857 (301)443-6245

**$ Given:** $5,040 per year; application form PHS-416-1.
**Deadline:** October 1, February 1, June 1.

**Restrictions:**
Biology, medical, psychology students doing biomedical/behavioral research training pertaining to drug abuse.

---

**Alliance for Engineering in Medicine and Biology**
Suite 700
1101 Connecticut Avenue, Northwest
Washington, DC 20036 (202)857-1199

**$ Given:** Unspecified number of $200 scholarships; prizes.
**Deadline:** June 15 thru 30.
**Contact:** Executive Director.

**Restrictions:**
Students enrolled in accredited institution must either submit paper expressing original idea or be nominated by faculty advisors or Dept. heads.

---

**Marshall H. and Nellie Alworth Memorial Fund**
c/o Dr. R.W. Darland
604 Alworth Building
Duluth, MN 55802 (218)722-9366

**$ Given:** 400 grants ranging from $1,200 to $22,000.
**Deadline:** March 1.

**Restrictions:**
Residents of northern MN studying science, math, and pre med. Most awards are given to high school seniors.

---

**American Foundation for Aging Research**
**University of Missouri Scholarship Program**
117 Tucker Hall
Columbia, MO 65211 (314)882-6426

**Restrictions:**
MO residents studying biology, medicine; 10 to 15 scholarships per year.

# 148·FREE MONEY

**American Museum of Natural History Collections Study Grant**
Central Park West at Seventy-ninth Street
New York, NY 10024 (212)769-5467

**$ Given:** Stipend to study collections at the museum.
**Contact:** Office of grants and fellowships, Diane Menditto.

**Restrictions:**
Must live outside of NY.

---

**American Society for Microbiology**
Michael I. Goldberg, Ph.D., Executive Director 1913 I Street, Northwest
Washington, DC 20006 (202)822-9229

**$ Given:** 2 fellowships - up to $4,250 to cover tuition and fees and $5,000 stipend.
**Deadline:** May 11.

**Restrictions:**
Graduate students in PhD program in microbiology who belong to minority group.

---

**Brookhaven National Laboratory/Office of Educational Programs**
Student Summer Program
Building 490
Upton, NY 11973 (516)282-4503

**$ Given:** Weekly stipend of $200 and round trip travel expenses to assist scientists in research. (11 weeks)
**Deadline:** January 31.

**Restrictions:**
Junior or senior with "B" average. Research done in biology, botany, accelerators, chemistry, energy, engineering, environment, math, medicine, physics and science writing.

---

**Conservation and Research Foundation, Inc.**
**Conservation and Research Foundation Research Grants**
P.O. Box 1445, Connecticut College
New London, CT 06320 (203)873-8514

**$ Given:** $100-$10,000 grants. Renewable.
**Contact:** President at above address. Application in form of letter of inquiry.

**Restrictions:**
CT residents who are graduate students studying biology, environmental law. Submit references.

---

**Cystic Fibrosis Foundation**
**Grant Management Office**
Student Traineeships
6000 Executive Boulevard, Suite 510
Rockville, MD 20852 (301)881-9130

**$ Given:** $1,500.
**Deadline:** October 1, February 1.
**Contact:** Associate Medical Dir. or Grants Coordinator.

**Restrictions:**
Student, undergrad or grad for minimum of 10 week period of research to introduce them to C.F. research.

---

**The Grass Foundation**
77 Reservoir Road
Quincy, MA 02170 (617)773-0002

**$ Given:** Total grants $372,914.
**Contact:** Mary G. Grass, Secretary.

**Restrictions:**
Predoctoral students of biology, neurobiology, medicine (physiology and neurology).

# Biology·149

**National Campers and Hikers Association**
4804 Transit Road, Building #2
Depew, NY 14043 (716)668-6242

**Deadline:** March 25.
**Contact:** Scholarship Director at above address.

**Restrictions:** Members or their children; wildlife conservation, forestry, botany, geology, ecology. High school applicant must be in upper ⅔ of class. College student must have GPA of 3.0.

---

**Fellowship Office**
c/o National Research Council
2101 Constitution Avenue, Northwest
Washington, DC 20418 (202)334-2872

**$ Given:** Graduate fellowships; 500 awards of $12,300 each.
**Contact:** Fellowship Office.
**Deadline:** November 14.

**Restrictions:** Mathematics, biology, engineering, science students.

---

**The Rockefeller Foundation Graduate Study Awards in Population Science**
1133 Avenue of the Americas
New York, NY 10026 (212)869-8500

**Deadline:** November 15.

**Restrictions:** Post-doctoral students studying social science, biology, chemistry, or who are working on a dissertation.

---

**Slocum-Lunz Foundation, Inc.**
**Grice Marine Biological Laboratory**
205 Fort Johnson
Charleston, SC 29412 (803)795-3716

**$ Given:** $1,000-$2000, 12 grants totaling $21,144.
**Deadline:** March 31

**Restriction** Graduate and doctoral students in marine science.

---

**Smithsonian Environmental Research Center**
**Work/Learn Program**
P.O. Box 28
Edgewater, MD 21037 (301)798-4424

**$ Given:** Support including weekly stipend of $75-$90 and living accommodations.
**Deadline:** December 1, April 1, July 1.
**Contact:** Linda Chick, Coordinator

**Restrictions:** Students to work on specific projects in environmental research within disciplines of math, chemistry, microbiology, botany, zoology.

## 150·FREE MONEY

**Society of Actuaries**
500 Park Boulevard, Suite 440
Itasca, IL 60143 (312)773-3010

**$ Given:** Unspecified number of grants up to $5,000.
**Deadline:** May 1.
**Contact:** Dept. Chairman, Placement/Guidance Office or the Society, above address.

**Restrictions:** Member of minority (Black, Hispanic, Oriental, Native American. Also woman on graduate level). Must submit test scores and be nominated by Dept. Chairman.

---

**Society of Nuclear Medicine, Education and Research Foundation**
**Fellowship Awards in Nuclear Medicine**
136 Madison Avenue
New York, NY 10016 (212)889-0717

**$ Given:** $3,000, $2,000.
**Deadline:** December 15, May 1, July 1.

**Restrictions:** Undergraduate or graduate study in nuclear medicine.

---

## BOTANY

**Brookhaven National Laboratory**
**Office of Educational Programs**
Student Summer Program
Building 490
Upton, NY 11973 (516)282-4503

**$ Given:** Weekly stipend of $200 and round trip travel expenses to assist scientists in research. (11 weeks)
**Deadline:** January 31.

**Restrictions:** Junior or senior with "B" average. Research done in biology, botany, accelerators, chemistry, energy, engineering, environment, math, medicine, physics and science writing.

---

**Mycological Society of American Graduate Fellowships**
Louisiana State University
Department of Botany
Baton Rouge, LA 70803 (504)388-8485

**$ Given:** 2 awards of $1,000.
**Contact:** Merideth Blackwell.
**Deadline:** March 31.

**Restrictions:** Graduate student in mycology who will be a candidate for PhD.

---

**National Campers and Hikers Association**
4804 Transit Road, Building #2
Depew, NY 14043 (716)668-6242

**Deadline:** March 25.

**Restrictions:** Members or their children; students of wildlife conservation, forestry, botany, geology, ecology.

**National Council of State Garden Clubs, Inc.**
4401 Magnolia Avenue
St. Louis, MO 63110 (314)776-7574

**$ Given:** 22 scholarships per academic year.
**Deadline:** October 1 to State Chairman; December 15 to National Chairman.
**Contact:** Above address.

**Restrictions:** Permanent resident of sponsoring state. Undergraduate with "B" average. Demonstrate financial need.

---

**Smithsonian Environmental Research Center**
**Work/Learn Program**
P.O. Box 28
Edgewater, MD 21037 (301)798-4424

**$ Given:** Support including weekly stipend of $75-$90 and living accommodations.
**Deadline:** December 1, April 1, July 1.
**Contact:** Linda Chick, Coordinator

**Restrictions:** Students to work on specific projects in environmental research within disciplines of math, chemistry, microbiology, botany and zoology.

# CHEMISTRY

**ASMT Educational Research Fund**
330 Meadowfern Drive
Houston, TX 77067 (713)893-7072

**$ Given:** 1 $1,000 scholarship per year. (Clinical Chemistry).
**Deadline:** March 1.
**Contact:** Scholarship Program, above address.

**Restrictions:** Clinical laboratory practitioner or educator who fulfills requirements of admission and has been engaged in laboratory performance in clinical chemistry for 1 year.

---

**Marshall H. and Nellie Alworth Memorial Fund**
c/o Dr. R.W. Darland
604 Alworth Building
Duluth, MN 55802 (218)722-9366

**$ Given:** 400 grants ranging from $1,200 to $22,000.
**Deadline:** March 1.

**Restrictions:** Residents of northern MN studying science, math, and pre-med. Most awards are given to high school seniors.

---

**American Geological Institute Minority Participation Program Scholarships**
4220 King Street
Alexandria, VA 22302 (703)379-2480

**$ Given:** $500-$2,000.
**Deadline:** February 1.

**Restrictions:** Meteorology, geology, physics, chemistry, science, minority undergraduate or graduate students in geoscience.

# 152 • FREE MONEY

**Association of Official Analytical Chemists (AOAC)**
1111 North Nineteenth Street, Suite 210
Arlington, VA 22209 (703)522-3032

**$ Given:** 1 $500 scholarship. Renewable one time.
**Contact:** Administrative Manager.
**Deadline:** May 1.

**Restrictions:**
Chemistry students. Sophomore in college with GPA of "B". Show financial need.

---

**Joseph Blazek Foundation**
8 South LaSalle Street
Chicago, IL 60603 (312)372-3880

**$ Given:** 78 grants of $500.
**Deadline:** February 1 of high school senior year.

**Restrictions:**
Cook County, IL high school seniors, residents IL, studying engineering, mathematics, chemistry, physics. Submit ACT, SAT, and FAF.

---

**Florence H. Brown Trust**
c/o Bank of Delaware
300 Delaware Avenue
Wilmington, DE 19899 (302)429-1109

**$ Given:** Varies from year to year.
**Contact:** Jim Morris.
**Deadline:** May 10.

**Restrictions:**
Medical, dental, law, engineering, chemistry students (undergraduate).

---

**Institute of Paper Chemistry**
1043 East South River
P.O. Box 1039
Appleton, WI 54912 (414)734-9251

**$ Given:** 36 $6,750 fellowships. 36 $3,000 stipends per year.
**Deadline:** March 15.

**Restrictions:**
Citizens of U.S. or Canada with B.S. in chemistry, chemical or mechanical engineering, paper science or biology. GPA 3.0/4.0. Present GRE scores.

---

**IOTA Sigma Pi**
c/o Dr. Celia Menendez-Botet
Memorial Sloan-Kettering Cancer Center
Department of Clinical Chemistry
1275 York Avenue
New York, NY 10021

**$ Given:** 1 $200 award for undergrads, 1 $300 for graduate study per year.
**Contact:** Antoinette Hockman, Ph.D. Dept. Chemistry & Chemical Engineering Stevens Institute of Technology Hoboken, NJ 07030
**Deadline:** February 1.

**Restrictions:**
Woman. Senior chemistry student or full-time graduate student. Must be nominated by department.

# Chemistry · 153

**The George F. Johnson Foundation**
8522 South Lafayette Avenue
Chicago, IL 60620

**$ Given:** 87 grants totaling $42,749, ranging from $240-$988.
**Deadline:** August 31.

**Restrictions:**
IL residents, preferably college freshmen majoring in engineering, chemistry, physics, mathematics, medicine, law, dentistry.

---

**The Kosciuszko Foundation**
15 East Sixty-fifth Street
New York, NY 10021 (212)734-2130

**$ Given:** $500-$1,000.
**Deadline:** January 15.

**Restrictions:**
Undergraduate students of Polish background or descent studying journalism, chemistry, engineering, mathematics, business.

---

**National Pharmaceutical Foundation, Inc.**
**Minority Graduate Study and Research Fellowships**
1728 Seventeenth Street, Northeast
Washington, DC 20002 (202)829-5008

**$ Given:** 2 fellowships ranging from $2,500-$10,000.

**Restrictions:**
Black American or other socio-economically disadvantaged ethnic minority graduate students studying pharmacology, pharmaceutical/medicinal chemistry, biomedical sciences, administrative sciences.

---

**National Scholarship Trust Fund (NSTF)**
4615 Forbes Avenue
Pittsburgh, PA 15213 (412)621-6941

**$ Given:** Grants ranging from $1,500-$3,000.
**Deadline:** January 10.

**Restrictions:**
Graduate study in mathematics, chemistry, physics, engineering.

---

**The Rockefeller Foundation**
**Graduate Study Awards in Population Science**
1133 Avenue of the Americas
New York, NY 10022 (212)869-8500

**Deadline:** November 15.

**Restrictions:**
Post-doctoral students studying social science, biology, chemistry, or who are working on a dissertation.

## 154•FREE MONEY

**Sales Association of the Chemical Industry, Inc. (SACI)**
50 East Forty-first Street
New York, NY 10017 (212)686-1952

**$ Given:** Unspecified number of $500 awards per year.
**Deadline:** May 30.
**Contact:** Education Committee Chairperson.

**Restrictions:**
Must specialize in chemically-related field such as chemical sales, marketing, or purchasing.

---

**Harvey W. Wiley Scholarship**
Association of Official Analytical Chemists
1111 North Nineteenth Street, Suite 210
Arlington, VA 22209 (703)522-3032

**$ Given:** $500 for 2 years.
**Contact:** Administrative Manager.
**Deadline:** May 1.

**Restrictions:**
College sophomore studying biology, chemistry; "B" average or better.

---

## COMPUTER SCIENCE

**Hughes Aircraft Company**
Corporate Fellowship Office
Building C2/B168
P.O. Box 1042
El Segundo, CA 90245 (213)414-6711

**Contact:** Corporate fellowship office.
**Deadline:** February 1.

**Restrictions:**
Engineering, computer science, mathematics, physics students. For graduate study; GPA of 3.0 or better.

---

**Murphy College Fund**
National Bank of Warsaw Trust Department
P.O. Box 1447
Warsaw, IN 46580 (219)2677-3271

**$ Given:** 9 grants totaling $4,500, ranging from $300-$600.
**Deadline:** April 15.

**Restrictions:**
College freshmen or high school seniors who are residents of Kosciusko County, IN.

---

**National Radio Astronomy Observatory Summer Student Program**
Edgemont Road
Charlottesville, VA 22903-2475
(804)296-0211

**$ Given:** Salaries from $850-$1,100 per month for research assistantships.
**Deadline:** February 1.

**Restrictions:**
Students of astronomy, physics, electrical engineering, computer sciences. Undergraduates must have completed 3 years training prior to program; graduates must not have more than 2 years graduate school.

## 154·FREE MONEY

**State Farm Companies Foundation**
One State Farm Plaza
Bloomington, IL 61701 (309)766-2039

**$ Given:** 20 fellowships of $2,000.
**Contact:** Assistant Vice President, Programs.
**Deadline:** February 28.

**Restrictions:** College juniors and seniors studying business, computer science, science, economics, finance, mathematics, law. Must be nominated by the dean or department head.

# ENGINEERING

**Alliance for Engineering in Medicine & Biology**
Suite 700
1101 Connecticut Avenue, Northwest
Washington, DC 20036 (202)857-1199

**$ Given:** Unspecified number of $200 scholarships; prizes.
**Deadline:** June 15 thru 30.
**Contact:** Executive Director.

**Restrictions:** Students enrolled in accredited institution. Must either submit paper expressing original idea or be nominated by faculty advisors or department heads.

---

**Marshall H. and Nellie Alworth Memorial Fund**
c/o Dr. R.W. Darland
604 Alworth Building
Duluth, MN 55802 (218)722-9366

**$ Given:** 400 grants ranging from $1,200 to $22,000.
**Deadline:** March 1.

**Restrictions:** Residents of northern MN studying science, math and pre-med. Most awards are given to high school seniors.

---

**American Association of Cost Engineers**
308 Monongahela Building
Morgantown, WV 26505 (304)296-8444

**$ Given:** $50-$3,000 awards.
**Contact:** Financial Aid Office.

**Restrictions:** Engineering students of selected universities.

---

**American Consulting Engineers Council**
1015 Fifteenth Street, Northwest
Washington, DC 20005 (202)347-7474

**$ Given:** 24 awards worth $31,000 ($1,000-$5,000).
**Deadline:** February.
**Contact:** Appropriate member organization (by state). See ACEC directory from dean's office.

**Restrictions:** U.S. citizen working toward B.S. in engineering, interested in pursuing career in consulting engineering.

## 156•FREE MONEY

**American Institute of Steel Construction Education Foundation (AISC)**
400 North Michigan Avenue
Chicago, IL 60611 (312)670-2400

**$ Given:** $5,000 awards. Not renewable.
**Deadline:** March 1.

**Restrictions:** Students majoring in structural engineering; college senior or graduate student.

---

**American Nuclear Society**
**Chave Lamarsh Scholarship**
555 North Kensington Avenue
La Grange Park, IL 60525 (312)352-6611

**$ Given:** Varies each year.
**Deadline:** March 1.

**Restrictions:** Students who have completed 2 years of a 4-year nuclear engineering program; financial need.

---

**American Nuclear Society**
**John and Muriel Landis Scholarship Program**
555 North Kensington Avenue
La Grange Park, IL 60525 (312)352-6611

**$ Given:** $3,500.

**Restrictions:** IL handicapped engineering, science students.

---

**American Society of Civil Engineers (ASCE)**
**Student Chapter Scholarships**
345 East Forty-seventh Street
New York, NY 10017 (212)644-7667

**$ Given:** 12 $500 awards.
**Deadline:** December 1.

**Restrictions:** Undergraduate member of student chapter of the American Society of Civil Engineers.

---

**American Society of Heating, Refrigerating, and Air Conditioning Engineers, Inc. (ASHRAE)**
1791 Tullie Circle, Northeast
Atlanta, GA 30329 (404)636-8400

**$ Given:** Grants to $6,000 per year. Not renewable.
**Contact:** Manager of Research-Grant-In-Aid Program.
**Deadline:** February 15.

**Restrictions:** Graduate engineering students. Application must be submitted by faculty advisor.

---

**American Society of Mechanical Engineers (ASME) Auxiliary, Inc.**
345 East Forty-seventh Street
New York, NY 10017 (212)705-7745

**$ Given:** 4-6 $1,000 awards for college students; 3-4 $2,000 awards for graduate students. Not renewable.

**Restrictions:** Member of ASME, citizen of U.S. Enrolled in accredited mechanical engineering curricula.

# Engineering·157

| | | |
|---|---|---|
| **American Society of Photogrammetry (ASP)**<br>210 Little Falls Street<br>Falls Church, VA 22046 (703)534-6617 | **$ Given:** $4,000 per year. Renewable.<br>**Deadline:** January 15. | **Restrictions:**<br>Must have completed 1 undergraduate course in surveying or photogrammetry. Member of ASP or American Congress on Surveying and Mapping. Demonstrate financial need. |
| **Amoco Foundation, Inc. Scholarships**<br>200 East Randolf Drive<br>Chicago, IL 60601 (312)856-6111 | **$Given:** $3,400 for 4 years.<br>**Contact:** See Finacial aid counselor. | **Restrictions:**<br>Juniors or seniors in the science/math field. |
| **Associated General Contractors (AGC) Education and Research Foundation**<br>1957 E Street, Northwest<br>Washington, DC 20006 (202)393-2040 | **$ Given:** 25-30 $1,500 scholarships. Renewable.<br>**Deadline:** November 15. | **Restrictions:**<br>Undergraduates enrolled in civil engineering or construction studies. Demonstrate ability and financial need. |
| **Bell Laboratories Engineering Scholarships Program**<br>150 JFK Parkway, Crawfords Corner Road, Room 1E230<br>Homdel, NJ 07733 (201)949-4300 | **$ Given:** Full scholarship.<br>**Deadline:** February 1. | **Restrictions:**<br>Minority engineering students, undergraduate. |
| **Joseph Blazek Foundation**<br>8 South La Salle Street<br>Chicago, IL 60603 (312)372-3880 | **$ Given:** 78 grants of $500.<br>**Deadline:** February 1 of high school senior year. | **Restrictions:**<br>Cook County, IL high school seniors studying engineering, mathematics, chemistry, physics. Submit ACT, SAT and FAF. |
| **Boys Club of America**<br>3760 Fourth Avenue<br>San Diego, CA 92103 (619)298-3520 | **$ Given:** 1 grant of $2,000 for each area of study.<br>**Deadline:** May 15. | **Restrictions:**<br>Male high school seniors studying medicine, law, engineering, political science within a 250 mile radius of San Diego. |

**158•FREE MONEY**

**Florence H. Brown Trust**
c/o Bank of Delaware
300 Delaware Avenue
Wilmington, DE 19899 (302)429-1109

**$ Given:** Varies from year to year.
**Contact:** Jim Morris
**Deadline:** May 10.

**Restrictions:**
Medical, dental, law, engineering, chemistry students.

---

**Center for American Indian Alternative Education**
**American Indian Scholarship Program**
P.O. Box 18285, Capital Hill Station
Denver, CO 80218 (303)861-1052

**$ Given:** 6 grants of $250-$2,000.
**Deadline:** April.

**Restrictions:**
AZ, NM, CO, OK, KS and San Bernardino County, CA residents studying medicine, engineering, science, business, education.

---

**Conoco**
Employee Relations Department
Professional Staffing Section
1007 Market Street
Wilmington, DE 19898 (302)774-6116

**Contact:** Sandra Graves

**Restrictions:**
Students of science, business, engineering.

---

**Directorate for Science and Engineering Education**
**Division of Research Career Development**
Dr. Douglas S. Chapin, Program Director
Room 414
800 G Street, Northwest
Washington, DC 20550 (202)357-7856

**$ Given:** Stipends of $11,100.
**Deadline:** November 14.
**Contact:** Fellowship Office National Research Council 2102 Constitution Avenue Washington, DC 20418 (202)334-2872

**Restrictions:**
Citizens or nationals of U.S.; have not completed postbaccalaureate study in excess of 20 semester hours (this includes minority fellowships), for masters or doctoral degree in math, physical biological, engineering, social sciences, history and philosophy of science.

---

**Amelia Earhart Fellowship Awards**
c/o Zonta International
35 East Wacker Drive
Chicago, IL 60601 (312)346-1445

**$ Given:** 32 grants of $6,000.
**Deadline:** January 1.

**Restrictions:**
Female graduate students in aerospace, science, or engineering, and sometimes law, medicine, and computer science.

# Engineering·159

**Hughes Aircraft Company**
Corporate Fellowship Office
Building C2/B168
P.O. Box 1042
El Segundo, CA 90245 (213)414-6711

**Deadline:** February 1.

**Restrictions:**
Graduate engineering, computer science, mathematics, physics students. GPA of 3.0 or better.

---

**Indian Fellowship Program**
Department of Education
400 Maryland Avenue Southwest
Washington, DC 20202 (202)732-1909

**$ Given:** $600-$24,000
**Deadline:** February 6
**Contact:** Dorothea Perkins Room 2177 at above address.

**Restrictions:**
Indian students; financial need. For graduate study in medicine, psychology, law, education. Undergraduate and graduate in business, engineering, natural resources.

---

**Institute of Electrical and Electronics Engineers, Inc. (IEEE)**
**Charles Legey and Fortescue Fellowship Committee**
345 East Forty-seventh Street
New York, NY 10017 (212)705-7882

**$ Given:** $10,000, one award, not renewable.
**Deadline:** January 15.
**Contact:** Secretary, above address.

**Restrictions:**
B.S. in electrical engineering; prefer giving for first year of graduate work.

---

**Institute of Industrial Engineers**
25 Technology Park/Atlanta
Norcross, GA 30092 (404)449-0460

**$ Given:** $1,500-$2,000 awards.
**Deadline:** February 15.
**Contact:** Executive Director.

**Restrictions:**
Full-time students in any school in U.S., Canada and Mexico pursuing industrial engineering. Scholastic ability and financial need are considered.

---

**The Kosciuszko Foundation**
15 East Sixty-fifth Street
New York, NY 10021 (212)734-2130

**$ Given:** $500-$1,000.
**Deadline:** January 15.

**Restrictions:**
Journalism, chemistry, engineering, mathematics, business students of Polish background or descent.

---

**The James F. Lincoln Arc Welding Foundation**
P.O. Box 17035
Cleveland, OH 44117-0035 (216)481-4300

**$ Given:** $250-$2,000 awards.
**Contact:** Secretary at above address.

**Restrictions:**
Graduate or undergraduate with appropriate papers representing students work on design, engineering or fabrication problems.

## 160·FREE MONEY

**Joseph F. Meade Memorial Science Fund**
c/o Lincoln First Bank, NA Trust Dept.
P.O. Box 1412
Rochester, NY 14603 (716)258-5175

**$ Given:** $250-$1,500.

**Restrictions:**
High school students from Hammondsport, NY Central School District. See guidance counselor.

---

**Mobil Oil Corporation**
P.O. Box 5444
Denver, CO 80217 (303)298-2000

**$ Given:** 8 grants of $500-$1,500.

**Restrictions:**
Engineering, science, geology students. Apply through college or university.

---

**Murphy College Fund**
National Bank of Warsaw Trust Department
P.O. Box 1447
Warsaw, IN 46580 (219)267-3271

**$ Given:** 9 grants totaling $4,500 ranging from $300-$600.
**Deadline:** April 15.

**Restrictions:**
College freshmen or high school seniors who are residents of Kosciusko County, IN.

---

**National Association of Plumbing-Heating-Cooling Contractors (NAPHCC)**
1016 Twentieth Street, Northwest
Washington, DC 20036 (202)331-7675

**$ Given:** Unspecified number of $1,000 awards per year. Renewable.
**Deadline:** March 1.
**Contact:** Scholarship Trust Coordinator, NAPHCC Scholarship Trust at above address.

**Restrictions:**
High school senior or college freshman. Must be sponsored by NAPHCC member in good standing. Must pledge to remain in contracting branch of industry for 4 of the 8 years following graduation.

---

**National Consortium for Graduating Degrees for Minorities in Engineering, Inc.**
P.O. Box 537
Notre Dame, IN 46556 (219)239-7183

**$ Given:** Tuition and fees plus $5,000 stipend and paid summer work assignment—graduate study.
**Deadline:** December 1.
**Contact:** Executive Director.

**Restrictions:**
Native, Black, Mexican American or Puerto Rican in junior year in college.

---

**National Center for the Blind**
**Howard Brown Rickard Scholarship**
1800 Johnson Street
Baltimore, MD 21230 (301)659-9317

**$ Given:** $1,200.
**Contact:** Peggy Pinder.
**Deadline:** March 31.

**Restrictions:**
Legally blind law, medical, engineering, architecture, science undergraduate and graduate students.

# Engineering·16

**National Radio Astronomy Observatory Summer Student Program**
Edgemont Road
Charlottesville, VA 22903-2475
(804)296-0211

**$ Given:** Salaries from $850-$1,100 per month for research assistantships.
**Deadline:** February 1.

**Restrictions:** Students of astronomy, physics, electrical engineering, computer sciences. Undergraduates must have completed 3 years training prior to program; graduates must not have more than 2 years graduate school.

---

**National Scholarship Trust Fund**
4615 Forbes Avenue
Pittsburgh, PA 15213 (412)621-6941

**$ Given:** Grants ranging from $1,500-$3,000.
**Deadline:** January 15.

**Restrictions:** Graduate study in mathematics, chemistry, physics, engineering; must pertain to the publishing industry.

---

**National Science Foundation National Research Council**
2101 Constitution Avenue, Northwest
Washington, DC 20418 (202)334-2872

**$ Given:** Unspecified number of $11,100 fellowships. Renewable.
**Contact:** Fellowship Office.
**Deadline:** November 21.

**Restrictions:** Minority graduate students and students who have not completed more than 20 semester hours in the science or engineering field. Full time enrollment in areas specified by the NSF.

---

**National Society of Professional Engineers**
1420 King Street
Alexandria, VA 22314 (703)684-2800.

**$ Given:** $1,000-$4,000; also some full scholarships.
**Deadline:** December 15.

**Restrictions:** High school seniors who will be studying engineering; also special scholarships for minorities.

---

**Navajo Nation Department of Higher Education**
**Navajo Nation Scholarship Assistance Program**
P.O. Drawer S
Window Rock, AZ 86515 (602)871-5544

**Deadline:** April 30, June 30, November 30.

**Restrictions:** Navajo students who are or will be studying medicine, engineering, law, business and who will return to the Navajo Nation.

# E MONEY

**...ience, Engineering and Health Physics Fellowships**
University Programs, Oak Ridge
Associated Universities
P.O. Box 117
120 Badger Avenue
Oak Ridge, TN 87830 (615)576-3428

**Deadline:** January 30.

**Restrictions:**
Graduate students with B.S. degree in science, engineering, physics.

---

**Office of Indian Education**
United States Department of Education
400 Maryland Avenue, Southwest
Washington, DC 20202 (202)732-1923

**$ Given:** $2,300-$13,000.
**Deadline:** March

**Restrictions:**
Native Americans accepted or enrolled and working toward graduate degree in medicine, law, education, psychology or graduate or undergraduate degree in natural resources, business administration, engineering.

---

**Arthur and Doreen Parrett Scholarship Trust Fund**
c/o Peoples National Bank of Washington
P.O. Box 720, Trust Division
Seattle, WA 98111 (206)344-3685

**$ Given:** 9 grants of $800 and 4 grants of $350.
**Contact:** Janet Syferd, Trust Officer
**Deadline:** July 31.

**Restrictions:**
WA students of engineering, medicine, science, dentistry.

---

**RCA Corporation**
P.O. Box 2023
Princeton, NJ 08540 (609)734-9881

**$ Given:** Scholarships and fellowships with stipends.
**Contact:** Financial Aid Office.

**Restrictions:**
Undergraduate and graduate students studying engineering, physical sciences with a few for telecommunications. Fellowships in electrical engineering, electronics, journalism, solid state physics.

---

**The Refractories Institute**
301 Fifth Avenue, Suite 1517
Pittsburgh, PA 15222 (412)281-6787

**$ Given:** 34 $500 scholarships.
**Contact:** Above address for list of University Ceramic Departments.

**Restrictions:**
U.S. citizen. Qualified college student who is or will enroll in Ceramic Engineering/Science Curriculum. Preference given to student who plans to enroll in refractories.

# Engineering·163

**Schramm Foundation**
P.O. Box 625
West Chester, PA 19380 (215)696-2500

**$ Given:** 14 grants of $300.
**Deadline:** Must be recommended by high school in March.

**Restrictions:** Graduates of high schools in vicinity of West Chester, PA for business or engineering degree.

---

**Society for the Advancement of Material and Process Engineering**
National Business Office
668 South Azusa Avenue
P.O. Box 613
Azusa, CA 91702 (213)334-1810

**$ Given:** 2 $1,000 awards per year. Renewable.
**Deadline:** Last day in February.
**Contact:** Chairman, Scholarship Committee at above address.

**Restrictions:** Undergraduate pursuing degree related to materials and processes.

---

**Society of Mining Engineers of AIME**
Caller #D
Littleton, CO 80127

**$ Given:** 1 scholarship of $1,000. Not renewable.
**Deadline:** November 30.
**Contact:** Industrial Minerals Division Scholarships at above address.

**Restrictions:** Geology, engineering students. "B" average in major and overall "C" in other subjects.

---

**Society of Naval Architects and Marine Engineers**
One World Trade Center, Suite 1369
New York, NY 10048 (212)432-0310

**$ Given:** 5-8 $1,000-$12,000 scholarships. Not renewable.
**Deadline:** February 1.
**Contact:** Secretary and Executive Director.

**Restrictions:** Undergraduates and graduates studying naval architecture, marine engineering, oceanography.

---

**Society of Photographic Scientists and Engineers (SPSE)**
7003 Kilworth Lane
Springfield, VA 22151 (703)642-9090

**$ Given:** 1 $1,000 award. Renewable.
**Deadline:** December 15.
**Contact:** Executive Director at above address.

**Restrictions:** Full-time student; has completed 2 years of college before term of scholarship.

## 164·FREE MONEY

**Society of Women Engineers (SWE)**
345 East Forty-seventh Street
New York, NY 10017 (212)705-7855

**$ Given:** 35 scholarships of $200-$2,000.
**Deadline:** March 1.
**Contact:** Dean of Engineering or above address.

**Restrictions:**
NY female engineering or electrical engineering students.

---

**Society of Women Engineers**
**Olive Lynn Salembier Scholarship**
345 East Forty-seventh Street, Room 305
New York, NY 10017 (212)705-7855

**$ Given:** $500.
**Deadline:** Spring.

**Restrictions:**
Female engineering students who have been out of engineering job market for at least 2 years.

---

**Society of Women Engineers**
**United Engineering Center**
**Bertha Lamme Scholarship**
345 East Forty-seventh Street, Room 305
New York, NY 10017 (212)705-7855

**Deadline:** February 1.

**Restrictions:**
High school students who will be studying engineering in college.

---

**LTV Steel Corporation**
P.O. Box 6778
Republic Building
Cleveland, OH 44101 (216)622-5255

**Contact:** Dee Tripp, Secretary, Contributions Committee.

**Restrictions:**
Engineering, science students, sons and daughters of LTV Steel Corporation. Must apply in junior year of high school.

---

**United States Office of Education**
**Office of Indian Education**
**Indian Education Fellowships for Indian Students**
400 Maryland Avenue, Southwest
Washington, DC 20202 (202)732-1890

**$ Given:** Fellowships ranging from $2,300-$13,000, financial need.
**Deadline:** February 6.

**Restrictions:**
American Indians studying engineering, medicine, law, business administration, natural resources, education.

---

**Vertical Flight Foundation**
217 North Washington Street
Alexandria, VA 22314 (703)684-6777

**Deadline:** February 1.

**Restrictions:**
Undergraduate and graduate students pursuing careers in helicopters or vertical flight.

Geography • 165

| | | |
|---|---|---|
| **Zonta International**<br>35 East Wacker Drive<br>Chicago, IL 60601 (312)346-1445 | **$ Given:** 32 $6,000 fellowships.<br>**Deadline:** January 1. | **Restrictions:**<br>Woman. BA or BS for graduate work in aerospace or engineering. |

## FORESTRY

| | | |
|---|---|---|
| **Ki Sigma Pi National Forestry Honorary**<br>Forestry Department<br>251 Bessey Hall<br>Iowa State University<br>Ames, IA 50011 (515)294-1233 | **$ Given:** 10 $350 scholarships.<br>**Contact:** Local chapter or Department of Forestry Scholarship Chairman at above address.<br>**Deadline:** February 1. | **Restrictions:**<br>Junior in college, member of Ki Sigma Pi, nominated by local chapter. Demonstrate financial need. |
| **National Campers and Hikers Association**<br>4804 Transit Road, Building #2<br>Depew, NY 14043 (716)668-6242 | **Deadline:** March 25.<br>**Contact:** Scholarship Director at above address. | **Restrictions:**<br>Members or their children; students of wildlife conservation, forestry, botany, geology, ecology. High school applicant must be in upper ⅖ of class. College student must have GPA of 3.0. |
| **St. Regis Paper Company**<br>150 East Forty-second Street<br>New York, NY 10017 (212)573-6000 | **$ Given:** Unspecified number of $1,000 awards for students in junior and senior years in college.<br>**Contact:** Head of Forestry School or advisor. | **Restrictions:**<br>Second year forestry student. |

## GEOGRAPHY

| | | |
|---|---|---|
| **Gamma Theta Upsilon**<br>**International Geographic Honor Society**<br>University of Wisconsin at La Crosse<br>La Crosse, WI 54601 (608)785-8340 | **$ Given:** 1 $500 award for undergraduates, 2 $500 for graduate students.<br>**Deadline:** June 1.<br>**Contact:** Dept. of Geography at above address. | **Restrictions:**<br>Member of Gamma Theta Upsilon or Omega Alumni Chapter enrolled (or accepted) in a graduate institution's geography program. |

# GEOLOGY

**Marshall H. and Nellie Alworth Memorial Fund**
c/o Dr. R.W. Darland
604 Alworth Building
Duluth, MN 55802 (218)722-9366

**$ Given:** 400 grants ranging from $1,200 to $22,000.
**Deadline:** March 1.

**Restrictions:** Residents of northern MN studying science, math, and pre-med. Most awards are given to high school seniors.

---

**American Geological Institute**
4220 King Street
Alexandria, VA 22302 (703)379-2480

**$ Given:** $500-$1,500 awards per year.
**Deadline:** February 1.
**Contact:** Director of Education at above address.

**Restrictions:** Minority undergraduate or graduate students studying meteorology, geology, physics, chemistry, science.

---

**Amoco Foundation, Inc. Scholarships**
200 East Randolf Drive
Chicago, IL 60601 (312)856-6111

**$ Given:** $3,400 for 4 years.
**Contact:** See financial aid counselor.

**Restrictions:** Engineering, geology students. Apply through college or universities. Write for list of schools which offer this scholarship.

---

**American Congress on Surveying and Mapping**
216 Little Falls Street
Falls Church, VA 22046 (703)241-2446

**Contact:** Executive Director
**Deadline:** January 15.

**Restrictions:** Fellowships in surveying, cartography and photogammetry.

---

**Geological Society of America**
3300 Penrose Place
Boulder, CO 80301 (303)447-2020

**$ Given:** 100 $200-$1,200 grants per year.
**Deadline:** February 15.
**Contact:** Executive Director at above address.

**Restrictions:** Research in geology and related areas.

---

**Mobil Oil Corporation**
P.O. Box 5444
Denver, CO 80217 (303)298-2000

**$ Given:** 8 grants ranging from $500-$1,500.

**Restrictions:** Students in engineering, science, geology. Apply through college or university.

**National Campers and Hikers Association**
4804 Transit Road, Building #2
Depew, NY 14043 (716)668-6242

**Deadline:** March 25.
**Contact:** Scholarship Director at above address.

**Restrictions:**
Members or their children; students of wildlife conservation, forestry, botany, geology, ecology. High school applicant must be in upper ⅖ of class; college student must have GPA of 3.0.

---

**Society of Mining Engineers of AIME Industrial Minerals Division Scholarship**
Caller #D
Littleton, CO 80127

**$ Given:** 1 scholarship of $1,000.
**Deadline:** November 30.

**Restrictions:**
College student, "B" average in major and "C" overall studying geology, engineering.

## GEOPHYSICS

**American Geophysical Union**
2000 Florida Avenue, Northwest
Washington, DC 20009 (202)462-6903 ext. 262

**$ Given:** $500 awards.
**Deadline:** May 1.
**Contact:** Society Activities Manager.

**Restrictions:**
First year graduate student; undergraduate accepted for graduate study, or junior college student accepted in bachelor's degree program in field of the atmospheric sciences.

---

**Amoco Foundation, Inc. Scholarships**
c/o Amoco Foundation, Inc.
200 East Randolph Drive
Chicago, IL 60601 (312)856-6111

**$ Given:** $3,400 for 4 years.
**Contact:** See financial aid counselor.

**Restrictions:**
Juniors or seniors in the science/math fields. Write for list of schools which offer this scholarship.

---

**Lunar & Planetary Institute**
3303 NASA Road 1
Houston, TX 77058

**$ Given:** Undergraduate internships.
**Contact:** Director at above address.

**Restrictions:**
Undergraduates with research interests in relevant fields.

# 168·FREE MONEY

**Society of Exploration Geophysicist Education Foundation**
Box 702740
Tulsa, OK 74170 (918)743-1365

**$ Given:** Awards ranging from $100-$1,500.
**Deadline:** March 1.

**Restrictions:** Undergraduates or graduates who intend to pursue careers in geophysics.

## MATHEMATICS

**Marshall H. and Nellie Alworth Memorial Fund**
c/o Dr. R.W. Darland
604 Alworth Building
Duluth, MN 55802 (218)722-9366

**$ Given:** 400 grants ranging from $1,200 to $22,000.
**Deadline:** March 1.

**Restrictions:** Residents of northern MN studying science, math, and pre-med. Most awards are given to high school seniors.

**Joseph Balzak Foundation**
8 South La Salle Street
Chicago, IL 60603 (312)372-3880

**$ Given:** 78 grants of $500.
**Deadline:** February 1 of high school senior year.

**Restrictions:** Cook County, IL high school seniors studying engineering, mathematics, chemistry, physics. Submit ACT, SAT, and FAF.

**Directorate for Science & Engineering Education**
**Division of Research Career Development**
Dr. Douglas S. Chapin, Program Director
Room 414
800 G Street, Northwest
Washington, DC 20550 (202)357-7856

**$ Given:** Stipends of $11,100.
**Deadline:** November 14.
**Contact:** Fellowship Office, National Research Council, 2102 Constitution Avenue, Washington, DC, 20418. (202)334-2872

**Restrictions:** Citizens or nationals of U.S.; have not completed postbaccalaureate study in excess of 20 semester hours (this includes minority fellowships), for masters or doctoral degree in math, physical biological, engineering, social sciences, history and philosophy of science.

**Hughes Aircraft Company**
Corporate Fellowship Office
Building C2/B168
P.O. Box 1042
El Segundo, CA 90245 (213)414-6711

**Contact:** Corporate Fellowship Office.
**Deadline:** February 1.

**Restrictions:** Engineering, computer science, mathematics, physics. Graduate study; GPA of 3.0 or better.

# Mathematics • 169

**The Kosciuszko Foundation**
15 East Sixty-fifth Street
New York, NY 10021 (212)734-2130

**$ Given:** $500-$1,000.
**Deadline:** January 15.

**Restrictions:**
Undergraduate students of Polish background or descent studying journalism, chemistry, engineering, mathematics, business.

---

**National Scholarship Trust Fund**
4615 Forbes Avenue
Pittsburgh, PA 15213 (412)621-6941

**$ Given:** Grants ranging from $1,500-$3,000.
**Deadline:** January 15.

**Restrictions:**
Graduate study in mathematics, chemistry, physics, engineering. Must pertain to the publishing industry.

---

**The National Science Foundation**
c/o National Research Council
2101 Constitution Avenue, Northwest
Washington, DC 20418

**$ Given:** $6,900 a year and $4,000 for 3 years in lieu of tuition and fees.
**Contact:** Fellowship Office.
**Deadline:** Late November.

**Restrictions:**
Mathematics, biology, engineering, science.

---

**Smithsonian Environmental Research Center**
**Work/Learn Program**
P.O. Box 28
Edgewater, MD 21037 (301)798-4424

**$ Given:** Support including weekly stipend of $75-$90 and living accommodations.
**Deadline:** December 1, April 1, July 1.
**Contact:** Linda Chick, Coordinator

**Restrictions:**
Students to work on specific projects in environmental research within disciplines of math, chemistry, microbiology, botany, zoology.

---

**State Farm Companies Foundation**
One State Farm Plaza
Bloomington, IL 61701 (309)766-2039

**$ Given:** 20 fellowships of $2,000 each.
**Contact:** Assistant Vice President, Programs.
**Deadline:** February 28.

**Restrictions:**
Junior or senior undergraduates studying mathematics, computer science, science, economics, finance, law. Must be nominated by the dean or department head.

# METEOROLOGY

**American Geological Institute Minority Participation Program Scholarships**
4220 King Street
Alexandria, VA 22302 (703)379-2480

**$ Given:** $500-$2,000.
**Deadline:** February 1.

**Restrictions:**
Minority undergraduate or graduate students studying geosciences.

---

**American Meteorological Society (AMS)**
45 Beacon Street
Boston, MA 02108 (617)227-2425

**$ Given:** 1 grant of $500 and 1 of $1,000. Not renewable.
**Deadline:** June 15.

**Restrictions:**
Meteorology major with at least 54 credits. Must intend to make atmospheric science a career and be nominated by major department.

# OCEANOGRAPHY

**International Women's Fishing Association Scholarship Trust (IWFA)**
P.O. Box 2025
Palm Beach, FL 33480

**$ Given:** Unspecified number of fellowships. Renewable.
**Contact:** Secretary, IWFA Scholarship Trust at above address.
**Deadline:** March 1.

**Restrictions:**
None.

---

**Society of Naval Architects and Marine Engineers**
One World Trade Center, Suite 1369
New York, NY 10048 (212)432-0310

**$ Given:** Approximately 5 grants covering tuition for graduates; some grants for undergraduates.
**Contact:** Robert G. Mende, Secretary and Executive Director.
**Deadline:** February 1.

**Restrictions:**
Naval architecture, marine engineering, ocean engineering graduate students or related fields. Schools which award these scholarships are MIT, University of Michigan, University of California at Berkeley, State University of New York, Florida Atlantic University. Apply directly to school.

Physics and Physical Sciences•171

**Woods Hole Oceanographic Institution**
Wood Hole, MA 02543 (617)548-1400

**$ Given:** Salaried traineeships per semester or summer session.
**Deadline:** 2 months before starting date.
**Contact:** Dean of Graduate Studies at above address.

**Restrictions:** Minority undergraduate in U.S. college or university. Must have completed at least 2 semesters.

## PHARMACOLOGY

**American Foundation for Pharmaceutical Education (AFPE)**
Radburn Plaza Building
14-25 Plaza Road
Fair Lawn, NJ 07410 (201)791-5192

**$ Given:** $5,000-$7,000 fellowships.
**Deadline:** March 15.

**Restrictions:** Graduate students currently enrolled in a program in pharmaceutical sciences. U.S. citizen with a B.S. degree.

**Maryland State Scholarship Board**
**Maryland Professional School Scholarships**
2100 Guilford Avenue
Baltimore, MD 21218 (301)333-6420

**$ Given:** Grants ranging from $200-$1,000, renewable.
**Deadline:** March 2.

**Restrictions:** Undergraduate or graduate study in medicine, dentistry, law, nursing, pharmacology.

**National Pharmaceutical Foundation, Inc.**
**Minority Graduate Study and Research Fellowships**
1728 Seventeenth Street, Northeast
Washington, DC 20002 (202)829-5008

**$ Given:** 12 awards ranging from $500-$1,000, renewable. 2 fellowships ranging from $2,500-$10,000, renewable.
**Contact:** President at above address.

**Restrictions:** Black American or other socio-economically disadvantaged ethnic minority graduate students studying pharmacology, pharmaceutical/medicinal chemistry, biomedical sciences, administrative sciences. Submit ACT, SAT, CEEB, or GRE.

## PHYSICS AND PHYSICAL SCIENCES

**Marshall H. and Nellie Alworth Memorial Fund**
c/o Dr. R. W. Darland
604 Alworth Building
Duluth, MN 55802 (218)722-9366

**$ Given:** 400 grants ranging from $1,200 to $22,000.
**Deadline:** March 1.

**Restrictions:** Residents of MN studying science, math and pre-med. Most awards are given to high school seniors.

## 172·FREE MONEY

**American Geological Institute Minority Participation Program Scholarships**
4220 King Street
Alexandria, VA 22302 (703)379-2480

**$ Given:** $250-$1,500.
**Deadline:** February 1.

**Restrictions:** Minority undergraduate or graduate students studying meteorology, geology, physics, chemistry, science.

---

**The American Physical Society Corporate Sponsored Scholarships for Minority Students**
335 East Forty-fifth Street
New York, NY 10017 (212)682-7341

**$ Given:** 6 new grants and 12 renewed grants of $2,000.
**Deadline:** March 31.

**Restrictions:** Black, Hispanic and native American high school senior or college freshman or sophomore studying physics.

---

**Amoco Foundation, Inc. Scholarships**
c/o Amoco Foundation, Inc.
200 East Randolph Drive
Chicago, IL 60601 (312)856-6111

**$ Given:** $3,400 for 4 years.
**Contact:** See financial aid counselor.

**Restrictions:** Juniors or seniors in the science/math fields. Write for list of schools which offer this scholarship.

---

**Joseph Blazek Foundation**
8 South La Salle Street
Chicago, IL 60603 (312)372-3880

**$ Given:** 78 grants of $500.
**Deadline:** February 1 of senior year.

**Restrictions:** Cook County, IL high school seniors studying engineering, mathematics, chemistry, physics. Submit ACT, SAT, and FAF.

---

**Department of Energy
Oak Ridge Associated Universities
University Programs Division
Nuclear Energy Fellowships**
P.O. Box 117
Oak Ridge, TN 37831-0117

**$ Given:** $12,000 fellowships per year. Renewable.

**Restrictions:** Graduate students with BS degree in physical sciences, life sciences, math or engineering; be accepted for graduate study in health physics. Must not be or have been enrolled in full time graduate program. GRE scores required.

# Physics and Physical Sciences • 173

**District of Columbia Public Schools, Division of Student Services**
415 Twelfth Street, Northwest
Washington, DC 20004

**$ Given:** 1 scholarship of $1,000.
**Contact:** Guidance Counselor or above address.

**Restrictions:**
Black students pursuing careers in physical or natural sciences.

---

**The Electrochemical Society, Inc.**
10 South Main Street
Pennington, NJ 08534-2896 (609)737-1902

**$ Given:** 3 summer fellowships per year. One grant biennially, intended for studying overseas in recognized institute or university.
**Contact:** Executive Secretary.
**Deadline:** January 1; February 1.

**Restrictions:**
For fellowship: graduate student in U.S. or Canada who will continue studies after summer. For grant: graduating senior or graduate student, enrolled in U.S. or Canada.

---

**Hughes Aircraft Company**
Corporate Fellowship Office
Building C2/B168
P.O. Box 1042
El Segundo, CA 90245 (213)414-6711

**Contact:** Corporate fellowship office.
**Deadline:** February 1.

**Restrictions:**
Engineering, computer science, mathematics, physics students. Graduate study; GPA of 3.0 or better.

---

**National Radio Astronomy Observatory Summer Student Program**
Edgemont Road
Charlottesville, VA 22903-2475
(804)296-0211

**$ Given:** Salaries from $850-$1,100 per month for research assistantships.
**Deadline:** February 1.

**Restrictions:**
Students of astronomy, physics, electrical engineering, computer sciences. Undergraduates must have completed 3 years training prior to program; graduates must not have more than 2 years graduate school.

---

**National Scholarship Trust Fund**
4615 Forbes Avenue
Pittsburgh, PA 15213 (412)621-6941

**$ Given:** Grants ranging from $1,500-$3,000.
**Deadline:** January 15.

**Restrictions:**
Graduate study in mathematics, chemistry, physics, engineering; must pertain to the publishing industry.

**174·FREE MONEY**

**Science Talent Search—Science Service, Inc.**
1719 N Street, Northwest
Washington, DC 20036 (202)785-2255

**$ Given:** 10 scholarships per year totaling $33,625. Renewable.
**Deadline:** December 15.

**Restrictions:** Enrolled as senior in secondary school in U.S., Puerto Rico, Guam, Virgin Islands, American Samoa, Wake & Midway Islands. Complete college entrance qualifications by October 1. Submit 1,000 words on independent research project in social or physical sciences, engineering, mathematics or biological sciences. May not have previously competed for Science Talent Search.

# SCIENCE

**The American Dietetic Association Foundation**
430 North Michigan Avenue
Chicago, IL 60611 (312)280-5013

**$ Given:** Undergraduate $500-$2,500; graduate $500-$2,500.
**Deadline:** December 31.

**Restrictions:** Undergraduates and graduate students studying human nutrition and practice of dietetics.

**American Geological Institute Minority Participation Program Scholarships**
4220 King Street
Alexandria, VA 22302 (703)379-2480

**$ Given:** $250-$1,500.
**Deadline:** February 1.

**Restrictions:** Minority undergraduate or graduate students studying meteorology, geology, physics, chemistry, science.

**American Geophysical Union June Bacon-Bercey Scholarship**
2000 Florida Avenue, Northwest
Washington, DC 20009 (202)462-6903

**$ Given:** $500.
**Contact:** American Geophysical Union member programs.
**Deadline:** April 15.

**Restrictions:** Females who intend to make a career in the atmospheric sciences. Undergraduate and graduate.

# Science·175

| | | |
|---|---|---|
| **American Institute of Aeronautics and Astronautics Scholarship Program**<br>1290 Avenue of Americas<br>New York, NY 10019 (212)581-4300 | **$ Given:** $1,000.<br>**Deadline:** February 2. | **Restrictions:**<br>Second year science, engineering, aerospace students. |
| **American Nuclear Society Awards and Scholarship Program**<br>555 North Kensington Avenue<br>La Grange Park, IL 60525 (312)352-6611 | **$ Given:** Several scholarships from $500-$3,500.<br>**Deadline:** March 1. | **Restrictions:**<br>Undergraduate and graduate students studying nuclear science or engineering. |
| **American Society of Enologists**<br>P.O. Box 1855<br>Davis, CA 95617 (916)753-3142 | **$ Given:** Several grants ranging from $1,000-$3,000.<br>**Contact:** Secretary-Treasurer.<br>**Deadline:** March 1. | **Restrictions:**<br>Students of enology (wine and grape industry), viticulture, food science or horticulture. |
| **American Society for Metals Foundation for Education and Research Scholarship Program**<br>c/o Career Guidance Coordinator<br>Metal Park, OH 44073 (216)338-5151, Ext. 465 | **$ Given:** 33 scholarships of $500.<br>**Deadline:** June 1. | **Restrictions:**<br>Metallurgy, science students. |
| **American Vacuum Society**<br>335 East 45th Street<br>New York, NY 10017 (212)661-9404 | **$ Given:** 1 year fellowship of $1,500.<br>**Contact:** Secretary of AVS.<br>**Deadline:** March 31. | **Restrictions:**<br>Graduate student with major field in vacuum science and technology, thin film research vacuum metallurgy, surface physics, electronic materials and processing and fusion technology. |
| **Association for Women in Science Educational Foundation**<br>1346 Connecticut Avenue, Northwest, Suite 1122<br>Washington, DC 20036 (202)833-1998 | **$ Given:** 4 grants of $500.<br>**Contact:** Dr. Sheila Pfafflin, President.<br>**Deadline:** January 15. | **Restrictions:**<br>Female graduate science students enrolled in predoctoral program. |

# 176·FREE MONEY

**Association of Official Analytical Chemists**
111 North Nineteenth Street, Suite 210
Arlington, VA 22209 (703)522-3032

**$ Given:** $500.
**Contact:** Angie Cole.
**Deadline:** May 1 of sophomore year.

**Restrictions:**
Chemistry, agriculture, biology, medical, science students.

---

**Bausch & Lomb Science Award Committee**
One Lincoln First Square, Box 54
Rochester, NY 14601 (716)338-5469

**$ Given:** Unspecified number of $1,000-$7,500 awards per year.
**Deadline:** February 15.

**Restrictions:**
Must have been awarded Bausch & Lomb science medal in senior year of high school. Completed at least 3 science courses. Must enroll in University of Rochester.

---

**Joseph Blazek Foundation**
8 South Michigan Avenue
Chicago, IL 60603 (312)372-3880

**$ Given:** 12 grants of $500.
**Deadline:** February 1.

**Restrictions:**
Science students of Cook County, IL, graduating high school seniors.

---

**Automotive Booster Clubs International Education and Scholarship Foundation**
c/o Wayne Black
Sun Country Sales
2518 South Forest
Tempe, AZ 85282 (602)967-4076

**$ Given:** $500-$800.

**Restrictions:**
High school senior studying education and scientific programs related to automotive industry and planning to attend Northwood Institute of Michigan or Southern Colorado University in Pueblo.

---

**Center for American Indian Alternative Education**
**American Indian Scholarship Program**
P.O. Box 18285, Capitol Hill Station
Denver, CO 80218 (303)861-1052

**$ Given:** 6 grants ranging from $250-$2,000.
**Deadline:** April.

**Restrictions:**
AZ, NM, CO, OK, KS, and San Bernadino County, CA residents studying medicine, engineering, science, business, education.

---

**Conoco**
Employee Relations Dept.
Professional Staffing Section
1007 Market Street
Wilmington, DE 19898 (302)774-6116

**Contact:** Clark Phippen, Secretary.

**Restrictions:**
Students studying science, business, engineering.

# Science·177

**Directorate for Science & Engineering Education**
**Division of Research Career Development**
Dr. Douglas S. Chapin, Program Director
Room 414
800 G Street, Northwest
Washington, DC 20550 (202)357-7856

**$ Given:** Stipends of $11,100.
**Deadline:** November 14.
**Contact:** Fellowship Office National Research Council 2101 Constitution Avenue Washington, DC 20418 (202)334-2872

**Restrictions:** Citizens or nationals of U.S., have not completed postbaccalaureate study in excess of 20 semester hours (this includes minority fellowships), for masters or doctoral degree in math, physical biology, engineering, social sciences, history and philosophy of science.

---

**District of Columbia Public Schools, Division of Student Services**
415 Twelfth Street, Northwest
Washington, DC 20004

**$ Given:** Unspecified number of $1,000-$2,000 awards per year.
**Contact:** Guidance Counselor.

**Restrictions:** High school senior pursuing a career in science or technology. GPA of 3.0. Evidence of financial need.

---

**Amelia Earhart Fellowship Awards**
c/o Zonta International
35 East Wacker Drive
Chicago, IL 60601 (312)346-1445

**$ Given:** Approximately 32 awards of $6,000 each.
**Deadline:** January 1.

**Restrictions:** Female graduate student studying aerospace, science.

---

**Ford Foundation Scholarships**
**National Research Council**
Fellowship Office
2101 Constitution Avenue
Washington, DC 20418 (202)334-2872

**$ Given:** $1,800 to complete Doctoral dissertation.
**Deadline:** Apply in the fall, one year previous to award.

**Restrictions:** Mexican-American, Puerto Rican, Native Indian, Alaskans and Black graduate students in science or PhD students who are writing their dissertation.

---

**Kosciuszko Foundation**
**Stan Lesny Scholarships**
15 East Sixty-fifth Street
New York, NY 10021

**$ Given:** $500-$1,000.

**Restrictions:** Students of Polish descent studying engineering, mathematics, science.

---

**Mobil Oil Corporation**
P.O. Box 5444
Denver, CO 80217 (303)298-2000

**$ Given:** 8 grants ranging from $500-$1,500.

**Restrictions:** Engineering, science, geology students. Apply through college or university.

## 178 • FREE MONEY

**National Aeronautics and Space Administration**
**University Program**
400 Maryland Avenue Southwest, Code LEU
Washington, DC 20546 (202)453-8344

**Contact:** Above address, write for brochure listing all of the scholarships available.

**Restrictions:**
Science students.

---

**National Center for the Blind**
**Howard Brown Rickard Scholarship**
1800 Johnson Street
Baltimore, MD 21230 (301)659-9317

**$ Given:** $1,200.
**Contact:** Peggy Pinder.
**Deadline:** March 31.

**Restrictions:**
Legally blind undergraduate and graduate students studying law, medicine, engineering, architecture, science.

---

**National Environmental Health Association**
**NEHA Scholarships**
720 South Colorado Boulevard, Suite 970
Denver, CO 80222 (303)756-9090

**$ Given:** Two grants of $850.
**Contact:** Lawrence J. Krone.
**Deadline:** January 31.

**Restrictions:**
College juniors or seniors studying environmental health.

---

**National Geographic Society**
**Committee for Research and Exploration**
Seventeenth and M Streets, Northwest
Washington, DC 20036

**Restrictions:**
Graduate research in the sciences.

---

**National Institute on Alcohol Abuse and Alcoholism**
**Alcohol National Research Awards**
5600 Fishers Lane
Rockville, MD 20857 (301)443-4223

**$ Given:** $6,552.
**Deadline:** January 10, May 10, September 10.

**Restrictions:**
Pre-doctoral fellowships for study on alcoholism. Must pay back by doing health-related research after degree.

---

**National Institute on Drug Abuse**
**Drug Abuse National Research Service Awards for Research Training**
5600 Fishers Lane
Rockville, MD 20857 (301)443-6710

**Restrictions:**
Pre-doctoral of at least 2 years in a field related to drug abuse.

## Science • 179

**National 4-H Council**
7100 Connecticut Avenue
Chevy Chase, MD 20815 (301)656-9000

**$ Given:** 287 scholarships amounting to $280,000.
**Contact:** County or State 4-H office.

**Restrictions:**
Scholarships in some fields of science, 4-H members.

---

**The National Science Foundation**
**National Research Council**
2101 Constitution Avenue
Washington, DC 20418 (202)334-2872

**$ Given:** Unspecified number of $11,100 fellowships. Renewable.
**Contact:** Fellowship office.
**Deadline:** November 21.

**Restrictions:**
Minority graduate students and students who have not completed more than twenty semester hours in the science or engineering field. Full time enrollment in areas specified by NSF.

---

**The Northwest College & University Association for Science**
100 Sprout Road
Richland, WA 99352 (509)375-3090

**$ Given:** Approximately 100 awards annually: $175 per week for graduate and undergraduate students.
**Contact:** Program Director.
**Deadline:** January 10.

**Restrictions:**
U.S. citizens. Must be junior in college at time of participation; graduate student must have identified thesis topic.

---

**Nuclear Science, Engineering and Health Physics Fellowships**
**University Programs**
**Oak Ridge Associated Universities**
120 Badger Avenue, P.O. Box 117
Oak Ridge, TN 87830 (615)576-3428

**Deadline:** January 30.

**Restrictions:**
Graduate students with BS degree in science, engineering, physics.

---

**Arthur & Doreen Parrett Scholarship Trust Fund**
c/o People's National Bank of Washington
P.O. Box 720, Trust Division
Seattle, WA 98111 (206)344-3685

**$ Given:** 16 grants from $300-$900.
**Deadline:** July 31.

**Restrictions:**
For study in school of engineering, science, medicine, dentistry.

**The Renate W. Chasman Scholarship for Women**
Brookhaven Women in Science
P.O. Box 183
Upton, NY 11973

**$ Given:** Awards of $1,000, not renewable.

**Restrictions:** Women, 25 or older enrolled at least half-time in a degree-oriented program; must be senior undergraduate or graduate student. Must be citizens of the U.S. or permanent resident aliens; must be residents of Nassau or Suffolk counties of Long Island, NY.

---

**LTV Steel Corporation**
Republic Building, P.O. Box 6778
Cleveland, OH 44101 (216)622-5255

**Contact:** Dee Tripp, Secretary, Contributions Committee.

**Restrictions:** Engineering, science students, sons and daughters of LTV Steel Corporation. Must apply in junior year of high school.

---

**Science Talent Search**
Science Service, Inc.
1719 N Street, Northwest
Washington, DC 20036 (202)785-2255

**$ Given:** 10 scholarships per year totaling $33,625. Renewable.
**Deadline:** December 15.

**Restrictions:** Enrolled as senior in secondary school in U.S., Puerto Rico, Guam, Virgin Islands, American Samoa, Wake & Midway Islands. Complete college entrance qualifications by Oct. 1. Submit 1,000 words on independent research project in social or physical sciences, engineering, mathematics or biological sciences. May not have previously competed for Science Talent Search.

---

**Sigma Xi Grants-in-Aid**
345 Whitney Avenue
New Haven, CT 06511 (203)624-9883

**$ Given:** $1,000 (maximum). Average grant $400.
**Deadline:** November 1, February 1, April 1.

**Restrictions:** Research in any field of scientific investigation.

# Science · 181

**State Farm Companies Foundation**
One State Farm Plaza
Bloomington, IL 61701 (309)766-2039

**$ Given:** 20 fellowships of $2,000.
**Contact:** Assistant Vice-President, Programs.
**Deadline:** February 28.

**Restrictions:**
College juniors and seniors studying business, computer science, science, economics, finance, mathematics, law. Must be nominated by the dean or department head.

---

**Watertown Foundation**
**Herring College Scholarships**
216 Washington Street
Watertown, NY 13601 (315)782-7110

**$ Given:** $500-$2,500. $100,000 given in total.
**Contact:** Executive Director at above address.
**Deadline:** April 1.

**Restrictions:**
Resident of Jefferson County, NY studying science. Freshmen and Juniors.

---

**Wheelwright Scientific School**
c/o Chase & Hunt
47 State Street
Newburyport, MA 01950 (617)462-4434

**$ Given:** 28 grants totaling $62,629.
**Contact:** Secretary.
**Deadline:** April 1.

**Restrictions:**
Young, male, Protestant residents of Newburyport, MA studying science.

---

**National Wildlife Federation**
1412 Sixteenth Street, Northwest
Washington, DC 20036

**$ Given:** 20-25 $4,000 fellowships, renewable.
**Contact:** Executive Vice-President.
**Deadline:** November 30.

**Restrictions:**
Citizen of U.S., Canada or Mexico. Graduate student, principally engaged in research rather than course work.

---

**Wolcott Foundation, Inc.**
3681 Lindell Boulevard
St. Louis, MO 63108 (314)371-4070

**$ Given:** 9 to 12 awards of $6,660. Not renewable.
**Contact:** Chairman, 287 Avenue de Las Flores, Thousand Oaks, CA 91360.
**Deadline:** May 15.

**Restrictions:**
Graduate students in science at George Washington University, Washington, DC, with GPA 3.0 or better, preferably with Masonic background.

---

**Women's Seaman's Friend Society of Connecticut, Inc.**
**Scholarship Program**
74 Forbes Avenue
New Haven, CT 06512 (203)467-3887

**Deadline:** April 1, May 15.

**Restrictions:**
CT residents majoring in marine sciences; financial need.

# WILDLIFE CONSERVATION

**National Campers and Hikers Association**
4804 Transit Road, Building #2
Depew, NY 14043 (716)668-6242

**Deadline:** March 25.
**Contact:** Scholarship Director at above address.

**Restrictions:**
Members or their children; students of wildlife conservation, forestry, botany, geology, ecology. High school applicant must be in upper ⅖ of class. College student must have GPA of 3.0.

**National Wildlife Federation**
1412 Sixteenth Street, Northwest
Washington, DC 20036

**$ Given:** 20-25 $4,000 fellowships, renewable.
**Contact:** Executive Vice-President.
**Deadline:** November 30.

**Restrictions:**
Citizen of U.S., Canada or Mexico. Graduate student, principally engaged in research rather than course work.

**Sport Fishery Research Foundation**
608 Thirteenth Street, Northwest, Suite 801
Washington, DC 20005 (202)737-2145

**$ Given:** From $1,500-$6,000 funding for research or fellowship grants.
**Deadline:** March 30.
**Contact:** Secretary.

**Restrictions:**
Graduate student in good standing interested in fisheries and aquatic resource conservation.

**Rob and Bessie Welder Wildlife Foundation**
P.O. Box 1400
Sinton, TX 78387 (512)364-2643

**$ Given:** Unspecified number of $575 awards per month for M.S. candidates; unspecified number of $600 awards per month for PhD candidates.
**Contact:** John Wilder.
**Deadline:** April 1.

**Restrictions:**
TX graduate students studying wildlife conservation, zoology. Priority given to proposals involving research conducted on foundation's refuge area or localities near Sinton, TX.

**Wildlife Management Institute**
709 Wire Building
1000 Vermont Avenue, Northwest
Washington, DC 20005 (202)347-1774

**$ Given:** Unspecified number of $1,500-$3,000 awards per 12 month period. Renewable.
**Contact:** Vice President at above address.
**Deadline:** October 31.

**Restrictions:**
Graduate student, approved by supervisor.

# ZOOLOGY

**Allied Mills Inc.**
**Animal Science Scholarships**
10 South Riverside Plaza
Chicago, IL 60606 (312)930-1050

**$ Given:** $1,000.
**Contact:** State 4-H Leader.

**Restrictions:**
Junior zoology student in good scholastic standing, 4-H member; financial need.

**American Museum of Natural History**
**Collective Study Grant**
Central Park West at 79th Street
New York, NY 10024 (212)769-5467

**$ Given:** Stipend to study collections at the museum.
**Contact:** Office of grants and fellowships, Diane Menditto.

**Restrictions:**
Must live outside of New York.

**Continental Grains**
**Animal Science Scholarships**
277 Park Avenue
New York, NY 10172 (212)207-5578

**$ Given:** $1,000.
**Contact:** State 4-H Leader.

**Restrictions:**
Juniors studying animal science, 4-H members; financial need.

**Entomological Society of America**
**Scholarship Program**
4603 Calvert Road
College Park, MD 20740 (301)864-1334

**$ Given:** $1,000.
**Deadline:** June 15.

**Restrictions:**
Zoology, undergraduates studying field of entomology.

**National Zoological Park**
**Mary Sawyer Hollander**
**Friends of the National Zoo**
Washington, DC 20008 (202)673-4955

**$ Given:** $1,800, 12-week full term (or $900 one-half term) stipends for research trainees.
**Deadline:** February 15.

**Restrictions:**
Most programs require completion of 2 years of college.

**Smithsonian Environmental Research Center**
**Work/Learn Program**
P.O. Box 28
Edgewater, MD 21037 (301)798-4424

**$ Given:** Support including weekly stipend of $75-$90 and living accommodations.
**Deadline:** December 1, April 1, July 1.
**Contact:** Linda Chick, Coordinator

**Restrictions:** Students to work on specific projects in environmental research within disciplines of math, chemistry, microbiology, botany, zoology.

---

**Rob and Bessie Welder Wildlife Foundation**
P.O. Box 1400
Sinton, TX 78387 (512)364-2643

**$ Given:** $600 stipend a month for Doctoral students. $575 for Masters students.
**Contact:** John Wilder.
**Deadline:** October 1 for following year.

**Restrictions:** Zoology graduate students doing research on wildlife conservation.

# BIBLIOGRAPHY

*Annual Register of Grant Support, 1985-86.* 19th ed. Chicago: Marquis Academic Media. 1985. 899 p. (200 East Ohio St., 60611) $87.00.
Includes information on nearly 3,000 programs sponsored by funding sources, including government agencies, public and private foundations, educational and professional associations, special interest organizations and corporations. Covers a broad range of interests including academic and scientific research, publication support, equipment and construction support, in-service training, competitions and prizes, and travel and exchange programs. Organized by broad subject areas with four indexes: subject, organization and program, geographic, and personnel.

*Awards, Honors, and Prizes.* 6th ed. Volume I: United States and Canada. Paul Wasserman, ed. Detroit: Gale Research Co., 1985. Approx. 950 p. (Book Tower, 48226) $145.00.
Directory of awards in advertising, public relations, art, business, government, finance, science, education, engineering, literature, technology, sports, religion, public affairs, radio and television, politics, library science, fashion, medicine, law, publishing, international affairs, transportation, architecture, journalism, motion pictures, music, photography, theater and performing arts.

*Basic Facts on Foreign Study.* New York, NY: Institute of International Education, 1985. Approx. 6 p. (809 United Nations Plaza, 10017) Single copies free.
A guide for U.S. students planning study abroad.

*Bear's Guide to Funding Money for College.* John Bear, Ph.D. Berkeley, CA: Ten Speed Press, 1984. 157 p. (P.O. Box 7123, 94707) $5.95.

*Better Late Than Never: Financial Aid for Older Women Seeking Education and Training.* Washington, DC: Women's Equity Action League, 1985. 43 p. (1250 1 St., NW, Suite 305, 20005) $8.00.
Focuses on programs that provide financial aid for women who need to train or retrain for a career. Apprenticeships are also included.

*Chronicle Student Aid Annual.* Moravia, NY: Chronicle Guidance Publications, Inc., 1986. 416 p. (Aurora St., 13118) $18.75.
Contains information on financial aid programs offered nationally or regionally, primarily by noncollegiate organizations. Awards are for graduate, undergraduate and postdoctoral students.

*The CISP International Studies Funding Book.* Walter T. Brown *et. al.* ed. New York, NY: Council on International and Public Affairs, 1986. Unpaged. (777 United Nations Plaza, 10017) $50.00.

# 186·BIBLIOGRAPHY

*The College Blue Book: Vol. 5: Scholarships, fellowships, grants, and loans.* 20th ed. New York: Macmillan Information, 1985. 718 p. (866 Third Ave., 10022) $44.00.

Lists financial aid programs offered by agencies and institutions, excluding colleges and universities. Individual programs listed by grant-making organization and arranged under broad and specific subject areas.

*The College Financial Aid Emergency Kit.* Joyce Lain Kennedy and Dr. Herm Davis. Cardiff, CA: Sun Features, Inc., 1986. 48 p. (Box 368-F, 92007) $3.50.

*College Grants from Uncle Sam: Am I eligible & for how much? 1986-87.* Alexandria, VA: Octameron Associates, 1985. (P.O. Box 3437, 22302) $2.00.

*College Loans from Uncle Sam: The borrower's guide that explains it all—from locating lenders to loan forgiveness. 1986-87.* Alexandria, VA: Octameron Associates, 1985. (P.O. Box 3437, 22302) $2.00.

*College Money Handbook: The Complete Guide to Expenses, Scholarships, Loans, Jobs and Special Aid Programs at Four-Year Colleges.* Karen C. Hegener, ed. Princeton, NJ: Peterson's Guides. 1985, 550 p. (P.O. Box 2123, 08540) $8.95.

*Complete Grants Sourcebook for Higher Education.* 2nd ed. American Council on Education. New York: Macmillan Publishing Co. 1985. 608 p. (866 Third Ave., New York, NY 10022) $85.00.

A guide to grantsmanship and a directory to more than 500 funding sources for higher education.

*Directory of Financial Aids for International Activities.* 4th ed. Minneapolis, MN: Office of International Programs, University of Minnesota, 1985. Approx. 440 p. (55455) $20.00.

Covers grants to individuals interested in international activities or in studying abroad.

*Directory of Financial Aids for Minorities, 1986-87.* Gail Ann Schlachter, ed. Santa Barbara, CA: ABC-Clio Information Service, 1986. 345 p. (P.O. Box 4397, 93103) $35.00.

The Directory is divided into four separate sections: financial aids designed primarily for minorities, a list of state sources for educational benefits, an annotated bibliography of directories and five sets of indexes by program title, sponsoring organization, geographic location, subject and calendar filing dates. Over 1,500 references and cross references to scholarships, fellowships, loans, grants, awards, internships, state sources of educational benefits and general financial aid directories are included.

*Directory of Financial Aids for Women. 1985-1986.* Gail Ann Schlachter, ed. Santa Barbara, CA: ABC-Clio Information Services, 1985. 370 p. (P.O. Box 4397, 93103) $35.00.

Lists scholarships, fellowships, loans, grants, internships, awards, and prizes designed for women. Also includes women's credit unions and sources of state educational benefits. Also includes international programs, more than 1,100 references to scholarships, etc. Annotated bibliography; indexed by sponsoring organization, geographic location, and subject.

*Directory of Grants in the Humanities, 1987.* Phoenix, AZ: The Oryx Press, 1987. (2214 North Central at Encanto, 85004) $74.50.

*Directory of Research Grants, 1986.* Betty L. Wilson & William K. Wilson, eds. Phoenix, AZ: The Oryx Press, 1986. 748 p. (2214 North Central at Encanto, 85004) $74.50.

Information on almost 3,000 grants, contracts, and fellowships available from Federal and State governments, private foundations, professional organizations, and corporations for research projects. Lists grant programs by specific funding areas; indexed by sponsoring organization and grant name.

*Directory of Special Programs for Minority Group Members.* 4th ed. Willis L. Johnson, ed. Garrett Park, MD: Garrett Park Press, 1986. 348 p. (P.O. Box 190A, 20896) $25.00.

*Don't Miss Out: The Ambitious Student's Guide to Financial Aid, 1986-87.* 10th ed. Robert Leider. Alexandria, VA: Octameron Associates, 1985. 86 p. (P.O. Box 3427, 22302) $4.00.

Planning guide suggesting procedures and strategies for students seeking financial aid. Updated annually in September.

*Earn and Learn: Cooperative education opportunities offered by the Federal government. 1986-87.* 7th ed. Alexandria, VA: Octameron Associates, Inc. 1985. Approx. 20 p. (P.O. Box 3437, 22302) $2.50.

Includes sponsors, occupational fields, and participating colleges.

*Fellowship Guide to Western Europe.* 6th ed. New York, NY: Council for European Studies, 1985. Approx. 100 p. (1509 International Affairs, Columbia University, 10027) $5.00.

*Fellowships, Scholarships, and Related Opportunities in International Education.* Knoxville, TN: University of Tennessee, 1986. Unpaged. (Division of International Education, 205 Alumni Hall, 37916) $8.00.

*Financial Aid for College-Bound Athletes.* Marlene Lazar & Dr. Stephen H. Lazar. New York, NY: Arco Publishing, Inc., 1982. 323 p. (215 Park Ave. South, 10003) $8.95 pap.

850 colleges and universities covered. Entries include name of school, address, athletic director's name, teams (both men's & women's), conferences participated in, deadlines, and other scholarship information. Also an index by sport—under name of sport are the schools with awards in that sport.

*Financial Aids for Higher Education: A Catalog for Undergraduates.* 12th ed. Oreon Keesler. Dubuque, IA: William C. Brown Company Publishers, 1986. Approx. 750 p. (2460 Kerper Blvd., 52001) $32.95.

Lists over 3,200 programs intended for both college freshmen and advanced students. Index includes donor agencies and foundations, common program names, subject areas, types of awards, and special eligibility characteristics. Updated every two years.

# 188·BIBLIOGRAPHY

*Financing College Education.* 3rd ed. Kenneth A. Kohl and Irene C. Kohl. New York, NY: Harper & Row, 1983. 304 p. (10 East 53rd St., 10022) $5.95.
  A practical guide to scholarships, loans, grants, and work-study programs for both parents and students.

*Five Federal Financial Aid Programs, 1985-1986: A Student Consumer's Guide.* Washington, DC: U.S. Department of Education, 1984. 17 p. (Box 84, 20044) Free.

*Foundation Grants to Individuals.* 5th ed. New York: Foundation Center, 1986. (79 Fifth Ave., 10003) $18.00.
  Profiles the programs of about 1,100 foundations that make grants to individuals. The foundations described have made grants to students, artists, scholars, foreign individuals, minorities, musicians, scientists and writers. The book includes information on foundation sources of funds for scholarships, fellowships, internships, medical and emergency assistance, residencies and travel programs.

*Fulbright Grants and Other Grants for Graduate Study Abroad.* New York, NY: Institute of International Education, Annual. (809 United Nations Plaza, 10017) Free.
  Lists financial assistance programs available to U.S. graduate students for study abroad.

*Funding for Research, Study and Travel: The People's Republic of China.* Denise Wallen, ed. Phoenix AZ: The Oryx Press, 1987. 230 p. (2214 North Central at Encanto, 85004-1483) $27.50.

*Grants and Fellowship Opportunities of Interest to Philosophers: 1986-87.* Newark, DE: American Philosophical Association, 1986. Approx. 50 p. (University of Delaware, 19716) Approx $3.50.
  Annual publication lists fellowships and grant opportunities available from sixty different sources.

*Grants for Graduate Students, 1986-88.* Andrea Leskes, ed. Princeton, NJ: Peterson's Guides, 1986. 385 p. (Dept. 6608, 166 Bunn Dr., Box 2123, 08543-2123) $29.95.

*The Grants Register, 1985-1987.* Norman Frankel, ed. New York: St. Martin's Press, 1984. 870 p. (175 Fifth Ave., 10010) $29.95.
  Lists scholarships and fellowships at all levels of graduate study, from regional, national and international sources. Also includes research grants, exchange opportunities, vacation study awards, travel grants, all types of grants-in-aid, project grants, competitions, prizes and honoraria—including awards in recognition or support of creative work, professional and vocational awards, and special awards—for refugees, war veterans, minorities.

*Guide to Graduate Study in Political Science, 1986.* Rev., 12th ed. Patricia Spellman, comp. Washington, DC: American Political Science Association, 1986. 430 p. (1527 New Hampshire Ave., NW, 20036) $20.00 for non-APSA members.

Describes approximately 300 masters and doctoral programs in political science; includes financial aid information and faculty listing for each program.

*1986 Journalism Career and Scholarship Guide: What to study in college; Where to study Journalism & Communications; Where the jobs are & how to find them.* Princeton, NJ: The Newspaper Fund, 1986. Approx. 139 p. (P.O. Box 300, 08540) Single copies free; two or more at $.50/copy.

Annual guide to aid offered through schools and departments of journalism in U.S. and Canadian colleges and universities, by newspapers, professional societies, and miscellaneous sources. Section on grants specifically designed for minority students.

*Need a Lift? To Educational Opportunities, Careers, Loans, Scholarships, Employment.* Indianapolis, IN: American Legion Education and Scholarship Program, Fall, 1986. 144 p. (The American Legion, 1050, Need a Lift? P.O. Box 46206) $1.00 prepaid.

*Paying for Your Education: A Guide for Adult Learners.* 2nd ed. New York, NY: College Board Publications, 1986, 160 p. (Box 886, 10101) $7.95.

*The Scholarship Book: The Complete Guide to Private-Sector Scholarships, Grants and Loans for Undergraduates.* Englewood Cliffs, NJ: Prentice-Hall, Inc., 1985. 391 p. (West Nyack, NY 10995) $14.95 + $3.50 postage and handling.

*Scholarships, Fellowships and Loans, Vol.8.* S. Norman Feingold and Marie Feingold. Bethesda, MD: Bellman Publishing Co., 1987. 484 p. (Dept. 8, Box 34937, 20817) $80.00.

Lists a wide range of scholarships, fellowships, loans, grants, and awards not controlled by the college or university. Includes index which lists awards according to specific educational or occupational goals. Material is dated. Check with funder before applying.

*Scholarships Guide for Commonwealth Postgraduate Students, 1983-85.* The Association of Commonwealth Universities. London, England: John Foster House, 1982. 328 p. (36 Gordon Square, WCHOPF) $25.00.

A guide to scholarships, grants, loans, assistantships, and other aid open to graduates of Commonwealth universities who want to undertake postgraduate study or research at a Commonwealth university outside their own country.

*Scholarships for International Students, 1986-88.* Anna J. Leider, ed. Middleburg Heights, OH: Scholarship Research Group, 1986. 271 p. (16600 Sprague Rd., Suite 110, 44130) $14.95.

*Scholarships and Loans for Nursing Education, 1986-1987.* National League for Nursing. 65 p. (10 Columbus Circle, New York, 10019-1350) $8.95.

# 190·BIBLIOGRAPHY

*Study Abroad, 1987-1988.* 25th ed. Paris: UNESCO, 1986 approx. 1347 p. (UNIPUB, Box 433 Murray Hill Station, New York 10157) $12.95.

    Listing in three languages of scholarships and courses offered by foreign universities and international and national organizations and institutions. The term scholarship is used to include all forms of financial or material aid for study abroad.

*Women's Organizations: A National Directory.* Martha Merrill Doss, ed. Garrett Park Press, 1986. 302 p. (Garrett Park, MD 20896) $25.50.

    Lists over 1,500 funding sources for women seeking educational and career opportunities.

*Writer's Market: 1986.* Paula Deimling, ed. Cincinnati, OH: Writer's Digest Books, 1985. 1,056 p. (9933 Alliance Road, 45242) $19.95.